国际商务中国实践

中英文案例集

International Business of China Practice
——Bilingual Case Study

主　编：张洪烈
副主编：尹　豪

中国财经出版传媒集团
经济科学出版社
Economic Science Press

图书在版编目（CIP）数据

国际商务中国实践：中英文案例集/张洪烈，尹豪编著．—北京：经济科学出版社，2017.10
ISBN 978-7-5141-8647-5

Ⅰ.①国… Ⅱ.①张…②尹… Ⅲ.①国际商务-案例-中国-汉、英 Ⅳ.①F740

中国版本图书馆CIP数据核字（2017）第275238号

责任编辑：初少磊　杨　梅
责任校对：徐领柱
责任印制：李　鹏

国际商务中国实践
——中英文案例集
主　编　张洪烈
副主编　尹　豪
经济科学出版社出版、发行　新华书店经销
社址：北京市海淀区阜成路甲28号　邮编：100142
总编部电话：010-88191217　发行部电话：010-88191540
网址：www.esp.com.cn
电子邮件：esp@esp.com.cn
天猫网店：经济科学出版社旗舰店
网址：http://jjkxcbs.tmall.com
北京季蜂印刷有限公司印装
710×1000　16开　18.75印张　290000字
2017年12月第1版　2017年12月第1次印刷
ISBN 978-7-5141-8647-5　定价：48.00元
（图书出现印装问题，本社负责调换。电话：010-88191502）

前言

中国企业通过“引进来”和“走出去”两种方式，使国际化必然成为企业发展的战略选择。尤其是在“一带一路”倡议的引领下，企业国际化发展的环境不断改善优化，企业跨国发展的步伐也不断加快，在国际商务领域的中国因素逐渐发展成为中国要素，中国企业也从国际商务活动中的跟随者前进为领跑者。

时代在进步、企业在革新，经过三十多年的国际化发展，中国货物进出口总额已跃居世界第一位，中国企业的对外投资量也攀升至世界第二位，充分体现出中国企业的发展经验值得推广学习。但是，这些宝贵经验的取得也付出了高昂的成本和沉痛的代价，足以引起后来者的反思与借鉴。这也形成了本书写作的目的和动力。

云南财经大学在2000年开始引进国外优质教育资源，开展中美合作的国际商务专业的本科教育；2011年，开展国际商务硕士专业学位研究生教育；2014年，将国际商务专业输出到泰国，成为教育“走出去”的首批专业；2016年，国际商务硕士专业获批立项为云南省专业学位研究生联合培养基地建设项目；2017年，国际商务硕士专业获得教育部援外项目立项，成为使用援外资金进行专业建设和培养硕士学位留学生的国际化专业。

在专业发展的过程中，学科团队积极开展课程建设，先后有十门课程立项成为重点课程、实习实训课程、实验课程；2014年《国际商务》课程成为教育部立项的“来华留学英语授课品牌课程”，本书是该品牌课程的建设成果之一。

通过多年教学的积累，课程建设团队完成了《国际商务中国实践——中英文案例集》教材。教材的出版经历了教育资源从“引进来”到“本土化”再到“走出去”的国际化发展历程，突破了本土化教育资源缺乏的约束，提炼了中国企业跨国经营的珍贵成果，推广了中国企业国际化的先进经验。

本书内容包括六篇三十五个案例。具体篇章包括全球化、国际商务环境、国际贸易与投资、国际金融、国际企业的战略与组织、国际商务运营等六篇内容。案例涉及中国企业海外拓展的外向国际化案例、跨国公司在中国本土化的内向国际化案例、国际金融机构的跨国业务案例和国家间经贸合作案例等内容。

案例由教育部“来华留学英语授课品牌课程”的团队成员分工编写完成，并在成稿过程中经过多次教学使用和修改。具体编写人员有张洪烈、尹豪、刘美武、潘雪冬、段春锦、张俊婕、李恒敏。2012 级和 2016 级国际商务硕士研究生为案例资料的收集整理做了大量的准备工作。加拿大外教 Barbara Helm 对英文部分提出了宝贵的修改意见。谨对参加写作的各位作者和提供帮助与支持的各位领导和老师表示诚挚的感谢。

感谢教育部“来华留学英语授课品牌课程”项目和云南省专业学位研究生联合培养基地项目的资助。

中国企业在国际商务领域的实践不断推陈出新，发展日新月异。案例是对过去的总结，在案例的运用过程中仍需要不断更新与发展。限于编者知识的局限性，书中的疏漏和缺点敬请读者批评指正，并提出宝贵意见。

编　者

二〇一七年十月

Preface

By adopting two ways of "bringing in" and "going out", Chinese enterprises are making internationalization a necessary strategic choice for enterprise development. Especially under the lead of "the Belt and Road" initiative, the environment of internationalization development for enterprises is being optimized. The pace of international development of enterprises is also accelerating. China, in the field of international business, is gradually developing from an element to a necessity. Chinese enterprises are also moving from followers in international business activities to top runners.

Age is in progress, companies are in innovation. With thirty years of international development, volume of international trade of China has been staying in top one in the world. Volume of foreign direct investment of China has also climbed to the top two. It fully reflects that the development experience of Chinese enterprises is worthy of promotion and learning. But the acquisition of these valuable experiences has been costly with a price of pain. This should be enough to provoke the reflection and reference of the latecomers. This also forms the purpose and motivation of the book writing.

In 2000, Yunnan University of Finance and Economics began to introduce high – quality education resources from foreign countries, and started the undergraduate education of Sino – American cooperation major International Business. In 2011, started the education of professional master's degree of international business. In 2014, exported international business major to Thailand and it became one of the first majors of education's "going out". In 2016, the professional master's degree of international business major received approval to build a joint training base for professional postgraduates of Yunnan province. In 2017, the master's degree of international business major received a foreign – aid project of Ministry of Education. It became an international major in the field of professional construction and training of master's degree students using foreign – aid funds.

In the course of development, the team actively carried out curriculum construction, with ten courses be recognized as key courses, practice training courses and experiment courses one after another. In 2014, "international business" course became one of the "Brand English lecturing courses for foreign students in China", which was established by the Ministry of Education. This book is one of the achievements of this brand curriculum.

Through the accumulation of years of teaching, the curriculum construction team has completed the bilingual textbook of *International Business of China Practice*. The publication of this textbook experienced an internationalization development course from the "bringing in" to the "localization", and to "going out". It breaks through the lack local education resources, extracts the valuable achievements of Chinese enterprises transnational operation, and popularizes the advanced experience of Chinese enterprises' internationalization.

The book contains six parts with thirty – five cases. The specific parts including: globalization, international business environment, international trade and investment, international finance, international business strategy and organization, international business operation, etc. The cases involve with the outward internationalization cases of Chinese enterprises overseas, inward internationalization cases with the localization of multinational companies in China, multinational business cases of international financial institutions, and economic and trade cooperation among nations and so on.

The cases are written and compiled by the team members of the "Brand English lecturing courses for foreign students in China" of Ministry of Education, and has been used in teaching and modified for many times during the process. The compilers are Zhang Honglie, Yin Hao, Liu Meiwu, Pan Xuedong, Duan Chunjin, Zhang Junjie, and Li Hengmin. The classes of 2012 and 2016 international business master graduate students have done a great deal of preparation for the collection of case data. Barbara Helm, a Canadian foreign teacher, made valuable comments on the English part. We would like to express our sincere thanks to all the writers and teachers who have participated in the writing.

We thank the Ministry of Education for the program of "Brand English lecturing courses for foreign students in China" and the funding of the joint training base project for professional degree postgraduates of Yunnan province.

The practice of Chinese enterprises in the field of international business is constantly evolving and developing rapidly. As the case is the summary of the past, the use of cases still needs to be constantly updated and developed. Due to the limitation of the authors' knowledge, there may be omission and shortcomings in the book. Criticisms and valuable comments are welcomed.

Authors
October 2017

目录

Contents

第一篇

全球化

一、

同仁堂的国际化之路

中国北京同仁堂（集团）有限责任公司是北京市政府授权经营国有资产的国有独资公司。同仁堂创始于 1669 年，是中国历史最悠久的企业之一。北京同仁堂坚持“以现代中药为核心，发展生命健康产业，成为国际知名的现代中医药集团”的发展战略，以“做长、做强、做大”为方针，以创新引领、科技兴企为己任，形成了现代制药业、零售商业和医疗服务三大板块，构建了六个二级集团（北京同仁堂股份集团、北京同仁堂科技发展集团、北京同仁堂国药集团、北京同仁堂健康药业集团、北京同仁堂商业投资集团、北京同仁堂药材参茸投资集团）、三个院（北京同仁堂中医医院有限责任公司、北京同仁堂研究院、北京同仁堂教育学院）和两个储备单位的企业架构，拥有三家上市公司。集团共拥有药品、医院制剂、保健食品、食品、化妆品等 1500 余种产品，28 个生产基地，83 条现代生产线，一个国家级工程中心和博士后科研工作站。

随着同仁堂的快速发展，品牌的维护和提升、文化的创新与传承也取得了丰硕成果，“同仁堂中医药文化”已列入首批国家级非物质文化遗产名录，同仁堂既是经济实体又是文化载体的双重功能日益显现。

2006 年中国北京同仁堂有限责任公司于中国香港特别行政区成立了第一个境外生产基地和研发机构，占地面积超过 10000 平方米，是香港最大的，也是设施最优、水准最高的生产研发基地。以安宫牛黄丸、破壁灵芝孢子粉胶囊为核心品种，2008 年推向市场后销售量节节攀升，成绩斐然。

同仁堂生产线已通过中国香港地区卫生署、日本厚生省、澳大利亚 TGA 的 GMP 认证、穆斯林哈拉认证和以色列洁食认证，为立足香港面向海外、打造境外制造的健康产品创造了充分条件，也为未来在欧美等国家建立本地化工厂提供了可资借鉴的经验。

同仁堂一直注重新产品开发和传统产品境外拓展，加快技术进步与管理升级。一方面，进行自主研发，倾力打造具有国际市场竞争力的现代养生保健产品，在品种群建设方面也取得进展。除在中国香港制造外，还在日本、韩国、新西兰、瑞士等地利用优势资源开发制造系列健康产品。另一方面，与国外知名院校及科研机构合作，开展重点品种的安全性和作用机理等研究，为中药产品进入西方主流市场积累技术和理论基础。

至2016年6月，同仁堂在25个国家和地区开设了115家包括零售终端、中医诊所和养生中心在内的网点。与此同时，开办了当地最大的中医养生保健中心，开创了养生保健发展的新模式。全球范围内的同仁堂医药从业人员获得了广泛的认可和信任，在同仁堂就医的人数累计已达3000万人次。

2015年10月10日，同仁堂国际跨境电子商务平台“天然淘”正式上线。这一平台奠定了同仁堂在互联网领域获得认可的基础。“天然淘”对所有海内外产品建立可追溯体系，每个产品上都印有二维码，消费者扫描便可查询商品从生产地直至销售各个环节的信息。

同仁堂国际利用全球优质健康和中医院资源，进军大健康领域，整合健康监测、健康云计算、移动互联技术为人们提供健康预防、保健、治疗、保险以及康复全流程的一揽子健康解决方案。平台由健康监测与咨询、跨境健康垂直电商、跨境中医药电商以及金融保险四大业务板块组成。

板块一：健康监测与咨询，防患于未然。健康服务生态平台以“治未病、预防监测”为核心，以更低的成本、更高的效率降低医疗健康信息的不透明，防患于未然，并基于用户检测数据，整合全球中医师资源，为用户提供养生调理、跟踪管理于一体，高水平、个性化、便捷化的养生保健咨询服务。

板块二：跨境健康垂直（专注健康领域）电商，全球优质健康资源引进来。启动中国首个聚焦健康垂直领域的跨境电商平台，实现当地直采、无中间环节、100%正品，为全球消费者提供高品质专业化的健康产品与健康服务。

板块三：跨境中医药电商，中医药健康服务走出去。立足传统中医药，借助跨境电商平台，整合海内外中医药、植物药等优质资源，作为中医药海外“输出”的重要平台，服务于中国及全球消费者。

板块四：金融保险，蓝海创新。基于用户健康检测数据，将以“中医健康保险”市场为突破，开发响应国家政策倡议的中医治未病健康保险产品，并针对电商交易，延展互联网责任类保险产品的创新。

“互联网+”核心并不在于“互联网”，而是在于“+”。如果只是就事论事地在传统行业基础上强加互联网，是做不出什么大名堂来的。唯有深刻理解互联网，才能真正深化传统行业和互联网的关系。

同仁堂在将中医药推向全球的过程中，为了从知名度跨越到忠诚度，生产到售后各个环节都应始终把顾客的利益摆在首位，真正做到“同修仁德，济世养生”，为消费者提供信得过的优质产品。同仁堂的国际化是本着“有华人的地方，就有同仁堂”。首先选择境外华人聚集地开设门店作为突破，这种“乡情故土”的营销，为同仁堂走向国际市场开了个好头。通过与中国香港和记黄埔合作，整合境外研发、销售终端和生产基地，并在境外坚持采用“名医+名牌+名药”的品牌之路，名医不仅有高超的医术，对中医药文化、同仁堂的历史也具有深刻的理解，同时力求借助当地的研发机构开发适合当地需求的新产品，从而提高了运营效率和中药在国际市场的认知度。同仁堂的国际化过程是展现老字号品牌所承载的中医药文化魅力的过程，也是一场中国传统文化的突围过程。这一模式基本上是围绕华人圈进行，只有少量单味中药以保健食品身份进入欧美主流市场。

在同仁堂推进国际化的过程中，有一条宝贵经验就是“以医带药”，也就是用中医来带动中药，这是密不可分的两件事情，只有让中医在国际上得到认同，才能进一步让国际市场接受中药。当然，各地方文化不同，使其他地区接受中药和中医都不那么容易，所以，首先要让中医的理论能够被患者理解，才能让中药更快传入。中药离开中医，就成为无源之水，无本之木。因此，中医在国际市场推广中的作用显而易见，也不可或缺，除了帮助患者恢复健康，同时能更好地传播我们的中医文化。在不知不觉中，加强其他地区对中医理论的了解，进而更加信任中医，接受中药。

案例讨论题：

1. 同仁堂走向全球市场的驱动力是什么？
2. 同仁堂走向全球市场的阻碍是什么？
3. 同仁堂如何顺应全球化的趋势，如何应对反对全球化的抗议？

伊利的全球化发展

内蒙古伊利实业集团股份有限公司是中国乳品行业龙头企业，是北京2008年奥运会唯一一家乳制品赞助商，也是第一个赞助奥运会的中国食品品牌。2009年5月25日，伊利成功联手2010年上海世博会，成为唯一一家符合世博标准，为上海世博会提供乳制品的企业。

在全球乳制品行业国际化和一体化的背景下，乳业产业链上的优质资源在加速流动，中国乳业对全球乳业的影响力日益增强，中国乳业逐步融入世界乳业的发展进程。中国乳业的国际化至少包括三个方面：资源、标准和研发。在这些方面，伊利也不断布局，加速推进。在资源上，伊利已经在新西兰建立了全球最大的一体化奶业生产基地；在标准上，与瑞士通用公证行（SGS）、英国劳氏质量认证有限公司（LRQA）和英国天祥集团（Intertek）这些国际质量机构达成战略合作，升级质量安全管理体系；在研发上，和欧洲、大洋洲等的知名大学共建了研发中心。

2013年7月初，伊利与美国最大的牛奶公司 Dairy Farmers of America Inc（简称 DFA）签署战略合作协议，伊利全球化的雄心充分显现。DFA公司总部设在美国密苏里州堪萨斯城，是全美最大的牛奶公司，拥有遍布美国48个州的18000个大型农场，在美国本土独立拥有21个大型奶品生产加工基地，出口市场遍布墨西哥、欧洲、中美、南美、亚洲、中东以及太平洋周边国家。这次中美两国最大的牛奶公司的合作，成了中美乳业合作的一件大事。

在全球化的浪潮中，伊利的全球化表现在以下方面：品牌全球化、技术全球化、资源全球化。

对于品牌的全球化，伊利集团步步推进，品牌全球化的足迹越来越坚实。2007年，伊利集团生产的28.8吨黄油出口埃及，实现了中国固体乳制品的首次出口，而且是出口到乳制品生产历史较为悠久的中东国家。这是一次重要的产品出口生意，检验了伊利产品的品质。在当年的乳品行业中，还缺乏真正享誉海外的中国品牌，通过这次出口，伊利认识到在全球范围提升品牌知名度的重要性。2008 年和 2010 年，伊利先后通过北京奥运会和上海世博会走上世界舞台，出现在国外消费者的视野中。2010 年年底，伊利进行了全面的品牌升级，确立了“成为世界一流的健康食品集团”的企业发展愿景。品牌全球化战略使世界认识了伊利，也使越来越多的世界级行业伙伴与伊利合作。从 2011 年开始，伊利展开了与美国迪士尼为期 5 年的全面合作，这次大型品牌的跨界合作使得伊利全新品牌形象释放出了国际属性的鲜明信号。通过迅速积累品牌知名度，伊利让全世界的消费者在短短两三年的时间内认识了这个来自中国内蒙古的乳品企业。这种品牌能量的爆发力，在全球的乳业格局中十分罕见，这也吸引来了更为重量级的国际合作伙伴——美国 DFA 公司。

在技术全球化上，伊利所采取的行动都针对自身的发展做出了切实可行的调整。早在 20 世纪 90 年代，中国乳业就开始了国际先进生产技术的应用。伊利等中国顶尖乳制品企业都采购了国际先进设备，在生产设备层面与国外乳企没有差距，甚至有的比国外还先进。在技术和管理等方面，伊利也不断与国外同行交流和合作。当年学习和引进国际先进技术还是站在国内市场赶超国际先进水平，而现在的技术全球化则已经是融入全球产业链的要求和必然选择。技术全球化是伊利全球化战略的重要内容，也是乳业发展的必然趋势。伊利和 DFA 的战略合作也包含牧场管理服务。DFA 拥有世界上最优秀的奶源管控经验和最具科技含量的加工技术，与之交流合作对于中国奶源管理水平的进一步提升会有较大的促进作用。此外，DFA 拥有大量现代化牧场，具有丰富牧场管理经验，对伊利建设现代化、专业化牧场有积极的借鉴作用。双方达成合作关系，伊利将获得 DFA 在奶牛养殖理念方面的指导和技术方面的支持，这将进一步提升伊利牧场的牛奶产量和质量水平，促进伊利的现代化牧场建设。

资源全球化使得伊利的优势更优。伊利将长期战略采购作为与 DFA 合作的主要内容之一，这体现出伊利全球化战略的一项重要内容就是将全球的优质资源为我所用。在奶源建设方面，伊利集团是行业内第一个完成全国性奶源布局的企业。在20世纪90年代，伊利就开始布局奶源，形成了呼伦贝尔、锡林郭勒和新疆天山三大黄金奶源带的生产基地网络，并成为中国唯一一家掌握“三大黄金奶源基地”的乳品企业。用全球的资源做全球的市场已经是行业共识和大势所趋，从这个意义上说，伊利是先行一步。DFA是美国乳业最大的上游原材料供应商之一，DFA的奶酪、乳清粉、大包装奶粉等产品在国际上拥有巨大优势，并长期为星巴克、卡夫等众多知名食品企业提供乳品原料。中国奶制品的市场需求增长迅速，而原料奶供应不足，尤其是奶粉的重要原料乳清粉，基本上都是来自进口。伊利与DFA合作，可能获得其稳定、低价的原料供应，将有助于进一步提升伊利在奶源方面的竞争优势。

从全球化海外战略来看，伊利集团采取的是“优势更优”的思路，即不断加强自己的奶源优势，注重从根本上进行品质的提升，意在夯实上游，意在对上游产业链的掌控。中国乳制品行业的结构调整，是众多奶制品企业进行产品升级，提升自身产品质量的契机。作为伊利国际化战略的重要一步，与DFA的合作是新的开始。

案例讨论题：

1. 哪些便利因素促进了伊利奶业的全球化？
2. 伊利集团的全球化发展有哪些好处？有什么弊病？
3. 全球化是好事还是坏事？请详细分析。

第二篇

国际商务环境

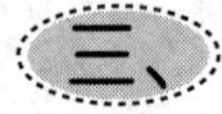

华为：拒绝海外市场的机会主义

在经历了金融危机、被美国调查等各种事件后，华为在海外市场仍有不俗的表现，甚至是捷报频传。2012 年，华为收入 2202 亿元人民币，按照固定汇率，同比增长 8%；净利润 154 亿元，同比增长 33%。华为的产品和解决方案已经应用于全球 150 多个国家，服务全球运营商 50 强中的 45 家及全球 1/3 的人口。

从某种意义上说，全球金融危机为华为等中国制造商拓展海外市场创造了新的机会。在市场低迷的行情下，海外企业资产价格大幅缩水，给了中国企业难得的淘“便宜货”的可能，这对于那些需要“走出去”以谋求国际化发展的中国企业来说，是一个难得的机遇。

华为通过海外扩张极大提升了国际市场地位。华为不仅在亚洲、非洲和中东地区获得了不菲的业绩，还成功进入了一些欧洲国家的市场。例如，华为在欧洲多个国家已经获得许多合同，并陆续突破了日本、北美等全球最高端市场。在非洲等新兴市场，华为已在南非、尼日利亚、肯尼亚等十多个国家设立了代表处。为进一步贴近客户，华为在非洲设立了南非、东非和西非三个地区部，提高对客户需求和服务的响应速度。经过十余年的市场培育和耕耘，华为已全面进入南部非洲大多数国家市场，并成为当地的主要通信设备供应商。

但是，在美国市场的拓展上，华为表现得还不尽如人意。美国市场竞争激烈，新进入者往往碰到很多竞争壁垒。2007 年下半年，华为希望以少数股东身份与美国私人资本运营公司贝恩联手收购美国 3COM 公司，以实现华为在美国的扩张。但这项交易最终未能通过美国政府对外资投资于敏感行业的审查程序。2011 年，华为被迫接受美国外国投资委员会的建议，撤销收购三叶公司特殊资产的申请。2011 年 10 月，美国商务部阻止华为参与国家应急网络项目招标。

华为在全球通讯行业的地位不断提高，其开发的各种产品销量的国际市场份额也排在全球前列，质量得到客户认同。现在，华为海外业务的营业额占到集团全部营业额的2/3。作为一个中国本土的高科技公司，华为必须思考在国际化过程中如何体现特色，如何提升品牌，如何进入高端国际市场。

以往华为在国际市场上成功的主要优势仍是低成本和低价格。但是，做国际市场不能仅仅靠价廉物美，因为国际对手可能规模更大、价格上更有下降空间。事实上，华为也已经开始意识到，走向国际市场更重要的是要形成自己的特色和品牌。比如，华为曾用3个月的时间为香港特区的固网运营商和记开发出号码携带业务；同样的业务，欧洲老牌的设备商此前花了6个月尚未完成。华为的交付成本和交付效率开始在业界形成良好的口碑，促进了华为形成一个快速响应的品牌形象。

全球化的征途不可能一蹴而就，市场需要不懈的开拓和耐心的培育。华为在全球化的征途中根据企业本身的情况和行业状况，将自己的全球化征程分为三个阶段：第一阶段是屡战屡败阶段，即屡战屡败、屡败屡战，直到零的突破。零的突破就是华为参与国际招标，是中标的突破，不是简单的产品销售的突破。第二阶段是突破阶段，即进一步派人到各个国家，哪一个国家人口多，电话需求大，就派人做市场；经过几年的艰苦努力，在2001年基本上实现了3个多亿元的销售。第三阶段是拓展欧美市场阶段，即蕴含着两条战线：华为在全球布网以后，在欧美以外的市场全面突破，并大力拓展欧美市场。

在全球市场的进入模式上，华为更是精心准备和考虑，针对不同时期、不同地区的不同需要，制定了相应具体的策略。在切入时机上，21世纪初，通信设备的关税相对较低，国内、国际市场竞争激烈。华为以“成本领先优势”进入国际市场。而国际电信巨头研发成本高，遭遇华为低成本战略，迫使其与华为开展战略合作。在切入方式上，华为在全球建立了12个研究所，研发系统实行CMM管理；通过这些研发机构引入国际先进的人才、技术，为华为总部的产品开发提供支持与服务，实现全球同步开发。在欠发达国家，依靠低价格策略进行自主品牌的建设；在发达国家，积极寻求与国际电信巨头的战略合作；积极进行代工贴牌生产的商务洽谈。而在市场选择上，华为还是沿用国内市场所采用的“农村包围城市”的先易后难策略，首先瞄准的是深圳的近邻香港特区，俄罗斯和拉美市场也是华为首先瞄准的目标市场。华为从电信发展较薄弱的国家开始经营，步步为营、层层包围，进军东南亚、中东以及非洲等区域市场；同时，延伸至发达国家，积极开拓欧美市场。

在全球化战略布局方面，华为也是不遗余力，尽最大可能以最低的成本取得最大的效率，在人力资源方面和资本方面都有很大的投入。华为在全球建立了 9 个地区部和 90 个代表处及技术服务中心。华为在全球悄悄布下的研发、生产、销售办事处已达到 50 多个，海外市场员工 4000 多人，实现了全球化的研发、生产和销售。

“海外市场拒绝机会主义”，华为总裁任正非的这句话一直被华为奉为开拓国际市场的圭臬。也正因为如此，华为通过一系列的海外扩张计划，充分准备、积极应对全球化征程中的挑战和机遇，努力克服阻碍，紧抓机遇，在海外市场的争夺战中抢到一席之地，拥有一个很不错的开局，华为的国际化之路将越走越宽阔。

案例讨论题：

1. 华为采取全球化战略的背景、动因和角色定位，从这三个方面进行深入分析。

2. 华为在全球化过程中遇到哪些困难，华为是如何解决的?

3. 在全球化的过程中，华为是如何实现管理水平全球化和资本运作全球化的?

4. 华为国际化发展的过程对中国制造型企业走全球化道路有哪些经验和启示?

四、肯德基的中国化

2010年3月，肯德基宣布，在上海8家餐厅率先推出两款米饭类产品，如果销售情况理想，肯德基将在中国市场开卖米饭。

在亚洲市场连锁餐饮业多元化经营之风盛行，例如，麦当劳的麦咖啡（McCafe）、肯德基的米饭、星巴克的茶等。毫无疑问，快速适应中国文化，顺应中国顾客的消费习惯，在竞争激烈的市场中争夺份额，正是这种多元化经营的根本动力。

肯德基创建于1952年，是来自美国的著名连锁快餐厅，主要出售炸鸡、汉堡、薯条、汽水等美式快餐食品。1987年在北京前门开设中国第一家餐厅到现在，肯德基已在中国1100多个城市和乡镇开设了5000余家连锁餐厅，遍及中国所有省、市、自治区，是中国规模最大、发展最快的快餐连锁企业。

自进入中国以来，肯德基为避免文化上的“水土不服”，一直致力于本土化的经营策略。2003年春节，肯德基的山德士上校一改平日白色西装的经典形象，开始在中国170座城市的800余家分店统一换上大红色唐装，头戴瓜皮小帽迎接顾客。以“嫁接”方式植入的中国用餐模式成为肯德基的重要措施。肯德基全球产品比例为新开发的当地产品占20%，传统产品占80%，但是在中国，新产品的比例可能已经达到40%多，尤其是单独提供的营养早餐，全球都没有先例。但肯德基的中国门店敢对异国风味进行中式改良。2008年1月23日，肯德基在北京宣布早餐时段开始卖油条。并宣称，肯德基油条没有添加明矾，却同样保持了外酥内软的口感，其健康卖点击中了中式传统油条的“软肋”。肯德基针对如何替代传统制作工艺，不依靠添加剂明矾而使油条膨松香脆等问题，进行了长达一年多的研究测试，最终推出了安心油条，售价每根

3 元，将作为肯德基早餐的长期保留产品。肯德基所推出的“安心油条”，可谓成就了“花式粥 + 油条”的最佳搭档组合。而对于喜欢创新的消费者，“油条 + 牛奶”“油条 + 奶茶”，或是“油条 + 咖啡”等新鲜搭配，肯德基认为也是不错的尝试。

早在 2002 年肯德基就在中国部分城市的部分餐厅开始供应早餐，并于同年推出了两款极具中国本土特色的花式早餐粥——海鲜蛋花粥和香菇鸡肉粥，以此正式拉开了中国肯德基加快产品本土化的序幕。肯德基产品研发负责人表示，肯德基重视本土化产品研发由来已久，一方面是品种、口味，另一方面是营养、习惯搭配。只要消费者有需求，肯德基早餐还会陆续推出具有中国特色的本土化产品。此后每年，肯德基都会推出一定数量符合中国消费者口味需求的本土化食品。除海鲜蛋花粥和香菇鸡肉粥外，肯德基推出的中式快餐还包括北京鸡肉卷、芙蓉鲜蔬汤、皮蛋瘦肉粥、川辣嫩牛五方、安心油条、牛肉蛋花粥、培根蘑菇鸡肉饭、巧手麻婆鸡肉饭等近十种产品。

对于肯德基的中国化之路，消费者也有不同的反应。一网站就肯德基卖油条一事进行问卷调查，有 26.69% 的人支持肯德基的入乡随俗；56.04% 的人对此表示无所谓；17.28% 的网友认为肯德基应该保持美国快餐的风格，不应该卖中国油条。可见，文化差异也会给产品的销售带来挑战。与其说跨国公司善于发掘当地文化的商业价值，不如说是当地居民忽视了本土文化中的自生财富。

事实上，其他跨国餐饮企业也在中国入乡随俗。从推出的新品到食品包装、店堂布置，不约而同刮起一股浓浓的“中国风”。如星巴克在咖啡饮品中加入中国茶，推出两款拿铁红茶饮料；麦当劳从 2008 年 1 月 23 日至 2008 年 2 月 19 日，给消费者连派四周红包。消费者凡在麦当劳购买任意一款鸿运三堡套餐或者中号、大号套餐，就能得“堡堡有宝”红包，100% 中奖。奖品包括由交通银行提供的现金，周大福提供的“丰衣足食足金福鼠”，还有标有“ILOVEU”的吊坠。棒约翰为迎合中国消费者的习惯，也推出了为中国消费者量身定做的比萨。这款比萨外形有点像中国的黄金大饼，在普通比萨的馅料上再覆盖了一层面饼，还撒上了一层芝麻。

案例讨论题：

1. 肯德基为何会在中国卖米饭和油条？商业行为背后有着怎样的文化伦理？

2. 跨国连锁快餐企业为何在中国纷纷穿上“唐装”？对中餐业有何借鉴意义？

3. 中国企业在国际化过程中，如何适应跨文化差异？

五、

国际手机巨头在中国陷入商务伦理困境

2007年以来，苹果公司以其时尚设计和创新技术，推出了iPad、iPhone等一系列IT产品，引发市场销售的狂潮。每当苹果新品推出的时候，在纽约、伦敦、东京、上海，大批粉丝甚至会彻夜排队，希望最先拥有和尝试这些产品。但是，在时尚靓丽的外表后面，产品的制造过程却有着不为人知的另外一面：污染、侵犯和毒害。这一面深深隐藏在其秘不示人的供应链中，很少为公众所了解。当公司不断刷新销售纪录的同时，生产产品的员工却遭受有毒化学品的侵害，许多中毒工人还在身体和精神的双重折磨中煎熬，劳工权益和尊严受到损害，同时周边社区和环境也受到废水、废气的污染。2010年连续爆发12起跳楼事件的富士康，也是苹果最重要的供应商之一。10条年轻生命的消逝至今仍令人心痛。由于苹果公司极少透露其供应商的情况，除了公司发出的一条简略声明，称苹果公司对此感到“悲伤和难过”外，很难了解更多。

事实上，苹果公司在对社会责任的贡献方面也是负面新闻频出。环保组织曾在《苹果的另一面》报告中揭示了苹果公司在中国的供应链存在的污染和毒害。此后，达尔文自然求知社、自然之友、环友科技、公共环境研究中心、南京绿石5家环保组织经过7个月的调查，又发现多达27家疑似供应商出现了环境问题。公共环境研究中心的马军介绍，根据调查，多家零配件供应商造成了严重污染，部分已对环境造成了严重的损害。在武汉名幸电子厂区东侧，有一条白白的水渠连通南太子湖，被当地人称为“牛奶河”。经过第三方环保监测站检测，排水渠水体中含有重金属铜和镍，均为该厂的指标性污染物。排水渠附近南太子湖比长江中游主要湖泊底泥中铜的含量高出56～193倍。马军表示，环保组织掌握有这些企业为苹果供应商的证据，之所以称“疑似”供应商，是因为苹果公司从来没有公开过自己供应商的具体名单。苹果公司对于环保组织的指控，一直以“我们长期的政策就是不披露供应商”来回复。

而苹果公司触摸屏的重要供应商联建（中国）科技有限公司爆出的丑闻，更是将苹果公司推上风口浪尖。联建科技原本使用酒精擦拭显示屏，但是，2008 年 8 月联建公司突然要求员工用正己烷取代酒精擦拭手机显示屏。在调查中工人们讲到，正己烷挥发速度明显快于酒精，这样就提升了工作效率；同时，工人们提到，使用正己烷的擦拭效果明显优于酒精，可以大大降低次品率。然而，这种为利润做出突出贡献的“神奇”材料却是一种毒剂。相关研究显示，正己烷会导致多发性周围神经病，出现四肢“麻木”等感觉异常以及感觉障碍和运动障碍。

苹果公司在其《供应商行为准则》中称：确保供应链有安全的工作条件。然而，联建公司在使用有毒有害化学溶剂之前，违反中国《职业病防治法》规定，既没有向有关部门申报，也没有告知员工，更没有向工人发放有效的防护设备。据部分中毒员工回忆，苹果公司的代表也访问过联建，但他们从来没有告知工人们正己烷有毒有害以及该如何防护。在中毒工人们漫长而痛苦的治疗过程中，苹果公司没有和他们做过任何交流，更没有探望过他们中的任何一人。

一波未平，一波又起。2010 年，苹果公司最大的代工厂富士康连续发生 12 起跳楼自杀事件，在令世人震惊的同时，也令中国社会开始反思如何给予劳动者应有的尊重，而不是让工人们如同机器零件一般在生产线上靠长时间加班去赚取看不到未来的可怜薪酬。

媒体曾披露过一份富士康员工的工资单：时间是 2009 年 11 月；底薪 900 元；正常工作 21.75 天，平时加班 60.50 小时，报酬 469 元；周六日加班 75 小时，报酬 776 元；工资总额 2145 元。这名员工当月收入的 60% 靠超时加班挣得，总计 136 小时的加班，比劳动法规定的最高加班时间整整多出 100 小时！而深圳市人力资源和社会保障局对 5044 名富士康员工的抽查显示，72.5% 的员工超时加班，人均月超时加班 28.01 小时。微薄的薪酬使得苹果代工厂员工陷入两难——不加班挣钱和攒钱就没有未来，而天天超时加班却失去了现在，而且有限的加班费依然不能让他们看到未来。

而另一家供应商广达集团下属的达富电脑（常熟）有限公司对员工的

“非人化”规定，更是将苹果公司推入商业伦理的泥沼。对此，江苏省、苏州市总工会进行的实地调查证实了，该公司确实曾有强迫女工解除腰带进行物检的行为，调查组明确要求企业依法成立工会，切实维护职工合法权益。

案例讨论题：

1. 苹果公司对供应商的社会责任行为确有严格要求，供应商不执行，苹果真的有责任吗?

2. 案例中，苹果公司商务活动中遇到的伦理问题有哪些？在面对这些问题时，苹果公司是如何应对的?

3. 结合不道德行为的根源，讨论跨国公司在处理产品外包的供应商选择问题上应如何决策?

六、中国铝业煤炭进口合同实施受阻

蒙古国位于中国和俄罗斯之间，国土面积为156.65万平方公里，多沙漠戈壁，自然环境恶劣，是世界上国土面积第19大的国家，也是仅次于哈萨克斯坦的第二大内陆国家，人口约为300万人。20世纪90年代蒙古爆发民主革命，于1992年颁布新宪法，并实行多党制政治制度，经济体制上开始向市场经济过渡。

“一带一路”倡议的实施，为沿线国家的经济发展增添了新动力，未来铁路、公路、航空、港口等基础设施建设将成为经济发展的新突破点，基础设施建设和设备制造将进一步拉动钢铁、有色、建材等高耗能产品的需求，继而拉动对煤炭的需求，促进国际煤炭贸易的发展。但是，在媒体大宗商品国际贸易的合作过程中，出现了项目合同实施障碍、跨文化整合困难等贸易壁垒问题。

2013年1月28日，中国铝业总公司（以下简称“中铝”）旗下中铝国际贸易有限公司证实，2013年1月11日，蒙古ETT公司（Erdenes Tavan Tolgoi LLC，ETT）主动提出毁约，称其不再履行向中铝供应煤炭的协议，要求对双方2011年7月签订的“TT东区煤炭长期贸易协议”进行重新谈判，ETT要求提高煤炭供应价格、减少供货量。ETT为蒙古最大的国有煤矿企业，位于乌兰巴托。根据TT东区煤炭长期贸易协议，中铝向TT项目提供3.5亿美元贷款，后者以一定价格水平的煤炭偿还债务。

中铝希望蒙古新一届政府及ETT新管理层认真研读合同，一旦毁约，中铝必将诉诸法律。ETT单方面要求毁约，折射出蒙古外商投资环境向不友好的方向发展。据统计，大约有5000家中资企业在蒙古有业务，但仅有50家左右能获益。

2012年8月，蒙古组建新政府。随后，ETT公司管理层改组。这些变动直接导致了“TT 东区煤炭长期贸易协议”实施受阻。2012 年 10 月，中铝派代表前往蒙古拜访 ETT 新首席执行官亚西尔·巴苏里，亚西尔·巴苏里当即提出要求提前偿还中铝的预付款，并要求就修改合同进行谈判。亚西尔·巴苏里的要求遭到中铝拒绝。2013 年 1 月 11 日，ETT 停止向中铝供应煤炭，理由是公司遇到资金困境，无力支付今年的煤炭仓储费用。面对 ETT 提出来的困难，中铝表示愿意代 ETT 暂时支付仓储费用。中铝愿意在资金上帮助他们渡过困难，帮助 ETT 支付直接成本，但对方的回应只有一个：更改合同。ETT 还与包括中国神华在内的多家企业洽谈煤炭供货合约。ETT 想和神华集团合作，因为神华集团是中国最大的煤炭公司，神华有煤炭行业的基础设施，又是一家国际化的大公司，中国铝业则没有相关煤炭业务。

中铝与 EET 公司签署的煤炭供应协议仅占塔本陶勒盖煤田储量的不到 1%。该煤田能够提供超过 10 亿吨高质量炼焦煤，但是蒙古方面尚未确定其他区块的开发权归属。在被叫停的 2011 年招标过程中，中国的神华集团、美国博地能源公司以及一个蒙俄联合财团参与投标。除非蒙古新政府能够证明其欢迎外国投资者，不会试图修改或通过法律限制外资在煤矿中的占有率，外国企业才会真正参与蒙古资源开发。但现实并不乐观，蒙古政府要讨好民众，维持脆弱的联合政府，很难创造稳定的法律环境。

ETT 称“中铝只是利用蒙古政府急切需要融资的机会获得了这笔交易，从正常国际贸易的角度来说，令人难以接受”。对此，中铝认为，ETT 的确面临资金困难，但“TT 东区煤炭长期贸易协议”是经过近一年的谈判达成的，两国政府均对此协议进行了批准。中铝出于长期合作的目的，在 ETT 并不具备融资的情况下，中铝仍同意给 ETT 提供 3.5 亿美元的预付款。这一合约一方面满足了中铝战略转型的投资需求，另一方面也满足了蒙古政府发展 ETT 的要求，是一个双赢的商业合作。中铝还认为，即使在蒙古煤炭价格低迷的时候，“TT 东区煤炭长期贸易协议”依然使 ETT 有盈利的空间，因为 ETT 的煤炭资源质量并不算很好，按照双方签订的协议价格，加上物流费用，成本基本与当时国际市场大宗商品价格持平。因此，中铝敦促 ETT 继续履行合同，否则将追索 ETT“无上限的责任”。

自 2012 年下半年以来，蒙古的能源矿产投资环境越来越不利于外商投资。蒙古的外商投资法案规定蒙古本国资本必须持有战略性资产的51%，这一法规曾直接导致中铝放弃收购蒙古南戈壁煤矿。不仅中铝与蒙古的合约面临蒙古的单方面毁约，力拓集团在蒙古的奥尤陶勒盖铜金矿也面临蒙古的单方面更改合约。

在中国周边国家中，蒙古的投资环境较差。很多企业在蒙古的投资项目都很难运行或难以收回投资。特别是遇到政府变更或者合作企业的管理层变更时，投资风险剧增，投资合作协议面临更改或终止的风险。蒙古的腐败问题也比较严重，导致在蒙古的投资成本难以预测，投资无法获利。而且中蒙口岸贸易秩序也较混乱，中国企业之间存在无序竞争现象，经常出现内部相互压价导致合约生变。这些因素也是中铝与ETT长期合约的现实威胁。

中铝方面称，一旦ETT毁约，将产生严重的法律后果，更重要的是，将对蒙古公司在国际上的声誉带来负面影响，从而会在相当长的时期内阻碍蒙古吸引外资。

中蒙煤炭贸易作为两国经贸合作的重要内容之一，受到中国政府的高度重视。在中铝公司的积极推动下，经过谈判协商，蒙古ETT公司最终在2013年4月同意继续履行合约，不作任何更改，中铝恢复煤炭进口。

案例讨论题：

1. 蒙古ETT煤炭公司单方面撕毁合同的政治和经济原因是什么？

2. 中国企业在蒙古国投资收益非常低的主要原因是什么？

3. 中国企业在对外投资的过程中需要注意哪些主要的国家差异？

4. 当对外投资过程中遇到因国家差异造成的障碍的时候，可以通过怎样的方式解决？

七、吉利收购沃尔沃公司

吉利控股集团始建于1986年，1997年进入汽车行业，多年来专注实业，专注技术创新和人才培养，目前资产总值超过千亿元，入选中国企业500强和世界企业500强，并跻身中国汽车行业十强，是国家“创新型企业”和“国家汽车整车出口基地企业”。吉利也是中国汽车行业中唯一一家民营轿车生产经营企业。2010年3月28日，吉利收购沃尔沃轿车公司的最终股权收购协议在瑞典哥德堡签署，获得沃尔沃轿车公司100%的股权以及相关资产（包括知识产权）。

沃尔沃是瑞典著名汽车品牌，该品牌于1927年在瑞典哥德堡创建。沃尔沃集团是全球领先的商业运输及建筑设备制造商。1999年沃尔沃集团将旗下的沃尔沃轿车业务出售给美国福特汽车公司。沃尔沃现在分为沃尔沃汽车分公司（Volvo Car Corporation）和沃尔沃集团（Volvo Group）两家，沃尔沃汽车曾是沃尔沃集团的部分家用轿车业务，沃尔沃公司于2010年被吉利收购，2010年后由吉利控股。

但是，在并购后期进行公司整合时，公司内部出现了一些问题。由于不同的历史及教育因素，中西方文化的传承、思想、道德观念、约束力等方面存在着相当大的不同。吉利汽车诞生于中国，濡染的是以儒家思想为主的中国文化，强调集体主义，中庸、平和、谦逊，注重人际关系；而沃尔沃集团是典型的欧美文化，崇尚个人英雄主义，注重工作的同时也追求生活质量，严格按照规章制度办事。瑞典是一个社会整体生活层次差别不大的国家，从从政人员到普通公民之间的财富差距都不大，汽车已经不再是宣扬财富的奢侈品，而只是一种交通方式；而中国自古以来便极为尊崇权力分层制度，从校园中的尊师重道，再到社会上的尊老爱幼，都显示出了中国与瑞典对于社会层次制度的不同观念。

但是，中国与瑞典在一点上有类似的特质，就是强调团队合作，集体利益高于个人价值。但在这一点上，两个国家也略有不同。瑞典人提倡为集体考虑，不突出个人价值；中国人则更讲究个人利益对集体利益的服从，利益的最高点是国家利益。瑞典人善于接受生活及工作的变数，相对于中国人更能对不同的、不确定的事情进行接纳和做出改变，更加乐观开放；中国人在工作生活中更习惯于制定规则，一切事务按照规章制度来执行，将可考虑到的变数都纳入机制当中，不习惯于接受未知的变数。中国的员工喜欢安稳舒适且变动不多的工作环境；而瑞典人则更能接受生活及工作中的变动或者临时的调配。

中国与瑞典在文化上的差距，给吉利公司收购沃尔沃汽车后进行整合加大了难度。中国与瑞典两个国家员工的文化背景差异巨大、行事准则背道而驰等，都导致两个企业的员工在工作中体现出不同的行为特质，包括工作中任务的传达，这不是单纯的培训及会议能够解决的，这是根深蒂固的难题。但是，吉利公司却找到了适合自己的解决这些难题的方法。

吉利公司在并购沃尔沃以后并没有急于强调自身品牌的重要性，而是吸取了一些并购过程中由于文化差异而导致失败的公司的教训。吉利公司恢复了沃尔沃汽车品牌在中国市场的知名度以及品牌深度。吉利公司也深知在公司跨国并购的过程中人员整合的重要性。吉利公司在公司正常进行财务及人力等方面并购的同时，最大限度地保留了对方的文化，包括继续使用其在瑞典总部及比利时的生产基地，同时将其管理层的自主权放宽到最大等。在最大程度保留双方文化的同时，吉利公司还对两家公司不同的文化进行了有效的隔离。吉利汽车以及沃尔沃的品牌定位不同，市场层面也难以匹配，如果硬将两种品牌混为一谈，同时竞争相同的客户市场人群是非常失策的，吉利公司成功地将两种不同的汽车品牌概念在市场上分开，以便在不同的客户市场上进行竞争。

吉利公司能够对双方的文化及管理制度取精去粕。吉利公司明白自己和沃尔沃公司来自不同的文化背景，对于相同事物的看法也各有不同，吉利看到这一点，经常安排双方的人员出差学习，互相到对方国家进行探讨科研，学习对方的先进技术文化，为自己培养更多的人才打下基础；同时发挥沃尔沃品牌的号召性，在完成并购后，将全球其他著名汽车公司的职业经理人、管理者招至麾下，这些能带来先进思想的管理团队为日后沃尔沃的发展打下了坚实的基础。吉利公司在保留沃尔沃公司文化的同时又制定了相应的规章制度，吉利公司与沃尔沃公司的员工、管理层分别进行会谈，就公司的新型管理监控制度以及日常的销售激励制度进行磋商，制定了适用于并购后的沃尔沃公司员工的考核机制。

吉利公司能够直视与沃尔沃公司在文化方面的差异，并对并购后的公司及时做出调整，在并购几年后，吉利公司实现了整体销售量的提高，以及品牌价值和认知度的提高。

案例讨论题：

1. 吉利公司在收购沃尔沃公司时产生的文化差异问题主要体现在哪些方面?

2. 吉利公司收购沃尔沃公司取得成功的关键因素是什么?

3. 吉利公司在成功收购沃尔沃公司后是如何将由文化差异带来的风险降到最低的?

八、金砖国家合作机制下中俄经贸关系重点领域的发展

近年来俄罗斯地缘政治状况剧烈变化，同时俄罗斯与金砖国家其他成员国间良好的战略合作基础，驱使俄罗斯选择金砖国家合作机制，并将其作为外交政策的优先方向之一。俄罗斯资源丰富，经济较为依赖自然资源，超过1/4的国民生产总值是通过原材料出口或者初级加工产品再出口获得，出口结构为资源依赖型。经济的原材料导向是俄罗斯在全球经济中的重要特点。如果不实现结构性改革，俄罗斯经济在严重依赖国际原料市场的情况下，必然存在一定的经济风险。乌克兰危机后，西方国家的制裁使得外国投资者对俄罗斯的投资热情降低。面对如此僵局，俄罗斯在维护自身利益的基础上开始将目光转向东方，更加重视与金砖国家的经济往来与合作，以积极营造有利于自身发展的外部国际环境。

与此同时，中国提出的“一带一路”倡议，将其经济合作的主线贯穿中亚国家和俄罗斯等，将中国、俄罗斯与其他国家的经济发展紧密连接，这为俄罗斯对冲外部国际环境恶化的不利影响、再次融入全球经济提供了良好的契机，也与俄罗斯寻求新的对外合作经济增长点不谋而合，拓展了其与中国乃至其他金砖国家的合作深度与广度。经贸合作是金砖国家的核心议题之一。在金砖国家合作机制下，中俄两国的经济合作主要在能源、跨境电商贸易、货币金融合作方面展开。

在中俄能源合作发展方面，2014年5月21日，中国国家主席习近平和俄罗斯总统普京在上海共同见证中俄两国政府《中俄东线天然气合作项目备忘录》、中国石油天然气集团公司和俄罗斯天然气工业股份公司《中俄东线供气购销合同》的签署。根据合同，自2018年起，俄罗斯开始通过中俄天然气管道东线向中国供气，输气量逐年增长，最终达到每年380亿立方米，累计合同期30年。合同约定，主供气源地为俄罗斯东西伯利亚的伊尔库茨克州科维克金气田和萨哈共和国恰扬金气田，俄罗斯天然气工业股份公司负责气田开发、天然气处理厂和俄罗斯境内管道的建设，中石油负责中国境内输气管道和储气库等配套设施建设。

中俄东线天然气合作是在中俄两国政府直接指导和参与下，在双方企业长期共同努力下实现的，是中俄加强全面能源合作伙伴关系、深化全面战略协作伙伴关系的又一重要成果，充分体现了互信互利原则。双方将共同努力，落实相关工作，确保项目圆满实施。

中俄天然气合作将加快俄罗斯远东地区油气资源开发和经济社会发展，实现出口多元化。俄罗斯出口天然气的目标市场主要是中国东北、京津冀和长江三角洲地区，满足中国国内能源消费增长、改善大气环境、优化能源利用结构、促进能源进口多元化等需求，并带动沿线地区相关产业发展。

中俄跨境电商贸易方面，中国的电商平台拥有发展成熟且资金雄厚、日用品产能规模大，以及地缘上接近俄罗斯物流拓展便利等有利条件。俄罗斯拥有 1.42 亿人口，8000 万居民使用互联网，其中 4000 万人是网购用户，对各种日用消费品需求量大。俄罗斯消费者较成熟和理智，即使在收入水平有限的条件下，对商品质量的要求仍相对较高，更加追求性价比最大化，通过中国提供的跨境平台，俄罗斯消费者可以买到更多物美价廉的商品。在全球经济增速放缓的背景下，中俄跨境电商贸易迅猛发展，以每年 50% 的幅度增长。据俄罗斯电子贸易平台协会估计，2016 年中俄跨境电商贸易达到 25 亿美元。

中俄跨境电商贸易迅速发展也得益于两国政府的相关促进政策措施。中国政府的主要措施有：加强中俄两国海关、邮政和铁路部门间的合作，建立三方联系配合机制，支持通过中俄客运班列和中欧货运班列运输国际邮件，为国际邮件过境提供通关便利。同时加大两国银行和金融间的合作力度，大力推广人民币计价结算，有效防范进出口企业收付汇风险。俄罗斯政府的主要措施是：俄罗斯联邦海关对于进境包裹中一个月之内购买的、价值不超过 1000 欧元、重量不超过 21 公斤的商品实行免税。此外，两国海关还不断完善监管措施，以提高通关速度。这些措施在一定程度上改善了跨境电商贸易的经营环境，保障其高效运行，也促进了中国众多优质日用品进入俄罗斯市场。通过发展电子商务实现信息资源的有效整合，加强信息交流，使中俄双方充分了解两国经贸相关的政策法规，高效精准地了解彼此的市场动态和捕获市场需求。

中俄跨境电商快速发展的同时也存在着不容忽视的问题，比如，相关涉外法律法规制度的完善；汇率风险大，卢布贬值导致中国商品价格竞争力下降，影响中方的盈利水平；物流、支付及通关效率有待进一步完善；跨境电商人才短缺等。今后还要密切关注贸易保护的苗头，俄罗斯可能增税以保护本土企业。今后中俄双方应保持密切合作与交流，进一步促进贸易便利化，为跨境电商提供更广阔的发展空间。

在货币金融合作方面，中俄一直致力于推动国际货币金融体系改革。近年来，金砖国家经济与社会发展取得了巨大进步，在美国和欧洲经济低迷的背景下，金砖国家已成为拉动世界经济发展的重要力量。然而，金砖国家在国际货币金融体系中仍然处于较低的位置，缺少足够的话语权，金砖国家合作的重要目标是提升自身在国际货币金融体系中的地位，使之与自身快速增长的经济实力和综合国力相匹配。2013 年第五次金砖国家峰会上发表的《德班宣言》中提出，推进金砖国家开发银行和金砖国家外汇储备库建设。发展中国家获得的长期融资和外国直接投资特别是资本市场投资十分短缺，因而面临着基础设施建设的严峻挑战，严重阻碍了全球总需求的增长。实现为以金砖国家为首的新兴市场经济体和其他发展中国家的基础设施建设等项目筹措资金，维护金砖国家的金融稳定，创造有利于自身经济发展的环境以及推动全球金融体系的多极发展为期不远。金砖国家于2014 年7 月15 日发表《福塔莱萨宣言》宣布成立金砖国家新开发银行，初始资本为 1000 亿美元，由 5 个创始成员平均出资，总部设在中国上海。金砖银行的成立，预示着俄罗斯与金砖国家的合作正从一个“侧重经济治理、务虚为主”的对话论坛向“政治经济治理并重、务虚和务实相结合”的全方位协调机制转变。

由此可见，俄罗斯以加入金砖国家为契机，在经济方面通过不断拓展与深化同中国及金砖国家其他成员国在能源领域、经贸领域、货币金融领域的合作，达到促进本国经济发展、扩大全球影响力、推动国际货币金融体系改革、维护国家经济安全等目标。俄罗斯将通过与中国及金砖国家其他成员国间的广泛合作与交流，推进俄罗斯经济现代化发展进程，提升自身在全球经济体系中的地位与作用。

案例讨论题：

1. 中俄天然气项目对中国和俄罗斯的经济有怎样的影响？
2. 中俄跨境电商贸易存在哪些问题？
3. 金砖国家如何通过合作推动国际货币金融体系改革？

第三篇

国际贸易与投资

九、

新型国际分工与中美贸易

中国和美国是世界上经济总量排在前两位的国家，特别是中国加入WTO以后，中美之间的进出口贸易额大幅上升。中美两国成为世界上最大的贸易伙伴。2015年，中美贸易额达到5583.9亿美元，同比上升0.6%。

改革开放以来，中国的进出口贸易大幅增加，这对提升中国的国际影响力，促进国内经济的发展，以及促进产业结构调整和科技进步，都产生了巨大、深远的影响。随着中美经贸往来不断扩大，贸易不平衡也不断扩大。根据美国商务部与美国国际贸易委员会资料，1993年以来，美国对华贸易一直处于逆差状态，到2003年中国已经取代日本，成为美国最大的逆差来源国。2009年中美贸易逆差为1433.8亿美元，约占美国整个贸易逆差的1/3，2015年中美贸易逆差为2614亿美元。

就性质而言，中国对美国的贸易顺差主要是因中美双方的国际分工，而不是因中国实行保护主义政策所产生的。因此，仅用贸易逆差来作为衡量美国的全球销售额和企业竞争力的尺度是不合适的。

中美经济贸易摩擦问题较为突出，问题主要体现在贸易不平衡上。在1984~1992年，中国一直处于逆差地位，自1993年开始中国转为对美顺差。中国加入世界贸易组织后，对美顺差呈大幅上涨现象。根据美方统计，美国对中国贸易逆差在2000年上升至838亿美元，美国对华逆差在该年首次超过日本，中国成为美国最大贸易逆差来源国。中美贸易逆差的不断扩大已经成为中美两国发展正常经贸关系的阻碍，同时也成为美国对中国产品征收反补贴税、要求人民币升值、保护知识产权等问题的一个重要理由。根据商务部产业损害调查局统计数据，截至2015年，美国成为迄今为止对华发起贸易摩擦案件最多的国家之一。从近年来这一问题发展变化的角度看，其政治色彩要远远大于经济色彩，从而成为中美关系中的一个焦点。这种情况在美国已经引起一些不明真相的人和某些利益集团的不满和抨击。

但事实是，经济全球化背景下国际产业转移是中美贸易顺差的主要原因。20 世纪 90 年代初，中国开始大力发展加工贸易，中国对美贸易顺差开始出现。日本、韩国等东亚国家和地区，为了降低生产成本和规避与美国、欧盟的贸易摩擦，纷纷把与欧美贸易摩擦较大的产品组装工序转移到中国，在中国设立了大量的外资企业，中国从东亚等国和地区进口原材料、半成品，经过加工、组装后依赖原有的销售渠道再向美国、欧洲等传统市场出口。在对外贸易中，各国对进口商品的原产地认定以“实质性改变”为原则，加工产品的出口国就从上述国家和地区转移到了中国。中国现在对美国的贸易顺差很大程度上是从东亚其他国家和地区转移过来的，由于东亚其他国家和地区不断地把生产转移到中国来，中国对美国的出口只是取代了原先东亚和东南亚对美国的出口。因而，国际产业转移很大程度上造成了中美贸易顺差。美国产业结构内部调整使得与出口和国内消费相关的产业萎缩严重，非出口的服务业占主导。由于在生产性创新方面投资短缺，效率下降，加上人工成本高，美国在消费品制造方面已不具备生产优势，只能依赖大量进口，而中国为美国提供了大量的日常消费品。

另外，从造成中国对美贸易顺差的主要商品看，基本上属于中国与美国之间合理的国际分工，并由中国发挥两个比较优势——产业之间的比较优势与产业（行业）内部的比较优势所导致的结果。中美两国的贸易结构决定了双边贸易的不平衡。美国的优势在于资本技术密集型的高科技产业，而中国的比较优势主要是劳动密集型产品。由于美国从中国进口的商品以生活必需品为主，需求弹性较小，美国经济增长带动中国出口增加的效果显著，能有效扩大中国对美国的贸易顺差。中国从美国进口的商品以高科技产品为主，高科技产品的需求弹性较大，随着日本、韩国及中国高新技术的发展，美国的高科技替代产品逐渐增多，因此，随着中国经济的增长反而降低了对美国进口商品的依赖，从而也扩大了中美贸易顺差。

案例讨论题：

1. 作为世界上最大的发展中国家，中国有哪些独到的比较优势？

2. 国际贸易是国际分工的外在表现，如何从比较优势和要素禀赋理论来理解中美之间的国际分工？

3. 中国在加入世贸组织的承诺中对农业，服务业中的金融、电信等部门，工业中的汽车等部门适当地保留了开放市场的必要条件，请问这是为什么？

十、中国光伏产业应对欧美“双反”调查

困境中的中国光伏产业再度遭受连番打击，不但欧盟对华“反倾销”调查立案的过程有可能会加速，作为新兴市场的印度也有意跟随欧美的步伐，对中国光伏产品进行反倾销调查。多方围堵之下，中国光伏产业如何应对，成为关系光伏产业生死攸关的事情。

随着人们对化石能源供应危机的忧虑，以太阳能和风电等为代表的新能源受到追捧，并被誉为全球第三次产业革命的核心。欧盟和美国等相继出台多种举措支持光伏等新能源发展，欧盟甚至成为全球最大的光伏市场。但美国次贷危机及欧洲债务危机接连爆发，政府对光伏市场的补贴政策大幅削减，欧美光伏市场容量迅速萎缩，产能过剩矛盾开始凸显。因此，为阻挡迅速发展的中国光伏企业抢占国际市场，美国及欧盟部分企业不断申请对中国光伏产品进行反倾销调查。

2011 年 10 月，美国太阳能电池生产商 Solar World 要求对中国 75 家相关企业展开“双反”调查，当年美国即开始立案调查。2012 年 3 月 20 日，美国商务部反补贴初步裁定对中国输美太阳能电池产品征收 2.9%～4.73% 的反补贴税。2012 年 5 月 17 日，美国商务部反倾销初步裁定对从中国进口的光伏产品征收 31.14%～249.96% 的高额反倾销税。

美国商务部的反倾销初裁结果刚刚公布两个月之后，德国 Solar World 公司向欧盟正式提交申诉请求，要求对中国光伏企业进行反倾销调查。2013 年 6 月欧盟委员会宣布欧盟将对产自中国的太阳能电池板及关键器件征收 11.8% 的临时反倾销税，如果中欧双方未能在 8 月 6 日前达成解决方案，届时反倾销税率会升至 47.6%。

印度光伏电池制造商已多次向印度商会提交反倾销申诉书。但由于产品范围界定方面存在问题，印度政府已经让申诉方进行了多次修改。

受传统欧美市场及新兴印度市场的多方围堵，整个光伏产业负债增加严重，产业濒临生存困境。中国商务部等政府相关部门、新能源行业组织、光伏企业已经相继行动，采取多项措施应对危机。代表国内多晶硅产能80%的4家多晶硅企业——江苏中能硅业、江西赛维LDK光伏硅科技、洛阳中硅高科技、重庆大全新能源向中国商务部提出对来自欧盟的多晶硅实行“双反”调查，商务部已经受理此案。商务部认定，美国可再生能源产业的部分扶持政策及补贴措施存在贸易壁垒，根据《对外贸易壁垒调查规则》规定，商务部将依法采取相关措施，要求美方取消被调查措施中与世界贸易组织相关协定不符的内容，给予中国可再生能源产品公平待遇。

继中国机电产品进出口商会表达反对意见后，全国工商联新能源商会也在北京发布《中国工商界关于反对欧盟对华光伏反倾销立案的声明》(以下简称《声明》)。《声明》反对欧盟对华光伏产品反倾销立案，呼吁欧方尽快来华磋商，对话解决贸易争端。另外，33家光伏企业代表在参加国际半导体设备与材料协会中国光伏标准技术委员会2012年第三次会议时也商议了脱困之术。

中国在2011年从德国进口多晶硅材料的金额是7.64亿美元，占中国进口同类产品份额的20%，从德国进口光伏电池生产用的银浆原料的金额达到了3.6亿美元。中国累计从海外采购了约400亿元的光伏电池生产设备，其中从德国、瑞士等欧洲国家进口占到了45%。欧盟若对中国光伏产品设限，直接损害来自欧盟的进口。在德国默克尔总理率团访华并出席第二轮中德政府磋商期间，随访的德国环境部长彼得·阿尔特迈亚主动谈及欧盟对华光伏产品贸易救济调查事宜。默克尔总理虽不会谈及企业纠纷，但将敦促双方为德中企业在各自国家创造公平的竞争环境。

案例讨论题：

1. 案例提到的太阳能企业Solar World被看作中国光伏产品遭遇多方贸易壁垒的始作俑者，其不单发动了美国对中国光伏产品的“双反”调查，继而又在欧盟引发了新一轮的起诉，请调查研究这家企业的相关背景和事件起因。

2. 在美国商务部裁定中国光伏产品存在倾销和补贴后，中国同时面临来自于欧盟以及印度的“双反”调查，这样的指控是否合理？中国政府是否对该行业进行了补贴？如何看待中国光伏企业对外倾销的嫌疑？

3. 在美国裁定中国光伏产品存在倾销和补贴后，欧盟又对中国光伏产品提出了反倾销的申诉，一旦立案就会成为欧盟史上涉案金额最大的反倾销案件，请分别说明中国光伏产品频遭国际堵截的原因。

4. 面对国际贸易保护主义的抬头，中国光伏企业面临着来自各方的压力，中国企业应该如何应对？

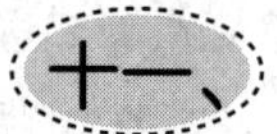

十一、中国与东盟的双边贸易发展

20 世纪 90 年代以来，区域经济一体化逐渐发展成为世界贸易合作的潮流，被大多数国家视为推动经济发展的新动力。而中国作为世界上最大的发展中国家，经过近 40 年的改革开放，经济实力已具备相当规模，已经成为世界上第二大经济体，同世界各国都有着密切地经贸合作。因此，为了维护中国的对外利益，推动对外经济持续快速发展，加入区域经济一体化组织是非常必要的。中国—东盟自由贸易区（CAFTA）是中国加入的第一个区域经济一体化组织，该组织包括 11 个国家，近 20 亿人口，是世界上包含人口最多的自贸区，也是发展中国家间最大的区域经济一体化组织。2010 年中国—东盟自由贸易区正式建成，标志着中国与东盟各国在商品贸易自由化的道路上迈出了重要一步。

2010 年中国—东盟自由贸易区建成以来，中国—东盟贸易增长迅速，2015 年中国与东盟贸易额达 4721. 6 亿美元。中国对东盟出口 2774. 7 亿美元，同比增长 2. 0%；自东盟进口 1946. 8 亿美元，同比下降 6. 5%，中方顺差达 827. 9 亿美元，是 2014 年顺差 637. 5 亿美元的 1. 3 倍。2015 年中国对东盟的贸易占中国对外贸易总额的比重为 11. 9%，比 2014 年（11. 2%）上升 0. 7 个百分点。自 2011 年以来，东盟连续保持作为欧盟、美国之后中国第三大贸易伙伴的地位，双方贸易占同期中国进出口总额的比重（贸易依存度）在近几年均维持在 10% 左右，中国则保持着东盟第一大贸易伙伴的地位。

2015 年，中国在东盟十国中的前三大贸易伙伴分别是：马来西亚、越南和新加坡。其中，马来西亚双边贸易额为 973. 12 亿美元，同比下降 4. 6%；越南双边贸易额为 959. 76 亿美元，同比增长 14. 9%；新加坡双边贸易额为 795. 59 亿美元，同比下降 0. 1%。

中国—东盟自由贸易区是世界上人口最多的由发展中国家组成的最大自由贸易区，和欧盟（European Union）、北美自由贸易区（NAFTA）并称世界上三大区域经济合作区。建立中国—东盟自由贸易区的设想是2000年11月在新加坡召开的中国与东盟领导人会议期间提出的。领导人会晤期间，针对东盟方面关注中国加入WTO对东盟的影响，朱镕基总理提议就中国和东盟之间建立自由贸易区的可行性进行研究。根据领导人的指示，成立了中国—东盟经济合作专家组。经过研究，专家组向领导人提出了建立中国—东盟紧密经济伙伴关系的建议，其中包括建立中国—东盟自由贸易区。2001年11月6日在文莱举行的第5次中国与东盟领导人会议上，双方就未来10年内建立中国—东盟自由贸易区达成了共识。2002年11月4日在出席第6次中国与东盟领导人会议后，中国国务院总理朱镕基和东盟10国领导人签署了《中国—东盟全面经济合作框架协议》，决定到2010年建成中国—东盟自由贸易区。此框架协议是中国与东盟全面经济合作的里程碑，它的签署标志着中国与东盟的经贸合作进入崭新的历史阶段。该协议规定，关于建立自由贸易区的正式谈判在2003年启动，2004年6月结束。2005年1月正式启动双方的关税减让计划。

中国—东盟自由贸易区于2010年1月1日正式建成。这是一个惠及近20亿人口、国民生产总值达6万亿美元、贸易额达4.5千亿美元的自由贸易区。中国—东盟自由贸易区的建立是国际经济合作的一个新的尝试，必将丰富区域经济合作的内涵。在探索性建设过程中，借鉴了欧盟和北美自由贸易区以及亚太经济合作组织的成功经验。自贸区的建立结合了区域经济的特点，做出了适宜中国与东盟现实的最佳选择。自贸区建立后，双方对超过90%的产品实行零关税。中国对东盟的平均关税从9.8%降到0.1%，东盟六个老成员国对中国的平均关税从12.8%降到0.6%。关税水平的大幅降低有力地推动了双边贸易的快速增长。

中国—东盟自贸区建成后，双边贸易发展迅速。2003年双边的贸易额还不到800亿美元，当时双方领导人商定使双边贸易额到2005年达到1000亿美元，结果提前1年，在2004年就突破了1000亿美元；双方领导人又商定将双边贸易额到2010年推到2000亿美元，结果提前3年，到2007年突破了2000亿美元。双边贸易额在2008年达到新高后，遇到金融危机，在2009年仍然保持在2000亿美元以上。2010年中国—东盟自贸区建成后的降税效应，把双边贸易额推到了一个新的高点，接近3000亿美元；2011年，双边贸易额达3623.3亿美元，创历史新高。其中，中国出口1698.6亿美元，同比增长22.9%；中国进口1924.7亿美元，同比增长24.7%。在东盟十国中，马来西亚、泰国、印度尼西亚和新加坡是中国与东盟贸易中的前四大进口来源地，2011年中国自上述4国进口额分别达到620.2亿美元、390.4亿美元、313.2亿美元和277.6亿美元，合计占中国自东盟进口总额的83.2%，同比分别增长23.1%、17.6%、50.9%和12.9%。

纵向观察，中国与东盟的贸易总额从1991年双方建立对话伙伴关系时的84亿美元、2002年签署《全面经济合作框架协议》时的548亿美元增加到2015年的4721.6亿美元，年平均增速为18.3%。2015年，中国与东盟的双边贸易总额出现了微小的降幅。其间，除1998年的亚洲金融危机、2008年世界性的金融危机以及2015年中国严峻的经济形势使区域贸易负增长之外，中国与东盟贸易总额均以较高速度增长。中国与东盟常年处在严重的贸易逆差状态，贸易逆差大约占双边贸易额的15%左右，在个别年份，中国—东盟贸易逆差甚至超过了20%。1996~2011年，中方对东盟都是处于贸易逆差的状态。这种中方对东盟常年逆差的状况，到2012年才得以改变，2012年双边贸易额是4001.5亿美元，其中中方出口2042.5亿美元，进口是1958.9亿美元，贸易顺差为85亿美元，占双边贸易额的2%。在2013年，这种趋势继续扩大，贸易顺差为444.8亿美元，占双边贸易总额的10%。自1991年以来中国的逆差居多，2011年更是达到了226.9亿美元，然而，自2012年以来，中国的贸易差额却急转为顺差，2015年中国顺差创下了827.9亿美元的新高。

中国与东盟之间的经贸关系正面临着进一步发展的有利条件。自贸协议的签订为双方存在的贸易投资等制度障碍扫清了道路。按照协议规定，中国近年来大幅度降低了关税，减少并取消非关税壁垒。中国的市场进一步开放，尤其是服务贸易领域的开放也将为东盟投资者提供广阔的商机。东盟已经连续10年成为中国第五大贸易伙伴，是中国在发展中国家中最大的贸易伙伴，而且双边贸易增长速度远远高于其他主要贸易伙伴。

中国与东盟签署的《中国—东盟全面经济合作框架协议》，更是中国与东盟关系发展中的里程碑。随着中国与东盟自由贸易区的建立，双方的经贸合作目标将更加明确，合作前景将更加广阔。

案例讨论题：

1. 简述中国—东盟自由贸易区的发展历程及现状分析。
2. 阐述中国与东盟建立自由贸易区的动机。
3. 分析企业在中国—东盟自由贸易区的投资环境。
4. 简述中国—东盟自由贸易区带给中国企业的机遇和挑战。

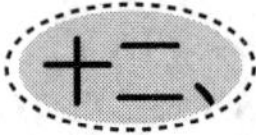

十二、红豆集团投资柬埔寨西港特区

纺织业是中国的传统支柱产业。随着中国经济的发展，纺织业出现产能过剩的情况，所面临的竞争压力越来越大，急需降低成本，转移剩余的生产能力。而国家商务部对企业投资建设的合作项目进行了宏观指导，在国别和产业指引、资本投资便利化、境外投资保障等方面提供支持，给一些境外投资的企业提供了便利和优惠。

红豆集团是纺织业的代表企业，总部在江苏无锡，以创民族品牌为己任，以优异的销售业绩稳居中国服装业百强亚军，成为集科研开发、生产制造、全球贸易于一体的大型民营企业集团。2015 年 6 月，世界品牌实验室公布了中国 500 个最具价值品牌排行榜，红豆品牌跻身百强。2016 年 8 月，红豆集团在“2016 中国企业 500 强”中排名第 265 位。

早在 2007 年，红豆集团积极响应国家“走出去”的号召，在中国商务部、财政部等国家部委及江苏省无锡市等各级政府部门的大力支持下，联合几家无锡企业与一家柬埔寨企业投资西港特区。红豆集团全权负责园区管理，将中方的管理能力和本地工人相结合，工厂中方管理人员不到 30 人，本地员工近 700 人。

2010 年，红豆集团旗下的红豆国际制衣入驻西港特区。2016 年，红豆制衣工厂开设两条西裤、两条西服共四条生产流水线，月产量分别达 30000 条和 55000 件。产品都已经通过西班牙、法国、意大利等国家的有关认证，客户订单绝大部分来自欧洲。

柬埔寨西哈努克港经济特区是江苏太湖柬埔寨国际经济合作区投资有限公司联合柬埔寨国际投资开发集团有限公司共同开发的经济特区。该特区总规划面积 11.13 平方千米，以纺织服装、五金机械、轻工家电等为主导产业，同时集出口加工区、商贸区、生活区于一体。首期特区已形成

5.28 平方千米区域的建设规模，建有 85 栋厂房，并建设了集办公、居住、餐饮和文化娱乐等多种服务功能于一体的综合服务中心大楼，柬籍员工宿舍，集贸市场，生活服务区等。另外，西港特区的建设和发展带动了周边经济的发展。莫德朗乡是紧邻西港特区的一个乡镇，这个贫困小镇正在迅速繁荣崛起。原先的泥泞小路变成了水泥公路，越来越多的新房拔地而起。莫德朗乡在特区工作的工人数占总人口的 30% 以上，村民在特区工作后，大大提高了收入水平。同时，特区的发展也给村民带来了多重商机，很多村民向工人出租宿舍或开小商店，拓宽了收入来源，成为当地“先富起来”的人。

红豆集团积极开拓海外市场、开展跨国投资是时代的要求，是企业发展的需要。中国经济发展进入新常态，积极推进国际产能合作，从本土向跨区域向境外发展，对民营企业而言，有利于企业不断提升技术、质量和服务水平，增强核心竞争力。企业要想国际化，在国际市场获得更多蛋糕，就不能限于单纯的产品走出去，必须要资本、品牌、市场、管理、人才等全面走出去，这是企业国际化发展的必由之路。

红豆集团在柬埔寨投资建厂可以获得更多的廉价劳动力。虽然中国人口众多，劳动力资源丰富，但是，随着中国经济的发展和高等教育的普及，劳动力成本提高了。而柬埔寨的经济发展仍在起步阶段，劳动力资源丰富，工资成本低。柬埔寨的年轻人口（10～35 岁）超过总人口的一半，为 750 万人，每年的增长率为 2.7%，还向马来西亚、韩国等国输送劳务，其劳动力就业领域主要分布在农业、成衣业、服务业。红豆集团在西港特区可以充分利用当地充裕、便宜的劳动力，获得生产成本上的优势。

通过海外投资，红豆集团转移了剩余生产能力，开拓了国际市场。纺织制衣业属于劳动密集型产业，进行标准化批量规模生产。中国市场对服装类的产品需求趋于饱和，该行业处在产品周期的成熟阶段。近年来，中国劳动力成本和物价上升，导致行业成本上升。企业也需要开拓其他的市场，转移国内剩余产能。此外，中国相对于柬埔寨的纺织制衣业来说，存在技术上的优势。这就使一部分企业家们寻找劳动力资源丰富密集、市场广阔的地方，以进一步降低成本，增强竞争力，获得更多的利润。

红豆集团在柬埔寨建厂后获得了多方面的优惠和优势。柬埔寨劳动力成本低，人工成本是每人每月 200 美元左右，折算成人民币约 1362 元，远远低于中国的工资水平。企业还获得了税收上的优惠，柬埔寨对进入特区的企业给予一系列税收优惠政策，例如免征收进出口关税、增值税等。红豆集团在西港特区生产的产品销往欧美国家，利用欧美国家的普惠制，能够获得更多的成本优势和更加广阔的消费市场，从而大大地提升了红豆集团的利润空间。

红豆集团将中国的纺织制衣技术和设备带入柬埔寨，继续延长该行业的生命周期，同时充分利用当地的一系列优惠政策，提高生产能力，减少成本，增加利润。

案例讨论题：

1. 红豆集团在西港特区的生产建设体现了哪些贸易理论？
2. 红豆集团在西港特区的生产建设对柬埔寨有哪些好处？
3. 哪些因素会影响中国企业继续进入西港特区？

十三、中国禽肉类产品出口欧盟

养禽业是中国畜牧业发展最早，产业化、规模化程度最高的产业，具有出口的价格优势。欧盟是中国出口禽肉类产品的主要贸易伙伴，但是早在2002年，欧盟筑起肉产品贸易的技术壁垒，以中国向其出口的部分动物源性食品中含有危害人体生命健康的残留素为由，除肠衣和公海捕获直接运抵欧盟市场的鱼类产品外，禁止中国的动物源性产品出口至欧盟。在2004年，更是由于禽流感的问题，中国禽肉熟制品遭受欧盟禁令。出口欧盟的市场被封，对中国的禽肉制品行业来说，既是一个沉重的打击，更是一个步入新生的重大转机。为了以全新的形象尽早重返欧盟市场，中国有关部门大量收集并翻译欧盟相关的法律法规及进口禽肉产品的卫生要求，对出口的企业从肉禽饲养、屠宰、熟制加工等环节严格按欧盟法规要求进行认真指导。禽肉出口企业也按照欧盟的要求和检验检疫的指导，投入大量资金，建立了全过程标准化体系和质量追溯体系，不断提升安全质量管理水平。经过政府和企业的通力合作，终于在2008年，欧盟批准其成员国恢复进口来自中国生产的熟制禽肉产品。

开禁之后，中国依然会面临许多问题，其中最值得注意的是欧盟在2009年提出的修改鹅肝或鸭肝制品、熟制鸡肉、熟制鸭肉等8个税号禽肉产品的关税减让表，并引入配额管理。根据GATT1994第28条第1款规定，如某一成员提出修改某项减让承诺，该成员需要与以下成员就补偿问题进行谈判：一是拥有最初谈判权的成员，二是具有主要供应利益的成员。此外，该成员还需要和在此项减让中具有实质利益的任何其他成员进行磋商。欧盟依照前三年的产品进口情况确定了与巴西、泰国等主要供应方进行谈判，但是中国却不在其中，因为当时中国正被欧盟封关。谈判结果却是将96%的低关税配额分配给巴西和泰国，中国与其他国家（地区）

只能分享其余4%的配额，超出配额部分需要缴纳高额关税。2013年开始发布和实施具体条例，这对于中国来说可以算是晴天霹雳。条例生效后，相当于欧盟再次利用配额管理对中国实行软“封关”。由于欧盟关税调整幅度过大，中国有关禽肉产品出口的价格优势就不存在了，一些客户可能不再购买中国的产品。

这意味着，中国的禽肉类产品会被巴西和泰国更具比较优势的产品挤出市场，中国辛辛苦苦再次打开的欧盟禽肉类产品的市场将会再次失去，之前所有相关企业和政府所做出的投入和付出将会付诸东流。欧盟的这一决定，不仅损害了中国国内相关企业的出口利益、妨碍了国内禽肉类行业的发展，而且还严重影响到中国相关行业从业人员的就业。禽肉产业的下游供应商都是农民，中国企业受到欧盟配额的限制，出口减少必将意味着减少国内的下游供应商的订单，从而导致农民不得不放弃养殖业而另谋生路。

2015年4月8日，中国向WTO秘书处提出与欧盟的磋商申请，涉及欧盟对部分家禽肉制品采取的关税配额管理措施，但磋商无果。中国为维护在世贸组织中的正常贸易利益，应国内禽肉产业的要求，经过和食品土畜进出口商会协商，决定在2015年6月19日，在WTO争端解决机构例会上，就欧盟影响部分禽肉产品关税减让的措施案（DS492）首次提出成立专家组的申请。中国提出理由是：受到欧盟修改部分禽肉产品关税减让措施的影响，其出口商目前面临高税率的困境，而且订单数量也在急剧减少，出口销售量大幅下降，市场份额削减严重。2015年5月，中国与欧盟就该争端进行了磋商，但未达成解决共识，中方随后向争端解决机构提出成立专家组的申请。欧盟认为，基于相关的进口统计，中国并没有实质性供应利益，也没有在90日内证明其作为大量供应商的利益。欧盟认为其做法遵循了恰当的程序。鉴于欧盟已于2015年5月与中国就该争端举行了磋商，欧盟认为中国此次提出成立专家组的申请过早，因此不同意设立专家组。据此，WTO争端解决机构将推迟就该案设立专家组。2015年7月20日，在争端解决机构例会上，WTO就中国诉欧盟影响部分禽肉产品的关税减让措施案（DS492）做出成立专家组的决定。在此次争端解决机构例会上，中国第二次就欧盟影响部分禽肉产品的关税减让措施案提出成立专家组的申请，中国希望通过争端解决程序，欧盟能够调整其受争议的相关措施。对此，欧盟表示，其措施符合 WTO 协定的规定，并已做好准备在专家组程序中做出抗辩。巴西、俄罗斯和美国将作为第三方参加该案专家组程序。

案例讨论题：

1. 欧盟先后用了哪些措施限制进口中国的禽肉类产品？欧盟采取这些措施的理由是什么？

2. 欧盟如何利用关税配额对中国实行软“封关”？

3. 为什么在欧盟的配额中中国与其他国家（地区）只能分享4%？欧盟的这一规定是合理的吗？

十四、蚂蚁金服投资印度“支付宝”Paytm

支付宝的母公司蚂蚁金服集团正式成立于2014年10月，在2016年4月完成了B轮45亿美元的融资，估值达到600亿美元。作为三大战略重点之一，蚂蚁金服从不掩饰自己在国际化方面的雄心，其总裁井贤栋在首届FTCC峰会上就表示未来四年内蚂蚁金服的用户50%在海外，50%在国内；未来9年，可以服务全球20亿消费者。事实上，从2015年开始，蚂蚁金服的国际化布局就已经明显提速。作为阿里巴巴集团的新锐力量，蚂蚁金服的业务覆盖了支付、理财、银行、保险、贷款、征信等泛金融板块。在海外，蚂蚁金服虽然业务不像国内那么普及，但还是频频传出收购的消息。

蚂蚁金服的境外布局主要围绕两大方向：一是支付宝，吸引中国出境游用户和海外华人在欧亚两地用支付宝购物；二是投资银行、保险和支付机构等。

在亚洲，支付宝还与泰国以及新加坡企业展开合作；在欧洲，支付宝与德国支付服务供应商Concardis以及珠宝品牌Wempe合作；此前，德国支付技术服务提供商WireCard也与支付宝展开了一系列的业务合作。蚂蚁金服在境外布局的第二大方向主要通过投资合作来实现。其投资布局的方向是保险类，实现通过互联网方式打造标准化、场景化的保险业务。

2016年，蚂蚁金服又通过阿里巴巴与安盛集团达成战略合作，以通过阿里巴巴全球电商生态系统来拓展安盛保险产品及服务的商业机会。另一投资方向是与支付强相关的公司，比如，在技术层面，蚂蚁金服投资了新加坡移动安全和加密技术公司V-Key，以加强自身产品的安全性。

在印度市场，蚂蚁金服大手笔投资了印度最大的支付平台Paytm及其母公司One97 Communications。Paytm全称“Pay Through Mobile”，是印度最大的移动互联网公司之一 One97 Communications 旗下的消费者品牌。2010 年成立之初，Paytm 只是一个手机预付网站；2014 年，Paytm 进入了印度的互联网金融领域并推出电子钱包，并提供电商服务给消费者。Paytm 已获得印度央行发放的首批支付银行牌照，允许其在印度开展支付、储蓄、汇款、转账等银行业务，为印度中小企业、低收入人群提供费率更低的在线金融服务。

2015 年年初，蚂蚁金服对 Paytm 进行了第一轮投资；2015 年 9 月，蚂蚁金服与阿里巴巴一起向 Paytm 进行了第二轮投资。两轮注资加上一系列在业务上的深度交流和合作，使 Paytm 正式成为蚂蚁金服的战略合作伙伴。从那时开始，双方的合作进入了快车道。两轮投资能助力蚂蚁金服抢占印度普惠金融的先机。入股 Paytm 后，Paytm 用户数在一年中从 2000 多万升到 1.5 亿，成为世界第四大电子钱包，也被称为“印度版支付宝”。

此后，蚂蚁金服有一支至少 20 人的跨部门团队每周飞赴在印度德里卫星城 Noida 的 Paytm 总部，从系统架构改造到风控体系搭建再到数据能力，全方位帮助 Paytm 提升平台能力。从技术、风控、产品到运营等各个环节，都和 Paytm 团队一起展开日常工作。同时，Paytm 也不断派出大量人员到杭州的蚂蚁金服总部，从业务内容到企业文化进行全面的学习。例如，蚂蚁金服刚刚参股时，Paytm 的风控架构只有十多条规则，经常遇到网络欺诈而束手无措，系统日常也只能承载一两万笔交易。经过一年的时间，Paytm 系统从百万级的处理能力，发展成可以承载亿级处理能力的架构；风险率从当初的百分之几，降到了万分之一。2015 年年初，在 Paytm 刚开始跟蚂蚁金服合作时，用户数大约是在两千万人左右，仅仅一年半之后，其用户数目已经翻了 6 倍，现在，Paytm 的用户已经达到了 1.4 亿，市场占有率比其他所有对手总和的三倍还多，来自线下的场景支付迅速达到了日均交易量的 50%。

拿蚂蚁金服和 Paytm 来说，二者在资本、底层技术、商业模式、企业文化等方面都有着深度的合作，这种协同效应是巨大的双赢。未来，双方计划将支付网络打通，这就意味着，支付宝的用户去印度可以刷 Paytm 的二维码，Paytm 的用户到中国乃至全世界，都可以刷支付宝的二维码，两国的人口数加总占世界人口数目接近 40%，这其中无疑蕴含着巨大的机会。

印度贫困人口的消费升级也将展现巨大的需求潜力。比如，目前，Paytm 用户中有一半生活在印度前十大城市，还有一半来自二线及以下城市和农村地区。就近期表现来看，二线及以下城市和农村地区用户数字增幅极快，体现了非常好的成长性。

蚂蚁金服目前已在美国、新加坡、韩国、英国、卢森堡和澳大利亚六个国家设立了分支机构，在东南亚、南亚地区，收购了泰国支付公司 Ascend Money 20% 的股份，投资 Paytm 母公司 One97 Communications，以及投资印度电子钱包 Paytm，进一步推进了蚂蚁金服的国际化进程。

国际化是中国互联网发展的必然选择，但国际化之路并不如想象中的平坦，百度折戟日本，微信在东南亚的尴尬处境等均是前车之鉴。在这场浩大的征途中，蚂蚁金服除了利用自己在中国积累下来的经验之外，虽然也在探索一些新的招数，如引进前高盛资深合伙人道格拉斯·费根等加强其国际化团队建设，但面对国际市场的复杂性以及各国政策的不确定性，未来的路，对蚂蚁金服而言，仍充满巨大考验。

案例讨论题：

1. 蚂蚁金服向海外扩张的动机是什么？

2. 为什么阿里巴巴对外扩张初期选择东南亚、南亚国家作为投资重点？

3. 为什么阿里巴巴选择入股当地企业的方式，而不是在当地建立独资企业或者其他方式进入外国市场？

4. 阿里巴巴在投资印度 Paytm 时有哪些优势？

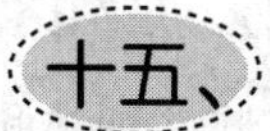

十五、中泰“蔬菜换石油计划”

中国和泰国于2008年6月，在商务部、云南省政府的提议和推动下，签订了一项《中泰蔬菜换成品油易货贸易总的框架协议》的贸易协议，该项目涉及云南西双版纳石化集团、云南欣农科技公司和泰国国家石油公司，旨在把云南的土豆、西红柿、荷兰豆等名优蔬菜运到泰国，然后等价换回泰国的成品油、热带水果和海鲜。该计划的产生可以说是非常符合云南同东南亚国家进行贸易的实际情况，也顺应了中国—东盟自贸区的建立和国家将云南发展成为面向东南亚开放的“桥头堡”的战略决策。协议中约定，由中方每年提供大约30万吨、总价值约1亿美元的蔬菜出口到泰国；作为交换，泰方每年向中国出口15万~20万吨同等价值的成品油。

该项目启动后，不仅有利于缓解云南成品油供应长期紧张的问题，而且还有利于打造“云菜”品牌，带动农民增收，可带动约10万农户生产，解决15万~20万亩蔬菜的销售问题，每亩可增收1000元。扩大城乡就业，蔬菜种植、加工环节可带动8万人，蔬菜、成品油的运输、物流、销售、服务等相关环节可带动就业7000余人。

对泰国来说，泰国每日蔬菜需求量在1.4万吨，一年近500万吨。而目前中国蔬菜在曼谷市场每日只有近百吨的销量，市场份额很小。由于泰国属于亚热带气候，不易种植蔬菜，故中泰蔬菜贸易前景非常广阔。

但是，该计划在执行的时候遇到许多以前没碰到过的问题。“蔬菜换石油计划”的执行主要有两种运输方式：其中，陆路运输是由泰国公司把油分批，按约定的时间，通过昆曼公路用油罐车拉到中国磨憨口岸，再由欣农公司利用和中石化的合作关系，将其供应给云南蔬菜流通行业协会的会员单位及种植基地、农产品运输户，以及广大农村地区；海运模式则是由PTT公司负责联系油轮，从泰国曼谷港出境，运到广东湛江入境，再由欣农公司把成品油运回来。

2009 年 6 月，因为连接两地的昆曼大道“通而不畅”，蔬菜换石油项目被搁置。从昆明到曼谷全程需要办理 4 次通关手续，经过 3 个国家，而办理通关手续的时间长短不一，收费种类和收费标准也不一样。20 多个小时的路程，即便是司机轮班倒，通关顺利，也至少需要两三天。很多企业因为成本高，宁愿绕道。

2010 年，由于泰国国内政治局势不稳定，泰国政府人员发生很大的变动，蔬菜换石油项目受到很大的影响。

在该项目达成协议的第二个年头，即 2010 年年初，在滇泰双方多部门的合力推动下，蔬菜换石油项目首次以陆路运输方式成功进口成品油。但因陆路运输仍存在诸多亟待解决的问题，至此又进入了程序协调中。2010 年“蔬菜换石油”项目实现了蔬菜出口 13 亿元，换回了 16 万吨泰国的成品油。

“蔬菜换石油”的成品油进口流程有陆运和海运两种方式。在欣农公司看来，海运方式尽管运量巨大，但由于票据、对外付汇等一系列问题，给该项目进展造成阻碍。

但有关决策层仍建议蔬菜换石油的成品油进口采用以海运为主，陆路为辅的进口模式。而此时，时间已进入 2012 年 10 月。云南省对此高度重视，省商务厅针对上述问题组织多个职能部门，包括国家相关部委在滇的派驻机构等一起召开联席会议，商讨、协调相关问题。在这次会议后的次月，即 2012 年 11 月，两艘设计运能力为 250 吨的油轮，经澜沧江湄公河，历时 22 天的水运过程，顺利运抵西双版纳州景洪市关累码头。

2013 年 3 月，云南省东南亚南亚经贸合作发展联合会召开了昆曼经济走廊“蔬菜换石油”项目商务访问团出访活动筹备会。此次出访，项目不仅与泰总理府和 PTT 公司取得了一致的认识，而且 PTT 公司还和云南联盟国际科技公司、云南欣农科技公司签订了 100 万吨的成品油购销协议，其中，柴油 80 万吨、汽油 20 万吨，泰国按照中国提供的成品油标准生产和供应，采取海运和多式联运方式运输。

为保障项目的进行，PTT 公司下属的运输公司还专门建立了为中泰贸易服务的跨国物流车队，并新购 100 辆沃尔沃运油车，中方也已新购 100 辆高标准拖头蔬菜冷藏车投入到这项工作中。

截至2014年6月，中国已经从泰国购进了4万吨柴油，这意味着商务部批准的8万吨“蔬菜换石油”项目的石油进口配额基本实现任务过半，云南“蔬菜换石油”项目进展较为顺利，按照市价换算，每出口1吨蔬菜，可换得近1.5吨柴油。

然而，这样一个本该对两国经济民生带来巨大利益的项目，8年来，虽然在部分细节上取得了一定成效，但由于存在体制、机制、管理、产业发展等方面的问题，以及传统交易方式的种种弊端，从签约至今，该项大宗农产品对外交易仍没有形成气候。再加上贸易过程中滋生的腐败现象，该项目现在已经全面搁置。

案例讨论题：

1. “蔬菜换石油”项目是哪种贸易方式？该贸易方式有何特点？
2. 该项目为什么多次被搁置，且收效不大？
3. 针对此项目的最终结果，探讨相关的商业伦理问题。

十六、
GMS 跨境电商合作平台企业联盟

次区域经济合作是20世纪80年代末、90年代初出现的一种全新的合作方式，是经济全球化和区域经济一体化的补充。1992年，在亚洲开发银行（ADB）的主导下，澜沧江—湄公河流域内的中国、老挝、缅甸、泰国、柬埔寨、越南6个国家共同发起了大湄公河次区域（GMS）经济合作，以加强各国间的经济联系，促进次区域经济社会协调发展，实现区域共同繁荣。大湄公河次区域拥有丰富的生物多样性资源、农业资源、水能资源、矿产资源、土地资源、人力资源、人文资源和旅游资源，区位优势特别明显，在资源和市场方面具有较强的互补性，充满着巨大的贸易和投资机会，具有极大的发展潜力。

中国自20世纪90年代初参加澜沧江—湄公河次区域合作以来，一直高度重视这一区域合作，GMS经济合作一直是中国—东盟自由贸易区建设的优先合作领域，GMS经济一体化对中国—东盟经济一体化起到了促进和催化作用。从大湄公河次区域经济合作开始，中国和东南亚国家之间的次区域经济合作不断深化和拓展，合作的领域不断扩大，合作的地域不断扩展，合作机制也不断完善，合作程度日益加深。经过20多年的发展，GMS各国各方面的合作卓有成效，不仅向次区域各国展现了更加美好的前景，而且对亚洲和世界的和平与发展做出了积极的贡献。

但是，在信息化的时代大背景下，传统的交易模式已经不能完全满足经济发展的要求。此时，电子商务作为全球化、开放化、高效化的新型商业模式，是各国增强经济实力、配置优势资源的有效手段。中国作为世界上电子商务最具活力的国家，现在已经有电子商务企业超过20万家，其中知名度较高的有5000家，跨境电子商务交易额2015年达到5.2万亿元人民币，开展跨境电子商务的企业超过25万家。随着海淘热的兴起，跨境电商平台也加速了在国内外的布局。对于跨境电子商务，李克强总理表示是用“互联网+外贸”的模式，进行大量的进出口业务，实现优进优出，带动实体店和工厂的发展，同时也带动就业。跨境电商实际上是让国内的工厂与国外市场对接起来。因此，跨境电商将是工业转型、市场开拓的重要工具。不光我国政府大力支持鼓励，大湄公河次区域其他国家的政府也十分关注电子商务的发展与跨境合作，并积极探索次区域跨境电子商务合作平台建设的新模式，研究和制定基础设施建设、法律框架保障、交易和支付体系完善、物流运输便利、人力资源培训以及保障网络安全的措施办法。因此，次区域内开展跨境电子商务合作，整合网络信息资源，促进信息流动，实现信息共享，加快跨境电子商务公共服务平台的建设是对区域内各国互惠互利的事。

2014 年 12 月，李克强总理在 GMS 国家领导人峰会上提出建立“GMS 跨境电子商务合作平台”，在 GMS 国家政府和亚洲开发银行（ADB）的支持下，“第 7 届 GMS 经济走廊论坛”在昆明举办并发表了《部长联合声明》，批准实施《GMS 跨境电子商务合作平台框架文件》，并确定在中国（云南）澜沧江—湄公河次区域经贸开发中心设立 GMS 跨境电子商务合作平台联络中心。

企业联盟为 GMS 跨境电子商务合作平台联络中心的分支机构，是由 GMS 成员国推荐各自电子商务促进机构、贸易促进机构和电子商务企业，在公平自愿的基础上，建立起来的更加紧密联系的非政府、非营利性的区域性国际合作组织，推动 GMS 国际跨境电子商务发展，共享次区域消费大市场。企业联盟在中国商务部国际司、GMS 其他成员国政府电子商务主管部门、云南省商务厅及 GMS 跨境电子商务合作平台联络中心的指导和支持下开展工作，企业联盟每年定期或不定期向 GMS 国家政府主管部门汇报相关合作进展情况。

企业联盟的原则是：“共建、共有、共享、共赢”。首先，企业联盟将建立具有 7 种语言的“GMS 跨境电子商务交易平台”“GMS 跨境电子商务培训及人才平台”“GMS 跨境电子商务虚拟孵化平台”，为 GMS 企业提供全方位的跨境电子商务服务，并每年举办“GMS 跨境电子商务对话会”促进区域电子商务的发展。这有效提升了 GMS 企业电子商务的应用水平。

其次，由于中国是全球最大的电子商务交易市场，电子商务是GMS各国企业尤其是中小企业进入广阔中国市场的最佳途径。而且GMS各国是东盟自由贸易区的成员国，近年来经济增长较快，与中国有较好的经济互补性，企业联盟在各国有良好的线上线下商务合作资源，是中国企业进入GMS各国市场的良好途径。因此，企业联盟促进了各国企业共享GMS及中国这个全球最大的电子商务零售市场。

再次，GMS跨境电子商务交易平台可以将GMS各国企业电子商务网站的内容自动翻译成中文、英文、法文、阿拉伯文等多种语言文字，促进各国企业开展面向全球的B2B电子商务，促进GMS企业开拓全球电子商务市场。

最后，GMS跨境电子商务交易平台作为GMS区域发展的重要平台和经济增长点，有效促进了大湄公河次区域的经济和贸易发展。

案例讨论题：

1. 大湄公河次区域合作带来的机遇和挑战是什么？
2. GMS跨境电商合作平台企业联盟在哪些方面可以发挥积极作用？
3. GMS跨境电商合作平台企业联盟如何促进次区域的经贸合作？

第四篇

国际金融

十七、

铜陵有色金属公司的套期保值策略

铜陵有色金属（集团）公司成立于1952年6月，是一个以铜金属采、选、炼、加工为主，集生产、经营、加工为一体的特大型国有企业。公司是全国300家重点扶持和安徽省重点培育的大型企业集团之一。2012年公司率先成为安徽省首家销售收入超千亿元的企业，进出口贸易总额连续14年保持全国铜行业首位，主要产品阴极铜产量位居世界铜精炼企业第五位。2015年铜陵有色金属公司生产的铜产量高达131万吨。

中国是一个缺铜的国家，每年需要从国外进口大量铜产品。从国外购买铜精矿，按照国际惯例，进口铜精砂采用的一般是点价制度。所谓点价，即买卖双方只谈数量，不谈价格，而价格以伦敦金属交易所（LME）的某一天或某一阶段市场价格为准，非常“期货化”。这意味着铜精砂从合同签订之日起就存在诸多不确定因素。为回避原材料及铜市价格波动和现货市场资信风险的冲击，铜陵有色于1992年便开展了境内期货套期保值业务。由于不能在国际市场直接套期保值，使其进口原料的保值效率难以实现最优化，故而申请从事境外期货套期保值运作，并于2003年4月经由国家批准。

2004年，针对铜价不断走高的市场情况，企业在境外进行了卖期保值操作。由于在保值平仓时期铜价格上涨，导致期货亏损，而在现货市场上获得超出套期保值利润640万美元，最终现货销售盈利弥补了期货市场的亏损。通过期货操作，企业规避了市场价格风险，锁定了原料成本，实现了预期利润。2004年，企业利润大幅增长，总额达5.5亿元，较上年增加5.3亿元。

铜陵有色在公司运营的过程中建立了风险规避的经营模式与运行方法。一是审慎运作的原则与程序。铜陵有色从事期货贸易仅限于对其主导产品电解铜进行套期保值。主要做法是：规范入场，强化内控。铜陵有色在国家完成期货市场整顿规范正式获准期货交易资格后，在指定银行设立期货专用账户。铜陵有色选定了四家具有不同优势的境外期货经纪机构作为境外期货保值业务代理商。同时，铜陵有色授权其下属四家全资子公司在期货市场以集团名义从事期铜套期保值业务，严格制定具体管理办法及操作规程，明确规定实行稳健操作的套保原则。二是恪守信用，控制流量。一方面是严守期货信用保证。期货市场实行的是保证金制度，铜陵有色则是由其境外期货经纪机构为之提供交易信用额度来替代期货交易保证金，并将其境外期货交易资金控制在其信用额度之内。另一方面是有效控制外汇资金运用额度。按照国家规定，境外期货交易汇出入资金由外汇局授权外汇开户行实行专户结算管理，对企业期货交易实行年度风险敞口管理。

随着金融领域的深化改革，铜陵有色公司使用新的套保工具来规避风险。2015 年 2 月 6 日，银行间市场清算所股份有限公司正式推出上海自贸区铜溢价掉期中央对手清算业务。同日，中国银行与铜陵有色下属子公司——上海铜冠贸易发展有限公司合作，率先完成了自贸区铜溢价掉期首笔交易，为该企业提供了代理清算服务。

2015 年 1 月 8 日，中国人民银行正式批准上海清算所开展铜溢价掉期业务。铜溢价掉期业务是以自贸区洋山铜溢价指数为标的，以跨境人民币计价、清算、结算的大宗商品金融衍生品，由经纪公司帮助达成交易，通过上海清算所提供中央对手清算业务。开展铜溢价掉期业务不仅能够满足铜陵有色公司的套期保值需求，还将吸引境外有此需求企业的广泛参与。

2015 年 2 月自贸区铜溢价掉期业务正式上线后，上海清算所再度与上海有色网合作，推出人民币电解铜掉期（CUS）产品。CUS 是在中国境内自贸区外的铜衍生品，针对内贸铜全价的一个掉期合约。由于升贴水的存在导致铜企业，不管是贸易商还是上下游企业，都没办法做到百分之百的价格保值。上海清算所推出 CUS 后可以把升贴水部分弥合掉，套保可以百分之百进行无缝对接，不会产生风险。CUS 除了采用点价加上升贴水的全价模式外，对参与者而言价格更加灵活、可把控。掉期和期货有点类似，但又有些核心的不同，CUS 必须有个指数提供方。CUS 以上海有色网发布的 1 号电解铜价格指数为标的指数，以人民币进行计价、清算以及结算。结算方式上，CUS 为现金结算，最终结算价格根据协议到期日上海有色网发布的境内电解铜的现货价格计算。根据作价方式，CUS 全价铜将以期货基准价加上现货升贴水。

发展铜金融衍生品，如铜溢价掉期和人民币电解铜掉期，为铜陵有色公司提供了更多有效的套保工具，从而公司可以规避价格波动风险，获得更多的利润。除此之外，铜金融衍生品也在帮助企业转型上起了一定的推动作用。

案例讨论题：

1. 铜陵有色公司在国际市场中面临的风险是什么？
2. 铜陵有色公司使用什么方法实现了风险规避？具体怎样实施的？
3. 铜陵有色公司使用的新的套保工具是什么？有何意义？

优酷和当当赴美上市

2010年12月8日，视频网站优酷网和电子商务网站当当网正式在纽交所挂牌上市。当日优酷以强劲的涨势收盘，涨幅161.25%，市值达34亿美元。这是互联网企业的成功，是互联网业发展里程碑式的标志。但这也只是阶段性的成功，其后优酷和当当都将面临更大的运营压力，成为公众公司后将面临更严格的监管。

优酷网是中国领先的视频分享网站。2007年，优酷网首次提出“拍客无处不在”，倡导“谁都可以做拍客”，引发全民狂拍的拍客文化风潮。经过多次拍客视频主题接力、拍客训练营，优酷网现已成为互联网拍客聚集的阵营。当当网由国内著名出版机构科文公司、美国老虎基金、美国IDG集团、卢森堡剑桥集团、亚洲创业投资基金共同投资成立，总部设在北京。1999年11月开通，以销售图书、音像制品为主，兼具发展小家电、玩具、网络游戏点卡等其他多种商品的销售。当当网目前是全球最大的中文网上图书音像商城。

优酷选择纽交所上市是因为纽交所是国际上的优质上市平台，优酷能和很多世界级的媒体公司、大集团公司在一个平台上市，具有历史意义，可以带给企业品牌增值、品牌美誉度和认可度。互联网企业倾向海外上市，美国投资人对中国互联网概念的认可不可或缺。更重要的原因在于：第一，国内上市成本高，上市过程烦琐，上市监管严格；第二，技术性门槛原因，中国对上市公司有一个盈利的硬性要求。

当当2009年才开始盈利，优酷在上市时还没有实现盈利，只是实现亏损额不断减少。按照中国中小板和创业板的相关标准，仅仅因为不符合财务标准一项，优酷和当当就不具备在中国上市的资格。而在美国上市有更多指标选择，美国纽交所有4种指标模式供企业选择，企业只要符合其中任何一套模式就具备上市资格。比如，优酷尚未盈利，则它就选择不包含盈利项目的指标模式，选择强调自己公司规模很大、所占市场份额大，以此为故事核心，成功打动投资者。而很多发展中的企业自身并无盈利能力，所需融资量却巨大，美国股市能看到的是对这些企业的预期。成熟股票市场中的股价反映的是对企业的盈利预期，面向的应该是企业的未来。

中国股市对企业上市前期的盈利性有强制要求，而且实行审核制，而非注册制，审核机制把关严格、不透明。在时间上，在美国企业上市只需要9个月，而在中国上市从准备到完成至少2年时间。中国市场不能满足需要快速融资的企业。中国股市对企业再融资审核严格，相当于再做一次新的IPO，而在海外则没有这样严格的要求。对资金需求量大的互联网企业来说，中国互联网概念已经被美国投资者接受，在美国上市融资是更好的选择。

在美国上市后，优酷和当当向世界展示了适应外国环境的中国互联网模式，这是中国互联网企业走向成熟和更高规格的标志。投资者看到的必然还有这些企业背后中国巨大的互联网市场。在美国上市前，两家公司在中国的上网人数已经超过4亿人，到2014年6月，中国上网人数达到6.32亿人。优酷的发展得益于中国互联网的快速发展。

不过，此后优酷和当当都将面临行业更激烈的竞争，国内其他几家视频行业公司56网、暴风影音、六间房等均表达了上市愿望。而当当也迅速受到了来自京东网和亚马逊的降价挑战，当当网CEO李国庆迅速宣称“将随时应对一切价格战”。

中国版权环境越来越严格，视频网站急需资金建立自己有版权的、优质的视频内容库。而优酷未来必然面临来自传统网站、大网站与传统电台结合的压力。比如，央视网会在有版权的视频内容库建立方面占有优势。又如，当当盈利的85%来自图书，模式单一；同时，数字图书未来对纸质图书出版的冲击将更大。此外，在美国上市以后，优酷和当当都将面临更严格的监管，如果信息披露不实或者不及时，都会引起投资者起诉、美国证监会的处罚，甚至公司管理人受到美国的刑事调查。因此，权衡去美国上市的利益得失，要审视自己的内部资源禀赋，企业要冷静决定去美国上市是否是自己的最优选择，不能光看别人的花开得好。

案例讨论题：

1. 优酷和当当分别是中国知名的视频网站和电子商务网站，为什么这两家公司都选择在美国上市?

2. 优酷和当当在美国上市后会有哪些机遇和挑战?

3. 这两家公司都是在全球资本市场上筹集资金，简要介绍与之相关的欧洲货币市场和全球债券市场。

十九、阿里巴巴集团美国上市之路

阿里巴巴集团于1999年在中国杭州创立。经过近二十年的发展，“阿里巴巴”已经成为全球著名的中国互联网品牌，公司的商业生态系统也覆盖到各行各业。公司主要业务和关联公司的业务包括：淘宝网、天猫、聚划算、阿里云、阿里妈妈、阿里巴巴国际交易市场、蚂蚁金服、菜鸟网络等。阿里巴巴相信互联网能够创造公平的竞争环境，让小企业通过创新与科技扩展业务，并在参与国内或全球市场竞争时处于更有利的位置。

2014年9月19日，经过多年的准备，阿里巴巴在纽约证券交易所成功上市（股票代码：BABA）。阿里巴巴赴美IPO的发行价为68美元，发行量为3.2亿股，为了满足投资者的强劲需求，阿里首次公开募股的承销商们（高盛、摩根大通、花旗银行、摩根士丹利等）还行使了超额配售权，使之正式以融资额250亿美元的规模成为有史以来最大的IPO。阿里登陆纽交所后，股价同市场预期一样持续飙升，最高达到120美元/股，使阿里巴巴成功超越Facebook成为仅次于谷歌的第二大互联网公司。在之后的半年时间内，公司的价值得到投资者的重估。

早在1999年10月，由高盛公司牵头，联合汇亚基金集团、瑞典银瑞达集团、新加坡科技发展基金等，向阿里巴巴注入500万美元天使投资。

2000年阿里巴巴引进第二轮融资，融资金额为2500万美元，其中软银提供了2000万美元，其他资金来自富达、汇亚资金、TDF、瑞典投资等五家风险投资机构。在二轮融资过程中，软银集团曾表示希望投资3000万美元占据阿里巴巴30%的股份，但被拒绝了。

2004年2月，阿里巴巴完成了第三次融资。此轮融资阿里从风险投资机构手中募集到8200万美元，其中软银出资6000万美元。融资完成后，马云及其创业团队仍然是阿里巴巴的第一大股东，占47%的股份；第二大股东为软银，约占20%；第三大股东为富达，约占18%；其他几家股东合计约占15%。

2005年8月，雅虎以10亿美元加上雅虎中国的全部资产兑换阿里巴巴集团39%的普通股（完全摊薄），并获得35%的投票权。交易完成后，雅虎成为阿里巴巴集团最大的股东，并获得其董事会四个席位中的一席。马云及持股高管丧失大股东地位，持股比例下降至31.7%。雅虎入股阿里巴巴后，风险投资商（如富达基金等）开始大规模退出。截至阿里巴巴集团B2C业务上市前，其他风险投资商基本“被清场”，阿里集团进入马云、雅虎、软银的“三足鼎立”时代。截至2007年阿里巴巴B2B业务上市前，阿里集团的持股比例为雅虎43%、软银29.3%，管理层和员工等持股比例为27.7%。2012年5月，阿里以71亿美元价格回购雅虎所持20%的股份。阿里集团给出的公告显示，阿里集团回购雅虎所持43%股份的一半。同时协议，如未来阿里集团进行IPO，阿里巴巴集团有权在IPO之际回购雅虎剩余持有股份的50%。

阿里巴巴旗下B2B电子商务贸易平台阿里巴巴网络有限公司曾于2007年11月6日在香港联交所主板挂牌上市，代码为01688.HK，发行价13.5港元，首日开盘价为30港元。当时，阿里巴巴市值达1996亿港元，一跃成为中国互联网业首家市值超过200亿美元的公司。

2012年2月21日，阿里巴巴集团和阿里巴巴网络有限公司联合宣布，阿里巴巴集团向旗下港股上市公司阿里巴巴网络有限公司董事会提出私有化要约，拟以每股13.5港元的价格回购公司股票。同年6月20日阿里巴巴（01688.HK）正式从港交所退市，阿里巴巴私有化计划完成。按照阿里巴巴集团的公告，私有化是为了业务战略转型，同时给中小投资者变现投资收益的机会。但是，有部分评论家认为阿里巴巴实则是在为雅虎股权的回购做准备，根本目的在于“控制权”回归以及集团整体上市。不过，阿里采用的退市价格13.5港元与发行价格持平，按10%的通胀率算，2012年终值是20港元，阿里不给利息白白借钱花，每股赚了6.5港元，就算除去股息也赚6港元。这次退市让美国雅虎和日本软银的收益最大化得到保障，却直接伤害了香港众多小股民的利益。

2013年7月，阿里巴巴集团CEO陆兆禧承认做好上市准备，市场随之传出其准备最早于9月赴港上市的消息。2013年8月，有意在香港上市的阿里巴巴集团公司向港交所提出了合伙人制度的上市建议。9月初，港交所因合伙人制度不符合香港证监会对投资者利益的保障，拒绝批准阿里巴巴破例以合伙人制度上市。2014年3月16日，阿里巴巴宣布，决定启动赴美上市事宜。6月26日，阿里巴巴决定申请在美国纽约证券交易所挂牌上市。9月19日，阿里巴巴在美国纽约证券交易所正式挂牌交易，股票交易代码为“BABA”。按照其68美元/ADS的发行价计算，其融资额超越VISA上市时的197亿美元，刷新了美国市场的IPO交易纪录，成为美国股票市场有史以来最大的IPO。首个交易日，阿里以92.70美元开盘，高出发行价36.32%，总市值达到2285亿美元。

案例讨论题：

1. 阿里巴巴为什么赴美上市？
2. 阿里巴巴赴美上市会对中国市场产生什么影响？
3. 比较阿里巴巴与腾讯的上市市值，并做出分析。

亚投行助力菲律宾基础设施建设

20 世纪 90 年代以来，世界各地金融危机频发，对地区乃至全球经济危害极大，国际金融秩序逐渐进入大挑战、大变革与大调整的新阶段。尤其是 2008 年的全球金融危机造成全球金融市场新一轮的剧烈波动，印证了全球经济复苏进程的脆弱性，也体现出加强全球经济和货币政策协调、进一步推动全球经济治理改革、重塑国际金融秩序的必要性。

现代全球金融治理始于布雷顿森林体系，由美欧等发达国家主导。经过半个多世纪的发展，这一体系的固有缺陷和不足日益暴露。一方面，该体系不能充分反映各国经济实力的增长变化，尤其是未能及时反映新兴经济体崛起的现实，发展中国家群体话语权严重缺失。另一方面，全球金融危机的频发很大程度上缘于美元的不稳定以及“华盛顿共识”的新自由主义。缺乏话语权的发展中国家群体维护货币体系的稳定性和汇率稳定十分困难。

2016 年 1 月 16 日，亚洲基础设施投资开发银行开业仪式暨理事会和董事会成立大会在北京举行，标志着亚投行正式启动运行。作为新时代下的区域多边金融合作机构，亚投行旨在为亚洲地区基础设施建设提供融资支持，推动区域互联互通，促进区域经济发展，推动世界经济增长。

亚洲基础设施投资银行是现有国际金融体系、多边开发机构和国际发展议程的有益补充，也是中国主动参与全球经济治理的有益尝试。亚投行的重点是推进基础设施互联互通和区域经济一体化，致力于实现亚洲经济的可持续发展。

作为一家新型区域性国际金融机构，亚投行之所以引起关注，不仅在于亚投行本身的功能是专注于区域基础设施互联互通和区域经济一体化，更在于全球经济版图快速重构的背景环境和现行国际金融秩序的不合理性。亚投行的设立得到了全球的广泛关注和参与，反映出现有国际经济秩序的不断演进和国际经济格局的历史性转变。

菲律宾的权威专家指出，发展是现阶段菲律宾最主要的任务，落后的基础设施和有限的融资渠道已经成为阻碍其经济发展的短板。在世界经济论坛发布的《2016—2017 年全球竞争力报告》中，菲律宾基础设施水平仅位列全球第 95 位；根据国际货币基金组织的研究，菲律宾的关键基础设施服务水平在东盟国家中排名末位。空中交通拥堵问题、马尼拉市区交通拥堵和公共交通运输难题都没有得到妥善解决，每天有近 50 万人挤入设计容量为 35 万人次的轨道交通车厢，国际航空运输协会也多次督促菲政府尽快确定新国际机场发展计划。

为此，2015 年底，菲律宾签署亚投行协定，以创始成员国身份加入亚投行，并分期出资 1.96 亿美元；2016 年 10 月 19 日，总统杜特尔特批准该协定；2016 年 12 月 5 日，参议院以 20 票赞成的绝对多数投票结果三读通过第 241 号决议。菲政经界普遍认为，亚投行在推动亚洲经济体持续增长、促进经济社会发展方面具有重要意义，有助于提升本地区应对未来金融危机和其他外部冲击的能力。同时，菲律宾作为亚投行成员国，将助力国家推进基础设施建设，为实现经济高速增长打开新局面。

正是由于亚投行首批项目的示范效应，杜特尔特政府计划开启菲律宾“基础设施建设的黄金时代”，预计任内总投资约 8 万亿比索（约合 1600 亿美元），其中包括棉兰老铁路、跨海大桥和供水等项目。杜特尔特对媒体表示，作为亚投行创始成员国，菲方希望获得更多融资，欢迎和鼓励中国公司和资本参与菲律宾基础设施建设。菲律宾国库署署长罗伯托日前表示，菲律宾将向亚投行提交快速公交系统和马尼拉防洪系统两个项目的贷款申请，希望在 2017 年申请到 3 亿 ~5 亿美元的贷款资金。

亚洲基础设施投资的市场潜力诱人，但风险也十分突出。绝大多数最需要基础设施投资的亚洲国家都存在政治社会不稳定，法治呈现真空状态，政府决策朝令夕改、信用不佳等现象。对亚投行而言，如何控制资金安全风险将是一个非常艰巨的运营挑战。亚投行在实际运营中应高度重视融资业务面临的各种风险与潜在挑战，在投资项目的选择上“戒急用缓”，既要吸取传统开发机构因苛刻的贷款条件和绩效评分机制而导致开发性投资供给不足的教训，尽量满足发展中国家所需开发性投资的可获得性，保障全球发展援助的有效性；也要坚持可持续发展原则，秉承项目的经济合理性，注重环境、劳工等社会敏感问题，融入可持续发展理念，在投资项目上考虑周全、慎重抉择。

案例讨论题：

1. 菲律宾如何利用亚投行开展基础设施建设？
2. 亚投行亟待解决的问题有哪些？
3. 作为国际金融组织的一员，亚投行如何参与到区域金融治理中？

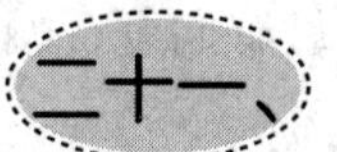

二十一、世界银行与国际发展援助

2013年1月，缅甸与世界银行对外宣布，缅甸已全部清偿对世界银行和亚洲开发银行的历史债务，双方要加快改革进程，开启新的合作阶段。世界银行集团以积极的姿态全面介入，通过制订发展规划、提供资金和技术援助，造福缅甸全体人民。世界银行集团目前正与缅甸政府讨论确定优先需求。2013年1月22日，世界银行执行董事会批准了一笔4.4亿美元的贷款，用于支持缅甸的“重新融入与改革支持”计划。该信贷将支持政府实施重要的改革措施，加强宏观经济稳定，改进公共财政管理，改善投资环境等。这笔信贷还将用于满足缅甸政府的外汇需求，包括偿还日本国际协力银行向缅甸提供的用于清偿欠债的过渡性贷款。

世界银行于1945年12月宣告成立，1946年6月开始办理业务，1947年11月成为联合国的专门机构。该行的成员必须是国际货币基金组织成员，但国际货币基金组织成员不一定都参加世界银行。自1945年成立以来，世界银行已从一个单一的机构发展成为一个由五个联系紧密的发展机构组成的集团。世界银行的使命也已经从建立初期的通过国际复兴开发银行（IBRD）促进“二战”后重建和发展，演变成为通过与其下属机构国际开发协会（IDA）和其他成员机构密切协调推进世界各国的减贫事业。世界银行其他成员机构包括国际金融公司（IFC）、多边投资担保机构（MIGA）和国际投资争端解决中心（ICSID）。

世界银行在成立之初，主要是资助西欧国家恢复被战争破坏了的经济。但在1948年后，欧洲各国开始主要依赖美国的“马歇尔计划”来恢复“二战”后的经济，因为美国根据“马歇尔计划”直接向欧洲国家贷款帮助其重建经济。那时，世界银行经历了第一次使命的转型。世界银行将注意力转向“经济发展”，即向发展中国家提供中长期贷款与投资，促进发展中国家经济和社会发展。20 世纪 50 年代，银行将重点放在公共项目上，对发电站项目、公路建设和其他交通运输投资项目有更多的偏爱。60 年代，世界银行开始通过提供大量的贷款来支持农业、教育、人口控制和城市发展。

在 1945 年世界银行建立之时，贫困和被战争破坏了的国家无法吸引到私人资本。因此，世界银行向那些信用等级通常较差的高风险客户提供低息贷款。随着“二战”后重建的完成，私人资本已经使公共发展援助相形见绌。世界在变化，世界银行也随之变化。当今世界银行的使命已成为“建立一个没有贫困的世界”。

很显然，世界银行不仅仅是一个银行。世界银行主要负责经济的复兴和发展，向各成员国提供发展经济的中长期贷款。但是，世界银行不是一个只包括贷款和赠款的银行机构，它的作用是在开放的国际体系下促进增长和协助减贫。世界银行处于一个独特的位置，可以通过贷款、知识和经验帮助各国设立更长期的发展战略。

世界银行行长金墉认为，世界银行同各国合作，以一种财政上健全和可持续的方式对基础设施和制度建设进行明智的投资。通过国际金融公司和多边投资担保机构，世界银行支持私营部门发挥催化剂的作用，私营部门占世界就业岗位总数的将近 90%。通过借鉴各股东国的经验，世界银行能够开发针对跨国问题的解决方案。为了推动投资者、企业和居民的信心和决策，世界银行积极促进公共财政透明和加强治理。公众的信任和信心是政府与制度的宝贵财富。为了应对十分脆弱的全球经济，首先要使民众相信经济制度和政策能够带来更可持续、公平和更具包容性的经济增长。

世界银行致力于为客户服务，特别是发展中国家的客户，而不是将之置之于旧观念中结构调整政策中。在概念的改变下，世界银行的思维方式也发生了转变。世界银行是解决方案的寻求者，而不是法令的传播者。如果最好的解决方案都无法符合客户的政治经济环境，世界银行便不会协助客户解决问题。

世界银行行长金墉表示，作为一个全球性发展机构，世界银行面临着经济和道义上的当务之急，亟须帮助解决威胁全球增长的风险，无论何时何地。全球经济强劲，所有国家都从中受益；全球经济疲弱，所有国家都不堪一击。欧洲各国要采取必要措施恢复稳定，因为它们的行动将影响到世界各地区的增长。近年来，世界银行将自己定位为解决方案的寻求者。发展中国家是世界银行的客户，世界银行为发展中国家的公共部门和私人部门提供服务。如果最好的解决方案都无法符合客户的政治经济环境，世界银行便不会协助客户解决问题。世界银行通过创新的渠道和融资工具来扩大资金基础。世界银行不仅用其资金来解决全球性问题，还将“负责任的利益相关者”概念融入其贷款流程。正如金墉所说，作为一个全球性发展机构，世界银行将同新老合作伙伴一起齐心协力，培育一个有效地响应不同客户和捐助方需求的机构；一个提供更强大的解决方案以支持可持续发展和帮助各国政府对公民负起更多责任的机构；一个将基于实证的解决方案置于意识形态之上的机构；一个驾驭和吸引最优秀人才的机构；一个扩大发展中国家的声音的机构；一个借鉴我们所服务的人民的专业知识经验的机构。

案例讨论题：

1. 国际货币体系是如何演化的？世界银行是在什么历史背景下产生的？其宗旨是什么？

2. 世界银行与商业银行有什么不同？

3. 世界银行的客户有哪些？2007 年至今，世界银行是如何通过为客户服务而实现其使命的？

4. “二战”后的重建早已完成，我们为什么还需要世界银行？

第五篇

国际企业的战略与组织

二十二、万达集团的国际化战略

中国万达集团创立于1988年，形成商业、文化、网络科技、金融四大产业集团，2015年资产6340亿元，收入2901亿元。万达商业地产是世界最大的不动产企业、世界最大的五星级酒店业主；万达文化产业集团是中国最大的文化企业、世界最大的电影院线运营商；万达网络科技集团专注线上线下融合，打造新一代物联网模式；万达金融集团致力于传统金融业务。

万达的企业文化是“国际万达，百年企业”。万达的企业文化是经过提升的，万达成立之初，企业文化是“老实做人，精明做事”。2003年前后，万达有了些盈利，对企业文化进行提升，企业文化是“共创财富，公益社会”。后来企业规模更大一点，第三次提升定的企业文化就是“国际万达，百年企业”，国际万达一定是国际化的，百年企业一定是常青的，为了实现宏伟的目标，万达必须国际化。

国际化可以分散风险，特别是民营企业，更需要国际化。企业国际化意味着减小企业经营风险。一个国家发展得再好，经济也有调整时期，但全世界经济同时出现大调整、大萧条，这种概率是极低的。中国政府也鼓励中国企业全球配置资源，利用全球市场。此外，万达需要靠国际化，通过国际并购才能做得更大。通过研究世界500强的企业，万达发现没有一家企业是完全靠自身生长成长起来的，没有一家企业在进入世界500强财富排榜前没发生过一次并购。

万达集团在2016年提出未来5年新的战略目标，即到2020年实现“2211”目标，就是到2020年，企业资产超过2000亿美元，企业市值超过2000亿美元，收入超过1000亿美元，净利润超过100亿美元，其中30%以上收入来自海外。有国际业务的企业有两种，一种是在本国生产产品，然后卖到世界各地，这只能算产品国际化；另一种是在一两个国家有投资，但是占全部业务比重小，管理方式、人才结构以及企业文化都没达到跨国企业水平。真正的跨国企业不仅要求企业规模足够大，至少有数百亿美元，而且企业收入至少30%来自海外。

正因为万达有远大的企业愿景，所以现在还持续保持着快速增长。2015年实现收入、资产、利润同比2014年增长20%，对万达来讲，这是多年来增速第一次掉到30%以下。在此之前，万达每一年都保持30%以上的增长，随着全球经济的重大调整，中国经济的持续放缓，万达的发展速度也降低了，但依然保持较快速度增长，这也是万达最终成为一流跨国企业的保证。

万达集团国际化战略的方式以并购为主、新设投资为辅。从英国工业革命到现在，世界市场特别是一些主要的市场领域，基本上都被先进入的企业瓜分了。万达要投资体育产业，但各种国际品牌体育赛事所有权、转播权基本都被老牌家族公司或跨国公司瓜分了，万达要参与进去，只能靠买。

万达国际化的重点在于"买得对"。万达有两条标准，一条标准是必须与万达现有产业有关联。万达国际化进入的产业都是万达已经进行的，不管是不动产，还是文化、体育、旅游，都是万达现在正在从事的产业。这样做的好处是使万达有一定的知识积累和人才储备，了解行业的具体情况。另一条标准是不管是跨国并购还是投资项目，都要求这些业务能移植到中国，能在中国获得更快发展。

2015年万达并购了世界最大的铁人三项公司——美国WTC，并购公司不到半年，铁人三项比赛就在中国厦门、合肥落地了。这项运动过去在中国是一个盲区，目前中国在这方面运动人数也少得可怜，只有200多人从事这项运动。万达在中国推广这项运动，至少可以做到几十万人参与。因为中国正进入健康时代、全民跑步时代，拥有巨大的发展空间。WTC在国外很难做到快速增长，一般有百分之几的增长就不错了，只有在中国才能获得更多增长点和更快的增长速度。

此外，万达国际化强调使用本土人才。2012年万达并购美国AMC公司时，由于它是电影终端渠道，美国政府对这种类型公司的并购有一定限制。

万达董事长王健林去拜访美国当时的驻华大使骆家辉先生，请他为万达向美国政府写一封推荐信。骆家辉先生问的一个问题是：万达是不是打算派中国人到美国去管理？王健林先生说不会，并购后如果原公司管理层全部离开，那其实意味着并购失败。最终万达并购 AMC 获得了美国政府的批准。万达并购 AMC 后，只派了一个联络员。万达并购的对象中，原来的股东都是大型跨国企业，并购企业最好的管理办法是留住原来的管理层，使之更好地工作。

万达集团到世界上任何一个国家去并购和投资，都是尽可能留住原来的管理团队，使用本土人才，想办法调动他们的积极性，而不是派中国人来管理。

万达国际化的进展从 2012 年开始，用了 4 年的时间，万达集团在全球 10 多个国家投资，投资额超过 150 亿美元，其中在美国就投了 100 亿美元。万达在英国投资了 12 亿英镑，有 2600 多名员工。2016 年 1 月斥资 35 亿美元收购美国传奇影业公司，是中国企业在海外的最大一笔文化收购。

万达国际化虽然时间不长，但步伐迅猛，而且进展比较顺利。没有失败就意味着离失败越近，万达在今后的国际化进程中不排除会摔跟头。但是，万达有一个原则：只要不发生颠覆性风险，就要去做这件事。事实上，勇敢迈出这一步才会觉得，国际化也没那么难。

案例讨论题：

1. 万达进入国际市场的方式以并购为主，万达集团是否可以通过其他方式进入国际市场，为什么？

2. 近几年来，万达不断拓宽国际市场，而且投资涉及多个行业，为什么万达要在多个行业同时投资？

3. 万达在国际化战略实施过程中遇到的问题有哪些，如何解决？

4. 万达集团的国际化之路对中国企业“走出去”有何启示？

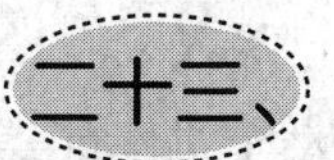

二十三、比亚迪新能源汽车的国际化战略

比亚迪股份有限公司成立于1995年，是一家高新技术民营企业，总部位于中国广东省深圳市。比亚迪最初从事电池的生产和销售，于2002年7月在香港主板发行上市。2003年，比亚迪收购西安秦川汽车有限责任公司，正式进入汽车制造与销售领域，开始了民族自主品牌汽车的发展征程。目前，比亚迪在整车制造、模具研发、车型开发等方面具有优势，拥有IT、新能源及汽车三大产业群，产业格局日渐完善，并已迅速成为中国最具创新的新锐品牌。比亚迪是目前中国唯一掌握车用磷酸铁锂电池规模化生产技术的企业，在世界上处于领先地位，其电池使用寿命长、成本较低而且具有良好的安全性能。比亚迪凭借其良好的战略成本管理能力，获得了一定的成本优势，市场份额不断提高。比亚迪在上海、北京、广东等地建有九大生产基地，并在印度、韩国、日本、欧洲、美国等国家和中国香港、中国台湾地区均设立有办事处或分公司，在职员工总数近20万人。

比亚迪的国际化整体战略包括资本国际化、国际质量管理体系、本土化制造与销售等方面，以创新技术和社会责任感填补欧美发达国家市场的空白。不同于大多数中国企业，比亚迪看到了世界的未来发展趋势，以前瞻性视野率先展开新能源汽车的研发及海内外推广。比亚迪电动汽车一改中国车企过往的模式，跳过亚非拉等传统目标市场，将它们推向美国加州、德国法兰克福以及以色列特拉维夫等。

比亚迪的新能源汽车K9是其自主研发的首款电动巴士，已逐步走向国际市场，在欧洲、北美、南美、亚洲的多个国家和地区通过了试运营，比亚迪的新能源国际化之路逐渐清晰。2014年，比亚迪把电动车运到美国加州，让挑剔的美国消费者真实体验新能源电动汽车。而加州恰恰是汽车排放法规最为严苛、对环保标准要求最高的地区。同年4月，3辆比亚迪

K9纯电动大巴，经检验检疫部门检验合格后顺利出口到美国。该批纯电动大巴共10辆，分批出口至美国，为美国加州斯坦福大学校内专用的穿梭大巴。在美国，保护环境的理念已深入人心，为电动车的推广使用提供了良好的基础。这也正是比亚迪电动车进军北美市场的原因之一，将从"点"的示范到"面"的铺开，最终达成比亚迪的"绿色梦想"。

比亚迪坚定地走电动汽车发展路线，继比亚迪K9之后，企业规划推出一款定位低于比亚迪K9的中型巴士。待该车推出后，将成为比亚迪旗下全新的入门级巴士，与目前市场上热销的丰田考斯特为同级车型，并将与其展开激烈竞争。比亚迪不仅仅是将绿色技术应用于汽车，而且是通过向城市推广城市交通电动化解决方案，得以在实现经济复苏的同时解决环境问题。这才是比亚迪在新能源方面的战略布局。

随着国际化步伐的加快以及国内市场的发力，比亚迪正在驶入"快车道"，并将布局的触角向外延展。早在2013年，比亚迪就已经获得欧盟的官方许可，具备在所有欧盟成员国销售电动巴士的权限。欧盟向比亚迪颁发了"欧盟整车车辆认证"（Whole Vehicle Type-Approval，缩写为WVTA认证）。这意味着凡是欧盟成员国，比亚迪均可在其境内销售电动大巴，而无需另外再获取该国的独立批准。比亚迪将欧洲纳入其纯电动大巴销售目标市场的范围，其电动公交车已行驶在英国、法国和荷兰的街头。

2016年6月，比亚迪与全球最大电力生产商之一的法国电力公司正式签署了战略合作协议。同年10月，比亚迪宣布斥资2000万欧元在匈牙利投资设立欧洲首个新能源电动车生产基地，2017年正式投产，初期主要生产零排放纯电动公交车和叉车，年产量可达400台，同时将设立欧洲研发中心。匈牙利政府对发展电动汽车十分重视，积极支持比亚迪投资建厂，并给予约340万美元的补贴。通过生产电动汽车，匈牙利希望带动该国的相关产业发展和当地就业，并将为落实气候变化的《巴黎协定》做出贡献。

市场扩大带来的规模经济效应，使得汽车生产制造的效率提高、单位成本降低。随着汽车生产规模的日益扩大，比亚迪在产品设计、工艺设计、自动化水平、生产组织方式等方面的经验逐渐累积，通过不断改进管理方法，提高了员工的作业效率。比亚迪在充电电池和零部件制造方面拥有先进的经验，员工的研发能力和实际操作能力也在不断提高。

新能源汽车的技术制约主要是动力蓄电池的能量储存能力和电池的使用寿命。纯电动车 E6 上市，标志着比亚迪在新能源车用蓄电池领域的技术水平得到进一步的提升。比亚迪实现了技术创新，有效地降低了企业的成本，保持了企业的竞争优势。因此，相较于其他企业，比亚迪拥有的核心技术能够减少发达国家企业的技术制约、降低专利费用，并能通过不断研发创新降低生产成本。

比亚迪利用新能源汽车的技术以及转型升级的时机，将国际化战略向纵深化推进。汽车电动化的浪潮已经在全球愈演愈烈，到目前为止，比亚迪纯电动车的足迹已经遍布了全球六大洲的 200 多个城市，包括伦敦、洛杉矶、纽约、京都等，接下来，比亚迪新能源汽车不仅要在全球做出更大规模的推广，而且在产品设计、供应链体系、生产制造的各个环节也更加体系化。比亚迪要做的是整合全球的资源，真正地把中国的技术推向全球。但同时，技术的升级转型伴随着产品、服务、品牌体系的建设，将会是比亚迪非常大的挑战。

案例讨论题：

1. 比亚迪的国际化战略为何一改中国车企的目标市场定位？它又是如何在美国顺利推进的？

2. 比亚迪在欧洲市场上拥有哪些有利条件？

3. 面对成本压力，比亚迪是如何做的？它有哪些战略优势？

4. 阐述比亚迪追求的是哪种国际化战略，这种战略选择能持续吗？如果不能又该做出何种选择？

二十四、

雀巢的中国本土化战略

2012年10月18日，世界食品巨头雀巢集团在中国发布2012年第3季度业绩报告，前3季度雀巢实现销售额676亿瑞士法郎，实现11%的销售增长。雀巢资料显示，雀巢公司前3季度在新兴市场取得了两位数增长，尽管发达市场整体经济萎缩，但是雀巢也取得了2.4%的增长。雀巢去年在大中华区的销售额为25亿元瑞郎，据此雀巢在大中华区市场的销售额将实现一倍以上的增长。在金融危机绵延难去的背景之卜，雀巢大中华区的表现却着实让人惊喜。雀巢的不凡业绩取决于其公司的全面本土化。

雀巢公司总部位于瑞士日内瓦湖畔，是世界上最大的食品制造商。拥有150年历史的雀巢公司由瑞士人亨利·内斯特莱于1867年创建的，它最初是以生产婴儿食品起家的。作为全球最大的食品制造商之一，雀巢自1984年进入中国，在中国经营22家工厂，雇员超过14000名，在中国累计投资超过70亿元人民币。自2006年任职中国区CFO的荷芬斯迪经历了中国市场的爆发性增长，他表示，雀巢中国的表现越来越让人兴奋，在雀巢全球中的地位也越来越重要。

如今，从原料供应到产品生产，从企业管理到人力资源，再到市场营销，雀巢彻头彻尾地执行着本土化。雀巢人都更愿意表示自己是一家中国公司。日前，雀巢大中华区总裁鲍尔公开对媒体表示，进入中国市场以来，雀巢公司与中国同呼吸、共命运，共同经历了社会、经济的高速发展期，也共同见证了全球经济危机，其公司已与中国成为一体，是中国大家庭的一员。

雀巢在中国销售的产品98%都是本地制造的，覆盖一系列按照国际上最高质量标准制造的产品。奶产品和冰激凌一直是雀巢的重头业务，在全球的总销售额中占比为18%，由此进入中国后不久，从1987年开始，雀巢先后在黑龙江、山东、内蒙古建立奶制品加工厂；作为雀巢拳头产品的速溶咖啡在中国市场一直占据 80% 的市场份额，雀巢为此在云南开辟咖啡种植区，目前雀巢每年从云南收购的咖啡豆超过 5000 吨。本土化的生产和制造除了使雀巢更加快速地融入中国之外，也带来了对原材料成本的控制以及市场扩大带来的规模效益。

雀巢中国的财务管理也在践行着本土化的宗旨。雀巢公司认为，由于各国的财务环境大不相同，贸然套用统一财务管理模式必会导致财务管理水土不服，因此，财务管理本土化最重要也是最基础的一点是尊重中国的法律法规，包括税法、经济法、财务会计、审计等多种制度。目前，雀巢中国 22 家工厂中有 20 家由中国本土人才管理，工厂的所有总工程师和各地区销售经理都由本土人员担任。荷芬斯迪自豪地表示财务也不例外。荷芬斯迪手下拥有一支高水准的本土财务管理团队，其中很多财务人员在雀巢内部工作了很长一段时间。荷芬斯迪表示，在制定重大发展战略时，他非常尊重和信任本土团队提出的意见和建议。为配合雀巢的培训文化，荷芬斯迪每年都要派中国同事到雀巢总部培训，效果也是显著的，其相关的培训项目已经帮助很多人达到了高层财务人员的标准。

此外，作为国际化和本土化战略并行的重要一环，为了更好地迎合中国消费者的需求，雀巢也实现了其产品本土化。为此，雀巢公司早在 2001 年就在上海建立了一个研发中心，专门针对中国消费者进行脱水烹调食品和营养食品的研究和开发，以生产出更符合中国消费者需要的产品。在产品的设计和生产上，雀巢公司主要以中国消费者的口味为导向。在中国销售的咖啡，其味道不同于美国市场或法国市场上的雀巢咖啡，而更贴近中国人的味蕾。雀巢公司在中国推出的“香蕉先生”“蓝熊嘟嘟”“布丁雪糕”和“荔枝冰冰”4 种冰淇淋，就是通过对中国青少年消费者口味的深入研究而开发出来的针对青少年顾客设计的产品。

为了迎合中国消费者的口味，雀巢迈进了它自己过去并不熟悉的保健茶领域。雀巢看准了保健茶在中国有很大的市场潜力，于是投入巨资与可口可乐联手开拓健康型饮料市场，包括各种茶饮料和草药类饮料。正如雀巢中华区前总裁狄可为所指出的那样，没有什么商品比食品和饮料更本土化了。狄可为指出，牛奶饮品在中国卖得很好，最受欢迎的是花生口味，其次是核桃口味。如果尝试在其他国家推出这类产品，是卖不出多少的。

案例讨论题：

1. 雀巢公司有着怎样的发展历程？它的全球化扩张战略是如何进行的？

2. 雀巢公司为何在外国市场要实行本土化战略？它有哪些本土化措施？它的战略成功吗？

3. 雀巢公司本土化对中国公司进入外国市场有何启示？中国公司如何借鉴？

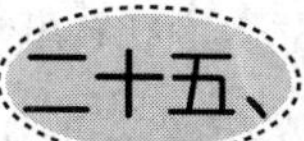

二十五、中兴通讯全球组织构架的演变

中兴通讯是全球领先的综合通信解决方案提供商。公司为全球 160 多个国家和地区的电信运营商和企业客户提供创新技术与产品解决方案。公司成立于 1985 年，在香港和深圳两地上市，是中国知名的通信设备上市公司。中兴通讯从 1995 年启动国际化战略，在美国、法国、瑞典、印度、中国等地共设有 18 个全球研发机构，近 3 万名研发人员专注于行业技术创新。2012 年，中兴通讯蝉联 PCT 国际专利申请量全球企业首位。公司依托分布于全球的 107 个分支机构，全球有 9 个交付中心，15 个培训中心，45 个本地客户支持中心，现有 10000 名售后人员遍布全球各地，在全球有超过 3000 多家外部合作伙伴，共同服务全球客户。

中兴通讯是著名的通讯设备制造企业，产品涵盖无线产品（CDMA、GSM、3G、WiMAX 等）、网络产品（xDSL、NGN、光通信等）、数据产品（路由器、以太网交换机等）和手机终端（CDMA、GSM、小灵通、3G 等）四大领域；中兴通讯的产品覆盖无线、核心网、接入、承载、业务、终端、云计算、服务等通讯产业链的相关领域；面向的客户是全球的电信运营商。

1995 年中兴通讯开始探索海外市场。1996 年 5 月，中兴通讯国际部正式成立。此时，中兴通讯主要采取的是典型的直线职能制。在企业的创业期及发展的初级阶段，需要一种集权式的组织结构以更好地发挥领导者能力以及企业统筹规划、协同整合的作用，而同时又需要部分兼顾各职能领域的具体特点，因此，直线职能型组织结构是中国企业乃至世界许多企业在发展初期普遍采用的一种组织结构。总裁领导下的副总裁（副总经理）负责制下设五大体系：市场体系、研发制造生产体系、财务体系、人事行政体系和综合管理体系。市场体系和研发制造生产体系为核心业务体系，直接由两位副总经理主管。

1998 年，中兴通讯开始推行事业部制，公司按照产品设立了网络事业部、移动事业部、本部事业部、CDMA 事业部、手机事业部、康讯公司（负责公司的采购）；同时按照客户设立了几个营销事业部，包括第一营销事业部、第二营销事业部、第三营销事业部（后来又增加了两个营销事业部）。在总部设立了六大职能中心：质企中心、IT 中心、市场中心、人事中心、财务中心、总裁办。各事业部是虚拟的利润中心，没有独立的财权和人事权。中兴通讯开始在海外本地设立生产基地。从 1999 年初开始，中兴通讯派出一小批员工进入电信市场欠发达国家拓展市场，在此阶段，中兴通讯通过自己在海外设立的部门在国际上直接寻找客户，开始走向自主的国际化道路。

中兴通讯从 2004 年开始实行产品经营团队，建立了跨事业部的团队进行产品开发，以期解决跨事业部之间的合作问题，但由于事业部下面没有直属的营销部门、供应链部门，实施效果不尽如人意。按照产品事业部管理方式，任何一个产品事业部没有能力提供整体解决方案，事业部之间沟通壁垒较厚，影响了向客户提供整体解决方案的反应速度。

从 2005 年开始中兴通讯进入突破期，在这段时期，一方面，通过在海外建立组织机构如研究所、办事处或者拓展处，招聘本地人才，实施本地化战略；另一方面，积极拓展海外市场、挖掘优质客户，加强和全球跨国运营商的全面、深入合作，建立 MTO 等机构。在公司内部对营销事业部的组织架构进行调整，把国内优秀的营销骨干员工派遣到国外拓展海外市场，同时，为了更好地贴近市场，服务于客户，促使市场管理公司把市场管理平台转移到海外一线，在全球成立了 14 个海外片区。

2006 年下半年开始，中兴通讯悄然进行了事业部转型，对事业部制进行了重大调整，建立以职能为代表的各个体系，如研发、物流、市场、销售体系等，在完善职能体系的基础上，引入矩阵式管理模式。总部同在一个城市的中兴通讯的竞争对手华为技术早在 1999 年就引进了矩阵式管理模式。

矩阵式管理是协调各职能体系的资源，打破职能体系之间的壁垒，组建跨体系的项目团队，在项目经理的统一管理下解决客户面临的问题，在大中型高新技术企业中越来越成为一种首选的管理模式。矩阵式管理把纵向的职能和横向的业务紧密结合在一起，快速对客户的需求进行反应。

在中兴通讯，原组织结构图中本部、数据、CDMA、网络和移动事业部已经消失，取而代之的是市场体系、销售体系、研发体系、物流体系。手机事业部没有参与调整，现在的组织结构图中依然保留了手机事业部。各个职能体系实际上就是中小企业的各个职能部门，只不过职能体系人数多，甚至多达上万人，职能更复杂。以职能体系为基础，在产品开发和提供通讯综合解决方案上，采用矩阵式管理模式。调整以后的中兴通讯建立了以职能体系为特征的组织结构，对各职能体系的职责进行了明确定义。

中兴通讯实施事业部制的矩阵管理。由于向各事业部下放了决策权，事业部的积极性和灵活性大为提高，管理化整为零，上下分工，具体产品的市场和客户的管理任务由事业部承担，总部从中脱身出来，集中精力于战略规划和协调管理。以产品管理为主线的矩阵管理所具有的灵活性，正好可以弥补事业部制存在的资源难以共享、协调难度大的弊端。矩阵式小组往往比固定的产品部门或事业部有更强的灵活性和协作优势。

2011 年 5 月中兴通讯对组织架构进行了部分调整，以适应当前不断变化的行业态势，赢得更多的市场。部分研发并入销售体系，为此，中兴把技术力量最大限度地前移，目前已把技术支持和宣贯前移到营销事业部，展开顾问式销售；同时还将研发体系的核心人物架构工程师前移到海外高端市场，与运营商一起把握用户需求；成立了云计算事业部，包括全球性的企业网销售体系。

2012 年起，中兴通讯又开始了新的组织变革的尝试，实行项目化组织运作。

第一，传统的组织都是科室或者部门、事业部制，但是在项目型的组织里，项目、任务是单元，不是以科室或者部门为单位。

第二，传统组织是由职位权威驱动，而在项目型组织里完全是由项目驱动。在一个项目里，所有参与的基层干部都要服从项目经理的指挥。

在中兴通讯的项目管理分级中，分为部门级、领域级、公司级、TOP 级；根据项目的特性，进一步分为项目、项目群、项目组合。可以将公司最核心的业务，即市场侧、研发侧都分解成项目，按项目管理的方法去设定项目目标、里程碑和项目资源配置，这样可以更好地进行资源配置。

案例讨论题：

1. 为什么中兴通讯之前的事业部是有效的？
2. 为什么事业部形式后来出现问题？
3. 为什么中兴通讯开始启用矩阵形式？

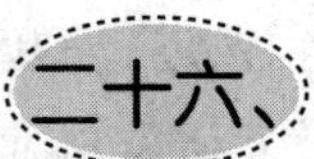

二十六、奇瑞公司拓展海外市场的困境

奇瑞汽车有限公司始建于1997年1月8日，是由安徽省芜湖市5个投资公司共同出资兴建的国有股份制企业。2016年奇瑞汽车集团全年销量达70.47万辆，同比增长28%，创历史新高。其中，出口88081辆，占同期中国乘用车出口量的约28%，连续14年位居中国乘用车出口第一。

奇瑞产品已覆盖全球80余个国家和地区，累计出口超过120万辆，并在海外建立了14个生产基地，近2000家经销网点和服务网点。同时，奇瑞也是国内第一个将整车制造技术和CKD散件出口国外的企业。奇瑞拥有员工13000人，其中研发人员超过5000人，外籍专家和管理人员超过210人。

奇瑞公司自创立之初就一直致力于海外市场的开拓。奇瑞的出口市场首先选择了中东、东南亚、非洲等发展中国家，然后，将触角慢慢伸向俄罗斯、东南欧和拉丁美洲。奇瑞已在俄罗斯、乌克兰、伊朗、埃及、马来西亚、印度尼西亚、乌拉圭等15个国家和地区建成了15个工厂，并与当地大型经销商集团结成联盟共同开拓当地市场。奇瑞的海外销售网络覆盖亚洲、欧洲、非洲、南美洲和北美洲五大汽车市场。

2004年12月16日，经过近8个月的谈判，奇瑞与美国梦幻汽车公司达成合作协议，奇瑞将以技术、厂房、设备作价投入3亿美元，梦幻公司将投入2亿美元的现金，共同在奇瑞公司建立研发生产基地。梦幻汽车公司将拥有奇瑞汽车五款新车在北美地区（美国、加拿大、墨西哥）的分销权，将按国际标准组织经销商队伍，建立250个规范的轿车销售网点，从2007年正式开始销售，保证在5年内完成100万辆的销量。

虽然美国是全球最大的汽车市场，但它同时也是标准最严格的市场。尽管奇瑞出口美国的5款车型外观设计已经相当成熟，但要符合美国的市场需求以及安全性能要求则仍需改进。2005年2月8日，梦幻公司宣布，已经聘请了前三菱北美公司的汽车研发总监丹尼斯·戈尔为总工程师和研发执行副总裁。丹尼斯·戈尔曾经在1998~2005年供职于三菱北美公司，在此之前则在本田北美公司和日产北美公司任研发部高管，除负责研发与改进技术之外，他在诸多日资公司的产品适应美国市场方面还具有丰富经验，这些经验，无疑将为奇瑞进入美国铺平道路。

尽管奇瑞对于进入美国市场雄心勃勃，但诸多因素注定了奇瑞在美国市场的开拓之路充满艰辛曲折。2005年4月底，美国通用汽车公司针对奇瑞英文商标“Chery”与通用旗下雪佛兰商标“Chevy”涉嫌雷同等问题向奇瑞发难，使奇瑞汽车进军美国市场的前景蒙上阴影。2005年4月底，美国通用汽车公司突然委托一位知名律师向奇瑞汽车的美国经销商——美国梦幻汽车公司致函，在该律师的信中，通用方面认为奇瑞的英文商标“Chery”涉嫌与雪佛兰的英文商标“Chevy”雷同，奇瑞不得用该商标在美国进行注册、销售、代理以及所有有关商业活动。除了品牌问题外，通用诉讼奇瑞还有另外三大“理由”：一是奇瑞QQ靠作弊通过的碰撞测试；二是奇瑞公司模仿和抄袭了Matiz车的外观；三是奇瑞QQ大多数零部件和雪佛兰Spark具有替换性。奇瑞与通用的商标之争只是一个导火索，通用的最大担心是奇瑞正在复制丰田等日系车通过低价策略在北美市场攻城略地的模式，进而影响到自己的市场份额。美国一家权威报纸评论称“中国汽车正在以一个危险的速度不断扩展，而奇瑞就是中国汽车工业中一只富有冒险精神的‘小老虎’”。

对于这些开拓海外市场的企业，失败的风险随时存在，比如一汽夏利在开拓美国市场不久就销声匿迹了。就在人们纷纷为奇瑞开拓美国市场的前景担忧之时，在2006年底的北京车展期间，美国梦幻汽车公司宣称，终止与奇瑞汽车的合作，并中断关于建立合资企业设计、制造并销售汽车的谈判。奇瑞认为，双方分手的主要原因是梦幻公司的资金迟迟没有真正到账；而布鲁克林称，奇瑞的汽车无法满足美国的质量及安全标准。

案例讨论题：

1. 分析奇瑞公司的国际化战略。
2. 奇瑞在美国市场失败的原因是什么？
3. 奇瑞在哪些市场取得了成功？这些成功经验能否复制到其他市场？

二十七、日产汽车公司的跨国进入战略

2012年9月，日产汽车在中国市场的销售量同比下降35.3%，其中，东风日产的轿车销量大幅下滑44.2%。日产汽车公司于2012年10月18日宣布，针对在抗议日本政府非法“购岛”的游行中意外受损的中国本地产日产汽车，推出全额补偿措施。日产公司推出该措施意在减轻车主负担，恢复在中国的汽车销售。

日产公司是1914年由田建治郎等人创建的，其前身是“快进社”，于1934年改为日产汽车公司。日产公司生产的轿车品牌很多。日产汽车公司是日本的第二大汽车公司，也是世界十大汽车公司之一，其总部位于东京，雇员总数近13万人。

从20世纪50年代末期开始，由于日本国内市场受到限制，日产汽车就制定了以出口为主的战略。1958年日产汽车的出口不足3000辆，但到1963年，日产汽车出口已达45000辆。1966年，日产汽车还在坚持扩大出口的基础上，提出了扩大出口方式的新思路——不单纯扩大出口，而是根据不同的市场环境，着眼于提高竞争力，并采取与出口市场相适应的经营策略。1960年，日产汽车在美国开办美国日产汽车销售公司，专门进口和销售小轿车、卡车及其零件；1965年，日产汽车又在加拿大开办日产汽车公司，销售小轿车和卡车。在坚持将日本生产的产品出口海外市场的同时，日产汽车还采取了新的市场开拓模式，就是实现产品的海外生产。80年代开始，日产汽车开始在美国建立生产厂，先是组建了小型卡车生产企业，后又成立了轿车制造企业；同时，日产在欧洲的跨国生产战略也正式启动；1983年，西班牙日产工厂开始生产日产途乐。

20世纪90年代，由于国际市场的开拓缓慢以及自身产品方面的原因，日产汽车在1999年之前出现了连续7年的亏损，亏损额在50亿美元以上。

1999 年 5 月 28 日，法国雷诺汽车以 54 亿美元收购了日产汽车 36.8% 的股权，成为该公司的大股东，组建了雷诺—日产战略联盟。雷诺汽车当年迅速采取行动，采用了“外科手术”式的改革措施，减少一半零部件供应商，由 1300 家零部件供应商减少到 600 家左右，3 年内使采购成本下降 20%，削减 20% 的销售成本和管理成本。公司在 3 年内裁员 21000 人，关闭 5 家工厂。关闭工厂的直接成果是日产的产能利用率得到有效提高，使日产汽车摆脱了困境。一系列措施使日产汽车在 2000 财政年度实现了“奇迹般”的 27 亿美元的运营利润。

2010 年 4 月 7 日，法国雷诺、日本日产和德国戴姆勒三家汽车企业在布鲁塞尔签署协议结成同盟，戴姆勒和雷诺将分别获得日产 3.1% 的股份。之后雷诺会将所持 1.55% 的股份交换日产 2% 的股份。通过联盟，戴姆勒公司认为，小型车市场竞争激烈，对价格反应敏感，因此，汽车厂商需要有效压缩成本。合并后形成的戴姆勒 - 雷诺—日产联盟有望节约数十亿欧元的成本，车型平台的共同开发、研发、包括在动力系统技术上的共享，都将实现成本的下降。

在中国市场，日产公司根据环境的变化适时调整了战略。20 世纪 70 年代，日产公司向中国直接出口公爵汽车，标志着日产汽车正式进入中国。随着中国改革开放进程的推进，1985 年，日产公司在北京设立办事处，并在 1986 年以技术授权的方式，向中国一汽公司转让 ATLAS 双排驾驶室技术。进入 90 年代，中国汽车市场加速蓬勃发展，日产公司开始实行本土化战略，独资运营其在中国的子公司。1993 年郑州日产有限公司成立；1994 年日产汽车（中国）有限公司在香港成立，主要经营进口车业务。进入 21 世纪，日产公司为抢夺市场先机，使用各种方式抢占市场份额。2002 年 9 月，日产公司与东风汽车公司建立战略联盟，建立了全面战略合作关系；2003 年 4 月，日产公司和东风汽车公司合资成立生产企业；2004 年 2 月，日产汽车公司驻北京的全资子公司——日产（中国）投资有限公司成立，与日产汽车公司总部一起管理在华投资。2010 年，日产公司的电动汽车——日产聆风也在北京国际车展上首次在中国亮相。

案例讨论题：

1. 日产公司为何要补偿受损的汽车？

2. 日产公司在进入欧美市场时，有着怎样的战略选择？

3. 日产公司为何要不遗余力地开拓中国市场？在进入中国市场的过程中，它又怎样因时制宜地调整战略？

第六篇

国际商务运营

二十八、欧莱雅在中国的营销

2015 年欧莱雅在中国的销售额达 149. 6 亿元人民币，较去年增长 4. 6%。而若以欧元计算，当年增速则超过 22%。至此，欧莱雅这家全球最大的化妆品公司已在中国保持连续 19 年销售增长的纪录。这也是继 2010 年销售额首次跻身集团内“10 亿欧元俱乐部”之后，欧莱雅在中国实现的又一个里程碑。

欧莱雅集团是世界上最大的化妆品公司，创建于 1907 年，总部在法国巴黎，是《财富》全球 500 强之一和《财富》“全球 50 家最受赞赏公司”之一。欧莱雅的各类化妆品畅销全世界，广受欢迎。除化妆品以外，该集团还经营高档的消费品，并从事制药和皮肤病研究。欧莱雅集团 2016 年实现全球销售 258. 4 亿欧元，同比增长 2. 3%，可比销售额同比增长 4. 7%。在中国市场，欧莱雅销售额增速远高于其他市场。持续的高增长使欧莱雅在中国的市场份额不断上升，并进一步巩固了中国作为欧莱雅集团全球前三大市场之一的地位。

欧莱雅的不凡销售业绩来自于不同凡响的销售策略。欧莱雅采取价值导向型定价方法，选择以“价格、档次”为区分的多品牌战略，产品所标榜的审美与品位以及由此决定的价格是品牌区隔的主要准绳，这一点主要体现在欧莱雅的金字塔品牌结构上。此外，欧莱雅的宣传渠道主要包括高档的时尚类杂志、街上的广告招牌、电视、网络等。欧莱雅对于不同的产品采用不同的广告策略，根据不同的目标顾客，欧莱雅采取了行之有效的促销方法。欧莱雅的广告策略向来讲究“张合有度”，在对旗下品牌的宣传中，欧莱雅善于赋予并展现出品牌不同的特性。例如，赫莲娜是精致而高雅，巴黎欧莱雅是可亲近的优雅，美宝莲是流行的时尚，小护士是亲和的大众形象等。这种品牌的鲜亮特色在持续的广告宣传中被反复强化，久而久之，也就沉淀在了消费者的心中。

除了对品牌理念坚持一贯的塑造外，欧莱雅还偏好于借助一句话的广告语。例如，“巴黎欧莱雅，你值得拥有!”“美来自内心，美来自美宝莲”等简洁而有力的广告语，冲击力强，给人印象深刻，这也为品牌的传播无形中增加了很多后续的广告影响力。此外，欧莱雅还为其品牌体系构筑了“梦之队”明星阵容，借助国际和本土当红明星的传播效应，塑造出欧莱雅自己的品牌明星方队。欧莱雅的高级管理人吉尔斯·韦尔曾说，“现在出口已经过时了，你必须本地化，并与本地一流的公司一样强，同时佐以国际化的形象和策略。”在欧莱雅的策略中，国际化和本土化是密不可分的。在宣传上，像美宝莲等国际性的品牌，欧莱雅在强调其国际形象的同时不忘与中国本土文化相融合，打造出“来自纽约的适合中国人皮肤的美宝莲”；而羽西等被收购的本土品牌，欧莱雅会在其原有内涵的基础上注入集团的新技术，使它超越本土，从而塑造出品牌的国际化形象。

大量的广告有时反而容易引起消费者的反感和抵触情绪，所以在运用广告之余，充分把握和利用一些公共沟通方式，往往可以起到意想不到的效果。而欧莱雅正是这方面的高手，例如，美宝莲 1998 年和 1999 年连续赞助世界精英模特大赛中国选拔赛，鼓励中国女性走向世界，展示东方女性独特的韵味，吸引了消费者的关注；2000～2002 年连续在全国高校举办“Beauty Night 校园巡回展示活动”，帮助在校大学生更好地理解内心美、塑造外形美，美宝莲首席化妆师为女大学生进行现场个人形象设计，引起了轰动。

公司通过与权威机构合作办理公益事项来扩大品牌效应。例如，与国际组织共同设立“欧莱雅—联合国教科文组织世界杰出女科学家成就奖”和“联合国教科文组织—欧莱雅世界青年女科学家奖学金”，每年评选一次，极大地提高了公司的地位和可信赖度。

此外，公司还利用社会焦点吸引消费者的注意。例如，国际护士节之日，欧莱雅（中国）有限公司正式通过上海市卫生局，将价值超过 100 万元人民币，且符合医护人员特殊需求的健康护肤品赠送给抗击“非典”一线的医护人员。

最后，公司通过参与权威机构的评选，提高产品的知名度。例如，参与国家工商行政管理总局和国家商标局等机构共同举办的第三届“中国商标大赛”，并被评为“2002年中国人喜爱的十大外国商标”之一。同属于欧莱雅集团的“美宝莲”品牌由于其唇膏销量占2002年中国市场第一而荣获“2002年最具市场竞争力的第一唇膏品牌”及“2002年唇膏市场上最受欢迎的品牌”。通过积极地使用公共沟通策略，欧莱雅集团成功地让其各种产品每天24小时尽可能出现在人们的视野中，无形中让消费者不断地认识或加深了对欧莱雅集团各个品牌的印象和好感。

案例讨论题：

1. 为何欧莱雅会有不俗的销售业绩？
2. 欧莱雅在中国运用了什么样的销售策略？效果如何？
3. 欧莱雅在中国与本土企业建立了什么样的关系？

二十九、东软集团引领中国嵌入式软件外包

作为中国最大的嵌入式软件提供商，东软集团与中国其他的软件企业一样，感受着嵌入式软件外包蓬勃发展带给它们的发展新机遇。

嵌入式软件在中国的发展潜力巨大。中国政府对于嵌入式软件产业的重视与扶持为其快速发展起了重要作用。完善的基础设施以及发达的通信与信息设施，也为 IT 服务产业的发展提供了诸多便利的政策与优惠。软件中的嵌入式系统技术能够广泛应用于国民经济的各个领域，形成多学科、多领域的交叉和融合。

中国制造业的发展将产生更多的软件开发与服务业务，软件已经成为许多设备中的部件，如通信设备，家电、汽车、医疗设备等，所有在中国制造的设备也将需要在中国制造软件部件，中国软件企业将会发展成为软件部件的制造者，也会成为这些产品在世界的销售、维护的服务提供者。目前，中国嵌入式软件外包业务的发展十分迅速，特别是日本企业对中国的嵌入式软件外包的业务需求越来越大，从手机、家电、汽车电子到半导体等，日本的电子制造业与中国的软件产业进行了很好的互补性合作。正是中国嵌入式软件产业良好的发展环境，为中国软件企业带来了新的机会和挑战。

东软集团是一家面向全球提供 IT 解决方案与服务的公司，致力于通过创新的信息化技术来推动社会的发展与变革，为个人创造新的生活方式，为社会创造价值。东软集团创立于 1991 年，拥有近 2 万名员工，在中国建立了 8 个区域总部，10 个软件研发基地，16 个软件开发与技术支持中心，在 60 多个城市建立了营销与服务网络，在美国、日本、欧洲、中东、南美设有子公司。东软以软件技术为核心，提供行业解决方案和产品工程解决方案以及相关软件产品、平台及服务。

东软集团创立初期的业务不是来源于国内，而是来源于国外市场，通过为国外企业提供软件开发外包而打下企业生存的基础，并由此逐渐扩大业务领域。其后，借助于国际市场服务所获得的经验与培养的能力，东软集团回师国内市场并发展壮大。同时，以国内市场的稳定为依托，东软集团逐步将其战略定位从国际化升级为全球化。

2011 年是东软集团成立 20 周年，在这一关键节点上，东软集团确立了全球化、基于互联网的多元化商业模式、以知识资产为拉动的业务增长模式和卓越运营改善计划等战略方向。其后 4 年来，通过技术、商业模式的创新和转型，东软集团成功构建了覆盖医疗机构、医院、企业、社区、家庭和个人的医疗健康产业群，打造了兴业、优政、惠民的智慧云城市解决方案与服务模式。在追求规模的同时，东软集团也在寻求可持续的竞争能力，为了提高利润空间，东软集团加快了全球化进程。

智能化设备是制造业未来发展的方向，智能化设备需要嵌入式软件的支撑，而嵌入式软件的开发是东软集团的技术优势。面对市场机遇，东软集团积极准备，为此建立了面向未来 3 ~5 年的人才战略规划。根据未来业务的发展，预测在不同的方向进行人才的培养和储备，重点开展骨干员工和管理团队的建设和培养。

在技术方面，建立并不断完善面向手机嵌入式软件的技术体系和员工能力模型，基于主流的手机软件平台（如 Symbian、Linux、Windows Mobile、高通、安卓平台等）建立东软集团在手机软件各个层次、各个软件模块方面的核心技术能力。

在管理流程方面，东软集团积极推行基于软件成熟度的质量管理体系；同时基于 ISO27001 标准建立了信息安全管理体系并通过认证。

东软集团通过多年的努力，已经建立起了同多个国际知名手机厂商的合作关系，所参与研发的手机产品面向中国、日本、欧洲和美国等国的多个运营商。在技术深度方面也涵盖了手机软件平台研发、应用研发和手机测试等各个层次，建立起了上千人的专业化的技术队伍。东软集团计划建设一支 2000 ~3000 人的专业化的手机软件研发团队，成长为国际一流的手机嵌入式软件服务提供商。

嵌入式软件具有的非标准化生产和客户定制程度高的特点，使得除了对技术及经验有特定要求外，在合作过程中的模式与融合也变得至关重要。经过多年的合作，东软已经适应了这些行业和产品开发的特点。特别是在汽车音响方面，东软集团与阿尔派公司保持了10多年的合作，成功的经验在于东软集团完善的开发流程和质量保证体系、成本优势和高质量的开发结果以及良好的服务意识和积极改善的态度。更重要的是，东软集团有着与客户求同存异、优势互补、共同成长、共赢的理念。东软与阿尔派的合作新模式是“两个公司、一个系统”。

东软集团以自身的实力取得客户的信任，使得双方的合作建立在同一平台上，是一种更平衡的合作方式；东软集团的QCD能力得到了客户的认可，也持续为客户创造了价值，东软集团承担软件构想、设计及开发的阿尔派产品多次在国际上获奖，为东软集团，也为阿尔派提高了知名度和品牌竞争力。这便是东软集团在与客户合作时能够融为一体的关键所在。双方未来合作的目标是以“无岸”的方式，共同推进产品的全球竞争力，互惠互利，追求更深意义的共赢。

东软集团的软件外包业务主要在应用软件和嵌入式软件两个领域。嵌入式软件是未来重点发展的业务。中国作为“世界制造工场”日益成熟，今后必然要向产品设计和软件开发的深度扩展，为此，东软早早进行了资源的准备和业务的尝试。

然而，与欧美市场相比，日本市场仍然是一块“小蛋糕”。北美和欧洲的IT服务与外包市场占全球市场的75%，并且将以每年60%的速度持续增长，这几乎是日本市场的两倍。当前，欧美国家也因研发成本、人才资源、开拓消费市场等原因，积极不断地将其研发和软件外包业务向中国转移。

过去，“中国制造”的奇迹改变了中国，也影响了世界。未来，中国还将成为在服务外包领域拥有巨大潜力的国家。而东软集团作为中国最大的软件外包服务提供商，必将抓住机会，使刚刚起步，具有巨大潜力的嵌入式软件外包成为东软集团发展的新引擎，来带动东软集团的未来向更广阔的方向发展。

案例讨论题：

1. 东软集团能够成为日本最大软件外包商的战略优势是什么？
2. 东软集团提供软件外包服务会获得哪些收益？
3. 比较软件领域自己开发与外包各自的优缺点。

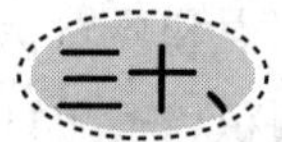

长安汽车的国际研发战略

作为中国自主创新领军企业之一的长安汽车，走向全球市场是其必然选择。长安汽车每年将利润的5%用于研发投入。长安汽车能够快速发展，成为世界上第一家在9年内达到年销售100万台乘用车的汽车企业也是得益于此。

长安汽车充分利用全球资源进行协同开发，在美洲、欧洲、亚洲等地都建立了研发中心，引入国际大型制造企业，以基于PDM的全球协同平台作为先进的协同管理理念，真正实现全球24小时不间断在线协同研发。2016年，长安汽车已经掌握了全速自适应巡航、车道保持、全自动泊车等智能驾驶核心技术，特别是结构化道路无人驾驶技术已通过实质性技术验证，为长安汽车在智能驾驶技术方面的快速发展迈出了坚实的一步。到2025年将实现真正的自动驾驶。

长安汽车全球研发体系涵盖重庆、上海、北京、意大利都灵、日本横滨、英国伯明翰及美国底特律，形成了由内而外稳固发展的研发格局以及全球研发体系。长安汽车的“五国九地”全球研发体系各有侧重，分工协作，形成一个协同体系。位于都灵的欧洲设计中心主要负责车身开发、造型研究、汽车内外饰件的研究；日本设计中心致力于工程化设计、模型制作、进出口商贸业务等；英国研发中心则侧重于发动机及变速箱的研发；美国研发中心专攻汽车技术最核心、难度最大的底盘研发。

长安汽车第一个海外研发中心于2003年9月在意大利都灵建立，主要进行汽车造型、可行性分析等设计工作。至2006年5月8日，长安汽车欧洲设计中心有限责任公司（简称长安欧洲）正式注册成立。其主要是利用意大利乃至欧洲的汽车设计、开发方面的优秀人才，采用当地的汽车设计理念和技术，在欧洲为长安公司进行造型研究、车身开发、汽车内外饰件的研究和开发等方面的活动，并与当地的有关公司、学校进行合作，建立长安公司的培训基地，为长安公司培养相关的技术人才。

欧洲设计中心已具备总布置设计、创意设计、数字化设计、软硬脂模型制作及模型后期加工等多项能力，涵盖了汽车造型设计全过程，拥有 6 个模型制作平台以及 1 个木工机加间、1 个喷漆间等配套设施。2006 ~ 2012 年，长安欧洲累计完成各项创意设计任务 800 余项，S4 级以上整车开发项目 23 个（产品项目及概念车项目总计）。尤其是在 2010 ~ 2012 年，共计承担了 11 个产品项目，4 个概念车项目。

2008 年 4 月 17 日，长安汽车日本设计中心在日本神奈川县横滨市港北区新横滨正式开业。主要从事汽车内外饰造型和工程化设计工作，包括造型部和工程部。其主要经营范围包括汽车内外饰造型设计、总布置及可行性研究、工程化设计、模型制作、样车制作、工程和生产支持与咨询等。成立该设计中心，正是要学习日本汽车设计的成熟理念和技术手段，充分依托日本一流的技术人才，快速提升长安汽车的设计能力，同时培养一批具有国际设计眼光与领先水平的研发人才。

2010 年 6 月，长安汽车英国研发中心在诺丁汉科技园区挂牌成立，随后又在英国 Fenn End、MIRA 设立办公地点。三地共同专注于先进动力总成研发。2015 年研发中心迁入伯明翰，伯明翰除了地理位置、交通便利的先天条件之外，也是英国汽车工业的黄金发展区，不仅汇集了众多知名汽车公司，也吸引了大量的汽车研发与制造相关的专业人才在此安家立业。

伯明翰被称为英国的底特律，英国汽车行业一直以发动机及变速箱的研发制造见长，日产、丰田、福特等全球汽车“大牌”均在英国设有研发中心。而长安汽车在英国建立动力研发中心，首先可以快速获取海外工程团队所能提供的体系和产品开发能力，利用这样一个模式，快速帮助长安缩短和世界一流汽车企业之间产品研发能力的差距。其次，还可以通过相互学习完成对母国人才的培养和知识的传承。

英国研发中心工程人员的平均工龄为 25 岁，超过 10% 的人员拥有博士学位。他们中的绝大部分都在捷豹、路虎、福特、宝马、劳斯莱斯、宾利等著名汽车企业中工作过。目前，英国研发中心总人数约为 150 人，海外人才比例占比约 90%。而在母国的动力研发团队在 1000 人左右。双方互有分工，各有侧重，中国研发中心负责从无到有，而海外研发团队负责从有到精。在这样一种体系下，通过海外团队先进的技术水平和创新能力，来带动培养企业团队能力，实现人才本土化的目的。

长安汽车美国研发中心 2011 年 1 月在“汽车之城”底特律正式挂牌成立。至此，继意大利、日本、英国等海外中心之后，长安汽车“五国九地、各有侧重”的全球研发布局基本完善。

长安汽车美国研发中心专攻汽车技术最核心、难度最大的底盘研发，其中包括底盘性能调校能力、底盘工程化设计、底盘技术研究以及底盘制造工艺等方向的研究。同时，美国研发中心还是长安汽车智能化发展的先导基地，而它就坐落在美国密歇根州最大的城市——底特律。依托美国研发中心作为智能化先导基地，以及 MTC 联盟全球的研发实力和会员权益的优势，长安汽车智能化领域的发展拥有更多的突围机会。从 2000 公里超长距离无人驾驶，到已经落地量产的停走式自适应巡航、自动紧急刹车、并线辅助/盲区监测等技术，长安汽车智能化领域在业界都处在领先水平，无人驾驶的量产计划更是领先行业水平 2 年时间。

长安汽车美国研发中心智能化团队的工作主要有两个方面：一是包括 ACC 和 APA 在内的驾驶辅助技术和自动驾驶技术；二是以 V2X 为基础的车联网技术。2016 年北京车展开幕前，长安汽车的无人驾驶汽车完成了从重庆到北京长达 2000 千米的远征，最终安全无损地抵达北京，堪称中国无人驾驶领域史无前例的壮举。但是由于成本、法规等方面的问题，自动驾驶技术距离实用化还很遥远。长安汽车美国研发中心计划在 2020 年实现三级自动驾驶技术的量产，当前的主要任务则是 ACC 自动巡航和 APA 自动泊车这两项技术的量产。

案例讨论题：

1. 长安汽车建立海外研发中心的作用是什么？
2. 长安汽车的海外研发如何与企业的持续发展结合起来？
3. 长安汽车建立全球联动研发网络的制约因素有哪些？

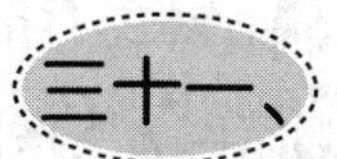

三十一、腾讯国际人力资源管理实践

腾讯是中国著名的互联网公司，其2004年上市时的股票发行价为3.7港元，2013年11月已经上涨到超过400港元，9年多以来的涨幅超过百倍。2017年4月，腾讯市值达到2790亿美元，成为全球第十大市值公司。

自2004年上市以来，腾讯的总收入、毛利和年度盈利这三项主要经营指标每年都保持两位数增加。在全球上市公司中，腾讯的长期财务表现仅次于亚马逊。优异的业绩揭示了腾讯在人才管理上的成功，其中最独到之处是以人为本、重视企业文化、强调包容和合作的精神。

目前，腾讯拥有超过2.4万名员工，其中30%以上拥有硕士及以上学位，60%是技术人员，中高级管理层实行全球化人力资源管理战略，吸纳欧美有实践经验的优秀人员加盟。平均年龄约29岁，男女比例大约3∶1。在全球范围内，腾讯针对硕士、博士、博士后，选拔具有技术特长的人才。在人力资源管理上，腾讯的做法不是靠人治，也不是靠政策，而是靠企业文化。企业文化是公司里经过长时间形成的一种共识和规范，它引导大家的一致行动。腾讯每年引进的人才非常多，既有来自谷歌、Facebook、甲骨文、微软、三星这些跨国企业的精英，也有来自投资银行、咨询公司、媒体的优秀人才，大家文化背景不同、经历各异，腾讯解决多元化人才的做法除了提供平台之外，主要还是靠企业文化，通过打造一种开放、平等和尊重的企业文化，靠企业文化的魅力解决个性差异和融合问题。

腾讯在员工待遇方面在国内IT企业里一直具有很高的评价。总的待遇分为激励薪酬和福利两大部分，前者包括固定工资、服务奖金、绩效奖金和专项长期激励；后者则包括作为法定福利的五险一金以及商业保险、各种体贴的带薪休假。在福利方面值得关注的有安居计划。为了帮助多年来与公司共同成长的员工早日安居乐业，腾讯设立了安居计划，为符合条件的员工提供首套购房首付款的免息借款，帮助员工解决后顾之忧，早日实现安居梦想。而腾讯提出的员工身心健康计划也是业内的一大创新，主要是提供国家级心理咨询师24小时在线咨询和面授来解答和舒缓员工的心理压力，与此同时，每双周定期邀请两名中医院主任级别的医生到公司为大家提供服务，这些举措在保障员工身心健康的同时，也大大提高了其工作效率。而作为一家非常重视人才的公司，腾讯在对员工的关怀上非常细节化，比如，为了减少员工通勤的时间，公司在深圳、上海、成都和北京四个城市提供免费班车，多达260条线路，年运流量在2010年已经高达200余万人次，这些都体现了腾讯作为国内网络IT龙头企业在待遇福利方面结构合理、内容丰富。

2005年后，随着腾讯的上市，公司也开始在国内外市场进行一系列的收购，从而正式开始了其国际化经营、多元化布局的道路。2015年12月18日，腾讯作为大股东收购了美国RIOT公司剩余全部股份，使其成为旗下全资子公司。腾讯对RIOT这家典型的美国公司的人力资源管理特点鲜明、过渡平稳，值得行业其他企业借鉴。腾讯所采取的方法就是充分尊重文化差异，作为一个以设计为主体的公司，腾讯给予RIOT几乎独立经营的自主权，在薪酬激励方面采取了欧美通用体系，而不是照搬国内模式，对于外国员工给予了舒适自由、极富创造力的工作环境，为RIOT注入了诸如顾客体验优先、注重团队建设、保持好奇心等腾讯引以为豪的企业文化理念，从而从企业文化和管理理念方面来保持国外子公司不偏离母公司的发展轨道。

在福利方面，RIOT提供具有竞争力的薪水，包括四种补贴：医疗保险计划、补贴视力保险计划、牙科保险计划、退休福利计划。除了这些，还有许多人性化的安排，比如灵活工作计时。公司设有全方位服务的自助餐厅，提供全面补贴膳食；咖啡吧、办公室厨房备有免费谷物、新鲜水果、小吃、茶和新鲜的磨碎咖啡；RIOT还为残疾员工提供合理的住宿。这些都体现了员工福利的细节，同时也展现了腾讯国际化中管理的包容程度之高。

腾讯对RIOT另一大改变则是让其十分重视公司员工的价值，开展了员工培训计划，为他们提供了进一步学习和成长的机会。这是腾讯入主后极力推崇的，因为腾讯坚信对于员工教育培训的投入是非常值得的，在未来会成倍的得到回报。而 RIOT 在腾讯入股后表现也节节攀升，在 2013 年营业额接近 10 亿美元，这对于一家游戏设计类企业来说是个相当可观的数字。

通过腾讯对 RIOT 的收购和人力管理的例子，充分说明了对跨国企业，尤其是高科技企业来说，文化的包容和对海外子公司的信任是多么的重要，在人力资源管理和薪酬待遇方面，想进一步取得改进的渴望是取得成功的不竭动力。

案例讨论题：

1. 腾讯人力资源管理的宗旨是什么？
2. 腾讯人员配备政策属于哪种类型？具体是什么？
3. 腾讯对海外 RIOT 公司的人力资源管理采取什么态度？效果如何？
4. 腾讯对 RIOT 的跨国管理有哪些值得借鉴的地方？

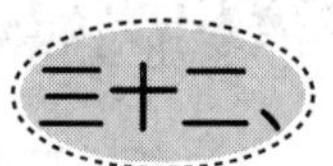

TCL国际人力资源管理战略

TCL集团股份有限公司创立于1981年，是全球性规模经营的消费类电子企业集团之一，旗下拥有三家上市公司：TCL集团、TCL多媒体科技、TCL通讯科技。2011年，TCL全球营业收入608.34亿元人民币，员工总数6万多名。

随着经济全球化和区域一体化的加速，企业间的竞争表现为企业核心竞争力的比拼，而人力资源管理已成为构筑企业核心竞争力的重要因素。对于大举开拓海外市场的TCL集团来说，企业所需要的员工的综合素质、对海外市场的适应能力都将有所提升。目前，TCL集团外籍员工占集团总人数比例为17%，未来3~5年，这一比例将进一步提高。这为TCL集团人才的选拔、培训提出了不同于以往的挑战。TCL集团的发展愿景决定了其对员工素质的要求不仅要具备出色的专业技能和管理能力，还要具备良好的自我激励、自我学习能力、适应能力、沟通能力和团队合作精神。

为提高集团管理人员的素质，适应人才国际化战略的要求，TCL采用内部提升和外部引进并重的人才战略。一方面，对现有的各级管理人员进行国际化企业经营运作能力的系统提升，有计划地选派部分人员到海外企业交流任职或到国际一流的商学院学习等；另一方面，以全球化视野，搜寻、吸纳具有国际化经营背景的高级管理人才和研发人才，迅速补充到关键岗位；并在国内引入具有潜质和一定经验，尤其是有外资企业工作经历的各类专才，作为国际化人才的后备队伍，加以培养锻炼。

2012年6月，TCL集团在广州召开了主题为“成就梦想创建具有国际竞争力的世界级企业”的新闻发布会，宣布集团2013国际化人才引入计划，计划招聘2200人，专业涉及电子、信息、通信、机械、营销、财会和人力资源等，招聘对象为有海内外知名企业工作背景和丰富经验的中高级人才，其中不乏事业部研发中心总经理、海外区域销售总经理等高级职位。招聘在美国纽约、硅谷和中国珠江三角洲、环渤海湾、长江三角洲等地举行。中高级职位占那次招聘的近 40%，研发型人才占了近 70%，TCL 汤姆逊项目和 TCL 移动通信的人才需求占到了 60%。

作为一个跨国集团，TCL 也面临着人力资源国际化带来的管理挑战。目前，TCL 的人力资源管理体系分为集团总部、各事业本部、各下属企业三个层次，其中多个事业本部的人力资源管理模式各不相同，有的采取矩阵式的管理，即一个事业本部设一个人力资源中心，横向联系各个事业部，纵向联系下属企业，实行人力资源派出制，被派出的专员接受直线经理和人力中心的双重领导。TCL 还采用直线职能制，即本部有一个人力资源部，各下属企业设有相应部门，仅这一级的人力资源经理就将近百人，大家各有一套工作方法，这样一来虽然人员比较庞大，但是运作起来却相对比较简单。

TCL 集团海外市场已覆盖东南亚、南美、中东、非洲、大洋洲、俄罗斯等多个国家。在海外员工的选用上，为增加各地分支机构的主动性和灵活性，应付市场环境变化，TCL 集团采用了因地制宜的管理方法。集团总部首先做出一套人力资源管理方案框架，由分支机构细化并实施。在人才的选用上，由当地负责人视东道国人力资源素质决定，并根据具体情况对东道国本土雇员进行相应培训，以使其尽快融入公司的工作。同时，依据东道国法律、风俗习惯与生活方式等，确定符合当地情况的薪资福利结构与工作时间；依据该国的工作习惯制定评估标准，依据实际业绩加以考核。集团总部人力资源部门经常派出工作人员到各分支机构指导工作，以确保各分支机构与集团总部人力资源部门的协调统一，保持较高的运作效率。

同时，TCL 在跨国人力资源管理上力求做到克服文化差异。多元化移民文化的价值观一直是 TCL 的骄傲，TCL 倡导“尊重学识、注重才能；鼓励创新、允许失败；敬业诚信、团队协作；包容文化、兼收并蓄”的人才成长环境，在进入全球市场时，这一文化将有利于来自不同文化背景的员工尽快地融合为一体，有效地开展工作，进而转化为强大的企业竞争力。

TTE 是 TCL 与汤姆逊合并整合后的跨国公司，目前全球拥有研发人员 1200 名，无论是哪个国籍的员工，都是 TTE 的一分子，将在各自的岗位上发挥才能并承担相应的责任。在制定 TTE 的薪酬标准时，企业综合了多方面因素，包括国际市场、国内市场以及 TCL 集团和汤姆逊的自身情况，以使来自不同国家、在全球不同地点工作的员工产生薪酬公正感。同时，对于那些在海外市场工作的中国员工，企业还须提供一定的奖金及激励，从而鼓励他们努力克服到一个陌生的环境中去工作和生活所必然面对的各种困难。

案例讨论题：

1. TCL 集团为什么在推进国际化过程中始终强调人的重要性？

2. TCL 集团在人员配备政策上采取了哪种政策？其中的优势和面对的困难有哪些？

3. TCL 集团如何降低外派经理的外派失败率？

4. TCL 集团在员工薪酬方面的做法有什么特点？

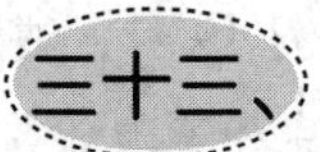

三十三、中国海外上市公司面临做空风险

2011 年 4 月 11 日，美国市场做空者浑水研究（Muddy Waters）对多元环球水务发布了“强烈建议出售”的报告，导致该股股价大跌。

浑水研究发布的报告显示，该公司土地资产入账金额过高，两份报告中有关在建工程项目的数据不相符，CFO 没有中国背景，其分销网络子虚乌有等。据此，浑水研究认为多元环球水务年收入不会超过 80 万美元，和其当初在美国上市时宣称的 1.544 亿美元相差甚远。这是浑水研究的惯用方法论：寻找公司在中美两份财务报表之间的差异，以此为线索展开调查。而原中方的审计报告是由一家本土的廊坊中天建会计师事务所出具的。

事实上，多元环球水务并非第一家因为会计制度差异而被外国公司做空的公司。2012 年 6 月 20 日，境外做空机构香橼（Citron）发表报告称，恒大地产以虚假信息及贿赂掩盖公司资不抵债。在香橼报告发出后，恒大地产的股票大跌，6 月 21 日恒大地产股价跌幅 11%，当天恒大市值缩水 76.26 亿港元；6 月 22 日再跌 3.53%。

2011 年 6 月 2 日，浑水研究发布了针对嘉汉林业的做空报告，指出嘉汉林业虚构资产和收入。报告发布后两天，嘉汉林业股价大跌超过 80%，市值蒸发 50 亿美元，最后被迫停牌接受调查。

2011 年 2 月 4 日，浑水研究发布了一份针对中国高速频道的研究报告，质疑该公司蓄意夸大盈利能力，并指出其向工商局提交的盈利数据与向美国证监会（SEC）递交的财报数据存在严重不符的事实，最终导致中国高速也被迫摘牌。

2010 年 6 月 29 日，浑水研究在其公司网站上发布了对东方纸业股份有限公司的研究报告，称其存在财务报表造假行为，如资产估值至少夸大了10倍，2009年的营收夸大了40倍等。报告带来的影响是股价暴跌：东方纸业的股价在一夜间下跌13%，在其后的六周中又狂跌32%。

甚至在更早前，2001年7月19日，纳斯达克声言由于网易公司未能以表格20－F的形式向纳斯达克和美国证券交易委员会呈报年度报表，因此违反了纳斯达克市场规则第4310（c）（14）条的规定，决定停牌。

调查显示，中国公司频遭调查做空，除了一些企业自身的财务问题外，也与中美两国的会计制度差异有关系。一些中国企业为了利润，会伪造银行对账单、捏造不存在的贷款、虚构资产、虚设销售合同、伪造库存清单从而达到增值税舞弊目的，等等。

虽然会计师事务所意识到中美会计制度存在差异，但还是无法做到中美两套财务报表完全一致。中国会计准则（PRCGAAP）是依照国际会计准则（IFRS）的规范制定的，而美国会计准则（USGAAP）在一些细节条款上与前者有一定差异。比较中美两套准则后发现，两者的差距主要体现在借款费用是资产化还是费用化、无形资产摊销方法、关联方认定和收入确认等多个细节上有差异。比如究竟是开票时确认收入还是货物离岸时确认收入，这些差异都会造成报表的不同。美国会计准则较国际会计准则更谨慎，对于公允价值采取更为谨慎的态度，在准则层面并没有什么“钻空子”的可能。近年来USGAAP逐步向IFRS靠拢，这意味着它和PRCGAAP之间的差距越来越小，有利于报表统一。

一些中国财务专家认为，中国的会计准则并没有需要特别改进之处，关键在于是否能够很好地得到执行。在美国，通常的审计做法是，美国的四大会计师事务所或者其他受美国公众公司会计监督委员会（PCAOB）指定的事务所接了某公司的IPO审计项目，然后委派一个合伙人或者高级经理来到国内，和国内同名下的兄弟事务所合作，由后者提供主要的审计团队。碰到审计收费比较小的项目，干脆就完全使用国内团队，只要在出具财报前给美国的事务所检查一下即可。如果碰到事务所没有国内团队，那么也可能和某一家国内事务所合作。国内会计师也很专业，但在稳健性原则上，和USGAAP有所出入。

中国的会计师在具体问题的操作上过于灵活。比如，账龄多久就必须提坏账准备，如果公司能够拿出一些证据，证明这笔钱一定能收回来，事务所也不强行要求其提坏账准备。多名会计师表示，在收入确认环节，造假比较容易。理论上能够戳破谎言的询证环节有时候也形同虚设，会计师也无法轻易察觉。

2010 年 7 月，PCAOB 和 SEC 联合发表官方警告声明称，对于由中国境内公司发布的财务审计报告必须小心谨慎对待。问题是，由于 SEC 没有权利传唤中国境内的公司，针对这些造假案件的调查显得捉襟见肘。不过，在中美第三轮战略与经济对话后，中美双方表示将首先加强在诸如打击盗版造假等领域加强审计对接。而 SEC 目前也有类似表态，希望通过跨国合作监管缩小灰色地带。不过，一些人认为，美国日趋严格的管控环境，也许会导致企业分流到其他市场。

案例讨论题：

1. 中国上市企业为何频遭外国调查公司攻击？中国企业为何频陷财务报告造假丑闻？

2. 国际会计准则的差异主要有哪些？对中国的海外上市公司造成了哪些影响？

3. 对在海外上市的中国企业来说，如何应对中外会计准则的差异？

海尔的海外融资

“年货”档期热度未消，海尔冰箱以14.8%的市场比重五次蝉联全球第一之后，继续主导市场格局。据互联网消费调研中心发布的分析报告显示，海尔冰箱凭34.0%的用户关注高居榜首，成为冰箱市场全民搜索的第一品牌。

1984年创立于青岛的海尔集团，从引进冰箱技术起步，通过技术开发，精细化管理、资本运营，兼并控股及国际化等一系列发展，如今已经成为全球第一大白色家电集团，在全球建立了29个制造基地，8个综合研发中心和19个海外贸易公司，全球员工超过8万人，用户遍布全世界。

从2006年开始，海尔集团继名牌战略、多元化战略、国际化战略阶段之后，进入第四个发展战略创新阶段：全球化品牌阶段。为了给这一战略提供坚实的财务资金后盾，海尔集团先后进行了借壳上市、互换筹资等一系列资本运作。

21世纪初，海尔有意通过上市和寻求国际方面的战略合作来保证资金流转和扩大发展规模。由于海尔集团资产庞大，国内资本市场运作规定烦琐、严格，海尔希望通过先在香港资本市场收购一家公司，再利用这家公司反向收购集团资产这种借壳上市的方式进入国际资本市场。海尔借壳上市的整个实施过程可分为三步。

第一步，借壳。海尔投资在香港选择了一家由香港商人麦绍棠控制的主营业务为婴儿卫生用品的上市公司中建数码作为壳目标。作为借壳的第一步，海尔集团和中建数码的大股东中建电讯集团先后合资组建了飞马香港和飞马青岛两家从事手机生产和销售的公司。其中飞马青岛的出资方为海尔投资和中建电讯，海尔投资控股51%；飞马香港则由香港富东公司（海尔控股77%）和中建电讯出资，富东公司持股49%。

第二步，注资。2001 年底，上市公司中建数码多媒体向中建电讯和富东公司分别收购其持有的全部飞马香港股权，其后又在 2002 年 8 月从海尔手中收购了飞马青岛 15.50% 的权益，全部交易都以这家壳公司中建数码的股权为支付代价，结束后，海尔投资在这家壳公司中的持股比例升至 29.94%，并且在 2002 年 1 月 23 日改名为“海尔中建”。2003 年 3 月，海尔中建剥离出全部的幼儿护理业务，移动电话的生产和销售成为其唯一主业。

第三步，更名。由于港交所发布新规——自 2003 年 3 月 31 日起视借壳上市为新公司上市行为，海尔借壳上市计划不得不提速，当年 6 月海尔计划完成向海尔中建注入洗衣机白色家电资产以及剩余的飞马青岛 35.50% 的股权，海尔中建则以 14.53 亿港元的新股及可转债、外加 5000 万港元作为支付代价。但该计划仍被港交所视为新上市，因而一再拖延，最终在 2005 年 1 月 28 日，最后一步注资终于完成，海尔集团总裁杨绵绵出任海尔中建的主席，海尔中建更名为“海尔电器集团有限公司”。

通过在香港特区借壳上市，海尔得以顺利进入国际资本市场，使其有了优质的资本支持；同时促进了海尔财务管理的国际化，特别是在内控建设、风险管理、会计准则、信息披露及审计等方面充分与国际接轨。海尔通过境外上市，不仅使海尔在国际产品市场上拥有了品牌影响，而且为海尔在国际资本市场上奠定了优秀的信用基础。在完成借壳上市后，互换筹资又被海尔提上日程。

从开始的单纯出口产品到海外本土化生产，海尔在不断地开拓海外市场，同时也注重对一些海外企业的并购。2009 年 5 月新西兰家用电器制造商费雪派克宣布将采用包销方式进行配股集资，并表示中国家电企业海尔集团将参股 20%。该公司称将至少筹资 1.89 亿新西兰元，其中通过向海尔集团首次配股融资 4600 万新西兰元。此外，该公司还将以先旧后新配股的方式从海尔集团筹资 1200 万新西兰元，以确保后者的持股比例达到 20%。这就意味着海尔集团需要筹集 5800 万新西兰元以入股这家电器公司，而在新西兰直接进行筹资就要受到当地法律和政策的各种限制，同时由于信用等级的原因，在当地直接筹资对海尔集团而言是不利的。

2009 年 5 月，1 新西兰元 = 4.6 元人民币，此时若正好一家新西兰公司需要筹资 26680 万元人民币在中国投资，同样，对于这家新西兰公司而言，在中国直接筹资会受到中国政府和银行等各种法律和规定的制约，不但会增大公司的筹资成本，而且会降低筹资效率。这时，海尔可以通过与这家新西兰公司进行货币互换来解决双方所遇到的问题。由于海尔集团与费雪派克公司在各自国家市场的信用等级不同，所以筹资的年利率不同。海尔集团在中国市场能以 6.5% 的固定年利率得到 5 年期人民币筹资，而在新西兰市场由于受知名度降低的影响，信用等级也比在中国市场的低，可以以 8.2% 的固定年利率得到新西兰元筹资。

这次货币互换分为三步：第一步，初始本金交换。海尔集团在中国市场借入 26680 万元人民币，费雪派克公司在新西兰市场借入 5800 万新西兰元，然后两家公司将各自所借入的资金互换。第二步，利息的定期支付。每年年末海尔集团向费雪派克公司支付规定利息，费雪派克公司向海尔集团支付规定利息，然后两公司将利息分别支付给各自国家的贷款者。第三步，到期本金的再次交换。第五年年末，海尔集团支付费雪派克公司 5880 万新西兰元，费雪派克公司支付海尔集团 26680 万元人民币，然后两公司将款项还给各自国家的贷款者。通过货币互换，两家公司避免了市场限制，顺利筹到资金，还规避了汇率风险。

案例讨论题：

1. 分析海尔集团在海外上市的利弊。跨国公司在全球资本市场上进行筹资时需要注意哪些问题？

2. 互换筹资如何为海尔集团规避汇率风险？

3. 列举跨国公司所能遇到的外汇风险类型，分析海尔集团的外汇管理模式。

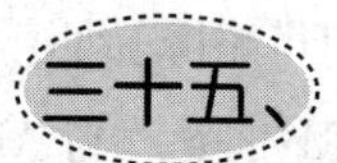

长虹国际业务风险管理

四川长虹电子控股集团有限公司始创于1958年，从军工立业、彩电兴业到信息电子的多元拓展，已成为集军工、消费电子、核心器件研发与制造为一体的综合型跨国企业集团，并向具有全球竞争力的信息与家电的内容与服务的提供商发展。

2016年长虹品牌价值达1208.96亿元人民币，继续稳居中国电子百强品牌第6位，在中国企业500强排名第152位，居中国制造业500强第64位。长虹旗下拥有四家上市公司：四川长虹、美菱电器、华意压缩、长虹佳华。

多年来，长虹坚持以用户为中心、以市场为导向，强化技术创新，夯实内部管理，积极培育集成电路设计、软件设计、工业设计、变频技术和可靠性技术等核心技术能力，构建消费类电子技术创新平台，大力实施智能化战略，不断提升企业综合竞争能力，逐步将长虹建设成为全球值得尊重的企业。

为更好地迎接各种挑战，长虹还根据复杂多变的市场行情，制定了自己的对策：高低结合，双拳出击。高端市场技术为王，低端市场质量为王。在决胜国内市场的同时，长虹放眼全球，积极参与到国际市场的大竞争中。直至2016年，长虹产品远销欧美、东南亚、中东、俄罗斯、大洋洲等地，出口创汇连续保持着100%以上的高速递增。公司已成功实现从产品出口到技术、资本输出的转型。

国际化发展的早期，四川长虹在国际财务管理中出现过重大失误。2001年，四川长虹开始与APEX发生业务往来，当年只有赊账没有回款，年末形成应收账款4184万美元。2002年是双方业务高峰，四川长虹销售给APEX公司6.1亿美元，但回款仅1.9亿美元，形成了4.62亿美元的应收账款。当年，四川长虹跟 APEX 公司的交易占全年彩电销售的 54%，占当年海外销售的 91.41%。2003 年，四川长虹又销售给 APEX4.24 亿美元的货物，回款 3.49 亿美元，销售略降、回款增加，但应收账款余额已增至 5.37 亿美元，折合人民币 44.51 亿元。与 APEX 公司的交易占四川长虹全年彩电销售的 33%，占当年海外销售的 70%。至 2004 年，四川长虹基本上结束与 APEX 的生意，仅向其销售 3559 万美元，同时加大回款力度，回款 1.09 亿美元。然而，四年生意下来，4.63 亿美元的应收账款已经形成。四年间，四川长虹共销售给 APEX 公司 11.13 亿美元，回款 6.49 亿美元。与 APEX 公司合作四年下来，这桩生意的坏账率高达 28.21%。最后，与 APEX 公司的官司结局针对最终形成的 4.63 亿美元的应收账款，除了可能回收 1.5 亿美元，没有回收更多的可能了。

经过此次坏账事件后，长虹公司汲取教训，在此后的国际贸易业务中，针对财务方面制定了严密的制度安排。强化客户信用管理，在与国外企业进行合作时，一定要通过多种途径对该公司的信用进行调查；建立客户资信管理制度，规范应收账款的日常管理和信用政策；建立健全财务制度，完善现行的财务核算制度、会计准则及内部控制制度；规范应收账款的方法和程序以及合格的保理公司。

保理公司是金融公司，金融企业对风险控制都有着极其严密的程序，国际贸易通过保理公司进行尽管安全，但由于有着复杂的运转流程，就会产生效率问题。比如，需要先向保理公司提出型号、数量的申请，然后等保理公司对承保货物进行风险审核后才能做出承保。遇到多批次、多型号、大数量的发货，保理公司审核过程就会制约交易的速度。另外，保理费也是一个问题。保理费分两种，有承保的保理收费和没有承保的保理收费，后一种仅代替企业回收货款，由于没有保证回款约定，因此收费较低，大约 3.5‰。家电产品毛利率低，基于成本考虑，四川长虹采用后一种居多。当货物大量销售时，有些账款就没进入保理账户，因此，四川长虹在这一环节十分重视。尽管货物发到了国外，但在转移给国外公司前，所有权属于四川长虹。货物经国外公司销售后，账款进入中间人保理公司账户，由保理公司划分金额，其中 10% 归海外合作公司，90% 归四川长虹。

除了此制度之外，四川长虹完善公司治理机构，建立起公司内部有效的制衡、约束和监督检查机制，建立严格的会计核算制度，内部正规管理。对于公司管理层，股东也制定了相应的制度来避免国际贸易中的失误。作为公司的财务总监，在应对公司应收账款没有收回时，首先应该及时向管理层建议立刻停止向该企业发货；其次，及时计提相应的坏账准备；再次，由内部业务员直接出面催收或者由公司专职机构出面催收或者委托收账公司代理追讨；最后，如果前面的方法依然没有收回应收账款，就使用法律武器进行追讨。

案例讨论题：

1. 应收账款在企业经营中的重要性如何体现？

2. 长虹应收账款事件产生的原因是什么？

3. 经过 APEX 公司事件后，长虹在应对海外业务时采取了何种策略防范风险？

参考文献

[1] 司建平．大健康背景下中医药国际化的策略选择 [J]．中医学报，2015 (5)：678 -680.

[2] 刘维军，王继斌．我国中药产品 2005—2012 年出口结构分析 [J]．现代药物与临床，2013 (4)：608 -611.

[3] 翁丽红，林丹红．北京同仁堂知识产权战略分析 [J]．福建中医药大学学报，2012 (6)：52 -54.

[4] 宋英杰，徐怀伏．我国中药产品对外贸易现状分析 [J]．现代商贸工业，2011 (1)：99 -100.

[5] 吴娅茹．从同仁堂的发展看中华老字号振兴之路 [J]．经济研究参考，2009 (37)：18 -25.

[6] 李江．全球化条件下我国乳业产业技术追赶的研究 [D]．北京化工大学，2010.

[7] 湛文倩．我国乳制品企业的品牌国际化战略研究 [D]．中国海洋大学，2012.

[8] 矫月．伊利集团海外业务成长战略研究 [D]．内蒙古大学，2013.

[9] 张剑秋．探索全球化浪潮中的中国乳业发展之路 [J]．中国乳业，2014 (9)：6 -7.

[10] 冯良．伊利高效增长与模式创新的逻辑关系 [J]．乳品与人类，2014 (6)：42 -49.

[11] 肖溢．经济全球化下国际贸易发展的趋势及我国应对策略 [J]．商业经济研究，2016 (1)：128 -130.

[12] 聂迎利，杜欣蔚，王礞礞等．年终盘点：2015 年中国乳业大事件回顾 [J]．中国乳业，2016 (1)：2 -17.

［13］何茂春，郑维伟．国际分工体系：中国、全球化与未来世界［J］．人民论坛·学术前沿，2016（9）：6－13．

［14］俞金尧，洪庆明．全球化进程中的时间标准化［J］．中国社会科学，2016（7）：164－188＋209．

［15］刘明．跨文化商务谈判中的中西文化差异研究［D］．长春工业大学，2010．

［16］伍巧芳．文化因素对商务活动的影响［N］．光明日报，2012－12－09（007）．

［17］陈奇．国际商务谈判实训方法、成效及改革建议——基于国际商务实训教学的思考［J］．市场论坛，2013（1）：102－103＋109．

［18］冯涛．中西方文化差异对国际商务谈判的影响［J］．哈尔滨商业大学学报（社会科学版），2013（1）：73－76．

［19］刘媛媛．企业并购后的跨文化整合研究［D］．对外经济贸易大学，2006．

［20］易蓉蓉．人民网．http：//gongyi.people.com.cn/GB/191247/214653/13977894.html，2011.02.22．

［21］自然之友 公众环境研究中心 达尔问．苹果的另一面．http：//114.215.104.68:89/Upload/201609021115599647.pdf．2011.1.20

［22］时海涛，于峰．吉利收购沃尔沃案例分析［J］．现代商业，2011（8）：250－251．

［23］张艳艳，周杏英．吉利收购沃尔沃案例的跨文化管理分析［J］．经济研究导刊，2012（8）：28－29．

［24］马佳彬，吴婷．当前中国汽车企业海外并购的可行性研究——基于吉利收购沃尔沃的分析［J］．现代物业（中旬刊），2012（12）：75－77．

［25］李丹．中国企业跨国并购中跨文化管理问题研究［D］．广西大学，2014．

［26］张国军．“金砖国家”合作意义的国际政治经济分析［J］．商，2013（14）：145－146．

［27］Г．托洛拉亚，谢周．金砖国家长期战略：俄方观点［J］．俄罗斯文艺，2014（1）：123－129．

[28] 郝宇彪，田春生．中俄能源合作：进展、动因及影响［J］．东北亚论坛，2014（5）：71－82＋128.

[29] 张博．中俄能源贸易发展研究［D］．东北师范大学，2014.

[30] 李兴，成志杰．中俄印——亚欧金砖国家是推动丝绸之路经济带建设的关键力量［J］．人文杂志，2015（1）：28－35.

[31] 陈元．深化中俄经贸合作筑牢两国关系基石［J］．管理世界，2015（1）：2－6.

[32] 贾中正，任琳．俄罗斯与“金砖国家”的经济联系研究［J］．俄罗斯研究，2015（5）：138－159.

[33] 朱杰进．金砖银行、竞争性多边主义与全球经济治理改革［J］．国际关系研究，2016（5）：101－112＋155－156.

[34] 李建岚．中美贸易失衡问题研究［D］．山西财经大学，2015.

[35] 郑云心．中美贸易摩擦成因研究综述［J］．西安建筑科技大学学报（社会科学版），2016（1）：37－41.

[36] 乔平平．中美贸易失衡的现状、原因及对策分析［J］．对外经贸实务，2016（5）：34－37.

[37] 黄达．中国—东盟自贸区的贸易与投资效应研究［D］．南京财经大学，2016.

[38] 李美莲，李红．2015～2016年中国—东盟货物贸易数量分析与预测［J］．东南亚纵横，2016（2）：3－7.

[39] 黄智铭，杨月元．“一带一路”战略中中国—东盟贸易发展的机遇及挑战［J］．沿海企业与科技，2016（2）：3－5.

[40] 周海江．红豆集团：打造西港特区“一带一路”合作共赢样板［J］．今日中国，2015（4）：88－89.

[41] 昌举，文华．西港特区：打造“海丝”新样板［J］．今日中国，2015（3）：88－89.

[42] 周海江．西港特区“一带一路”上的责任企业样板［J］．环球市场信息导报，2015（11）：13－13.

[43] 刘琳．中国境外经贸区建设模式——基于西港特区的案例分析［J］．经营管理者，2014（35）：162－163.

[44] 董彦．柬埔寨的“西港特区”是如何炼成的［J］．中国报道，2015（5）：32－33.

[45] 于景浩．把西港特区建成柬埔寨的“深圳”［N］．人民日报，2014－07－14（002）.

[46] 俞懿春．西港特区，“一带一路”上的示范园区［N］．人民日报，2015－10－11（003）.

[47] 罗蓉．中国贸易救济信息网．http：//www. cacs. gov. cn/cacs/newcommon/details. aspxnavid = C07&articleid = 131207

[48] 罗蓉．中国贸易救济信息网．http：//www. cacs. gov. cn/cacs/newcommon/details. aspx. articleId = 129514

[49] 中国报道《新浪财经》．http：//finance. sina. com. cn/world/gjjj/20090120/15475782804. shtml

[50] 董学清，许剑铭．《新华网》．http：//news. xinhuanet. com/fortune/2008－09/03/content_9764144. htm

[51]《大众日报．新华网》．http：//www. sd. xinhuanet. com/cj/2013－03/28/c_115187244. htm

[52]《人民网》．http：//world. people. com. cn/n/2015/0409/c1002－26819232. html

[53]《青麦田·同花顺财经》．http：//news. 10jqka. com. cn/20150410/c571671785. shtml

[54] 陶力．蚂蚁金服联姻正大集团 复制泰国版“支付宝”［N］．21世纪经济报道，2016－11－02（016）.

[55] 包慧，韩瑞芸．蚂蚁金服集团总裁井贤栋：从“全球化”到“领先于全球”有多难［N］．21世纪经济报道，2016－05－09（009）.

[56] 廖一凡．蚂蚁金服如何为阿里塑造金融架构?［J］．经理人，2015（3）：90－91.

[57] 陶力．觊觎印度市场 蚂蚁金服国际化探路［N］．21世纪经济报道，2016－04－14（016）.

[58] 侯云龙．阿里加速金融业务全球化布局［N］．经济参考报，2014－11－19（003）.

[59] 窦滢滢．蚂蚁金服加速“出海”意在国内市场［N］．中国经济时报，2014－11－25（007）．

[60] 李平．大湄公河次区域（GMS）合作20年综述［J］．东南亚纵横，2012（2）：34－38．

[61] 马晨．中国跨境电商的发展现状及今后对策研究［D］．对外经济贸易大学，2015．

[62] 闫新苗．我国跨境电商的现状及发展建议［D］．对外经济贸易大学，2015．

[63] 朱恺．中小企业应用跨境电商问题研究［D］．杭州电子科技大学，2015．

[64] 张卉．跨境电商发展的SWOT分析及对策［J］．山东工商学院学报，2015（3）：88－93．

[65] 顾若琪．云南积极布局跨境电商［N］．国际商报，2016－05－30（B04）．

[66] 马苗．GMS跨境电商平台企业联盟成立［N］．昆明日报，2016－06－12（002）．

[67] 郭曼．GMS经济走廊 从概念走向现实［N］．昆明日报，2015－06－15（T02）．

[68] 赵毛毛，晏建学．对于云南省跨境电商出口业务发展的思考［J］．电子商务，2016（10）：29－30．

[69] 中泰“蔬菜换石油”项目中方出口蔬菜货值过亿［N］．国际商报，2009－11－10（005）．

[70] 倪光清．蔬菜换石油铺就双赢路［N］．云南经济日报，2009－12－01（D02）．

[71] 陆昱．云南易货贸易发展研究——以“蔬菜换石油计划”为例［J］．学理论，2015（10）：103－104．

[72] 吴诚三．中泰两国蔬菜换石油协议正式“启航”［N］．中国水运报，2012－11－07（002）．

[73] 张子卓．蔬菜换石油项目启航［N］．云南日报，2012－11－01（001）．

[74] 米华. “蔬菜换石油”受阻泰国政局动荡 [N]. 第一财经日报, 2010-06-11 (B02).

[75] 中泰蔬菜换成品油项目潜力巨大 [J]. 时代金融, 2014 (19): 44-45.

[76] 云南“蔬菜换石油”项目进展顺利 [J]. 蔬菜, 2014 (7): 13.

[77] 云讯. 云南蔬菜进军泰国换石油 [N]. 中华合作时报, 2014-05-16 (A03).

[78] 马红民. 积极利用期货市场提高企业经营管理水平——谈铜陵有色金属 (集团) 公司套期保值经验 [J]. 有色金属工业, 2000 (11): 44-46.

[79] 窦登奎. 我国上市企业运用衍生金融工具套期保值的实证研究 [D]. 西南财经大学, 2011.

[80] 王志刚. 我国铜企业战略套期保值研究 [D]. 中国农业大学, 2014.

[81] 袁心慧, 姚丽琴, 曹若冰. 铜陵有色: 境外商品期货交易成功案例 [J]. 中国外汇管理, 2005 (10): 59-60.

[82] 梁洪流, 束亚君. 人民币汇率变化对铜陵有色公司的影响及对策 [J]. 中国有色金属, 2010 (S1): 167-170.

[83] 张津. 衍生工具套期保值与企业价值关系研究 [D]. 北方工业大学, 2013.

[84] 祝继高, 隋津, 汤谷良. 上市公司为什么要退市——基于盛大互动和阿里巴巴的案例研究 [J]. 中国工业经济, 2014 (1): 127-139.

[85] 杨狄. 上市公司股权结构创新问题研究——以阿里巴巴集团上市为视角 [J]. 现代经济探讨, 2014 (2): 43-47.

[86] 张诗阳. 阿里巴巴集团在美上市案例对我国上市公司法律制度的启示 [D]. 山西大学, 2015.

[87] 邹龙凤. 对《中国日报》与《纽约时报》关于阿里巴巴上市报道的批评话语分析 [D]. 鲁东大学, 2016.

[88] 文一墨. 阿里巴巴上市困局: 控制权的暗斗? [J]. 财会学习, 2013 (11): 10-12.

[89] 漆彤. 论亚投行对全球金融治理体系的完善 [J]. 法学杂志, 2016 (6): 13 -21.

[90] 徐奇渊. 亚投行怎样扎实走好下一步 [J]. 人民论坛, 2015 (12): 58 -59.

[91] 白秀兰, 赵非甦. 对亚洲基础设施投资银行的现实分析 [J]. 国际金融, 2015 (3): 75 -80.

[92] 张茉楠. 亚投行催生全球新金融治理架构 [J]. 党政论坛: 干部文摘, 2015 (12): 25 -25.

[93] 朱宏春. 中国如何应对亚投行治理和运营中的挑战? [J]. 南方金融, 2015 (6): 10 -13 +54.

[94] 王晓秋. 后危机时期提升我国国际金融话语权的对策研究 [J]. 改革与战略, 2012 (3): 71 -74.

[95] 孙思远. 万达集团并购 AMC 经济后果研究 [D]. 哈尔滨商业大学, 2015.

[96] 陈亚飞. 市场变化格局下的万达集团跨界转型发展初探 [D]. 上海师范大学, 2015.

[97] 谢玮. 王健林: 万达国际化的内在逻辑 [J]. 中国经济周刊, 2016 (20): 35 -37.

[98] 高湛诗琪, 史婧茹, 蒋函廷等. 中国万达集团并购美国传奇影业效应分析 [J]. 对外经贸, 2016 (7): 51 -52 +63.

[99] 中国万达集团: 着力打造国际化开放型的现代企业集团 [N]. 东营日报, 2011 -12 -12 (003).

[100] 张玉玲. 万达的国际化是否过于冒进? [N]. 光明日报, 2012 -09 -11 (014).

[101] 王健林哈佛谈国际化转型: 万达将继续体育并购 [N]. 北京商报, 2015 -11 -03 (B02).

[102] 郭腾江. 比亚迪公司新能源汽车竞争优势和基本竞争战略研究 [D]. 华东理工大学, 2014.

[103] 王洪生, 张玉明. 云创新: 新能源汽车产业发展新模式——以比亚迪新能源汽车为例 [J]. 科技管理研究, 2015 (23): 195 -199 +222.

［104］王宏起，汪英华，武建龙等．新能源汽车创新生态系统演进机理——基于比亚迪新能源汽车的案例研究［J］．中国软科学，2016（4）：81－94.

［105］向熳．比亚迪新能源汽车的市场竞争环境及战略分析［J］．中国市场，2016（32）：187－188.

［106］郭燕青，时洪梅．比亚迪新能源汽车开发中的创新方式研究［J］．管理案例研究与评论，2010（6）：469－478.

［107］雍君．比亚迪战略之变［J］．沪港经济，2014（6）：64－65.

［108］肖太明．比亚迪电动公交市场发展策略分析［D］．上海交通大学，2013.

［109］曾力．项目制，让中兴通讯组织"自运转"［J］．中外管理，2016（8）：112－113.

［110］乔英合．东软软件外包项目管理工作流引擎的设计与实现［D］．东北大学，2009.

［111］韩磊．企业物流外包供应商选择研究［J］．中国海洋大学，2010.8（3）.

［112］雷佳，魏泱，何建洪．我国企业构建全球研发网络的制约因素与动机激发——以长安汽车公司为例［J］．现代商业，2016（14）：123－124.

［113］两化融合：长安汽车研发协同模式创新［J］．企业管理，2015（9）：12－15.

［114］张宝林．政产学研用协同创新 打造中国汽车行业自主品牌［J］．中国科技产业，2014（1）：15.

［115］刘艺戈．基于企业家思想的企业战略与人力资源管理协同作用研究——以腾讯公司为例［J］．中国人力资源开发，2016（18）：92－98.

［116］彭剑锋．互联网时代的人力资源管理新思维［J］．中国人力资源开发，2014（16）：6－9.

［117］黎巍．腾讯公司发展战略研究［D］．上海交通大学，2010.

［118］任里．互联网行业知识型员工全面薪酬激励分析［D］．中国政法大学，2013.

［119］张杰．企业财务诊断方法研究［J］．行政事业资产与财务，

2012 (8): 57 -58.

[120] 吴世农.《CEO 财务分析与决策》[M]. 北京大学出版社, 2013.

[121] 王竹泉, 孙莹, 张先敏等. 中国上市公司营运资金管理调查: 2013 [J]. 会计研究, 2014 (12): 72 -78 +96.

Part I

Globalization

1.

The Internationalization of Tongrentang

Beijing Tongrentang (group) Co., Ltd. in China is a state-owned exclusively-funded venture which is authorized by the municipal government to operate state-owned assets. Tongrentang was founded in 1669. It is one of the longest historical standing companies in China. Beijing Tongrentang's development strategy has always been "with modern traditional Chinese medicine (TCM) at the core, to develop the health industry and to become an internationally renown modern TCM group". "To be longer, be stronger and be bigger" is its guiding development principle, and leading in innovation and enhancing the venture through science as its duty. Now it has formed three major divisions, i. e., modern pharmaceuticals, retail business and medical services. It also has established six secondary groups (Beijing Tongrentang Group, Beijing Tongrentang Technology Development Group, Beijing Tongrentang National Medicine Group, Beijing Tongrentang Health Pharmaceutical Group, Beijing Tongrentang Business Investment Group, and Beijing Tongrentang Medicinal Herbs Ginseng Antler Investment Group). Moreover, it has three institutions (Beijing Tongrentang TCM Pharmacy Co., LTD., Beijing Tongrentang Research Institute, Beijing Tongrentang Education College), and two reserve units of the enterprise. It now has three listed companies, with more than 1500 products, including drugs, hospital preparations, health food, food, and cosmetics. It also has 28 production bases, 83 modern production lines, one state-level engineering center and a postdoctoral scientific research workstation.

Brand maintenance and improvement, and cultural innovation and inheritance have also produced fruitful results in the development history of the company. "Tongrentang Chinese Medicine Culture" has made the first edition of the state-level non-material cultural heritage list. Tongrentang is both an economic entity and a cultural carrier. These two functions are becoming increasingly apparent.

In 2006, Beijing Tongrentang Co., Ltd. built the first overseas production base and research and development institutions in Hong Kong, S. A. R., covering an area of more than 10000 m^2. It is the largest production research and development base with top level facilities in Hong Kong. Its core products are Angong Niuhuang pills and capsule of broken spore of Ganoderma lucidum. Since these two products were first put in the market in 2008, the sales volume has continued to increase and sales have attained remarkable achievements.

Tongrentang production line has been certified by the Hong Kong Health Bureau, and the Japanese Ministry of Health, received GMP certification from Australian TGA, as well as Muslim Hala certification and Israel video certification. As a result, the production line is running at capacity in Hong Kong to supply health products for overseas markets. In addition, it provides Europe, the United States and other countries with experience for building local chemical plants in the future.

Tongrentang constantly focuses on new product development and overseas expansion of traditional products, speeding up technological advancement and upgrading management. It engages in independent research and development, in order to create modern health care products which are able to compete well in international markets. It has also made progress in the range of products. Apart from manufacturing in Hong Kong, China, it has also developed and manufactures a series of health products in Japan, South Korea, New Zealand, Switzerland, and other countries, using resources to their full advantage. Moreover, it has partnered with well-known foreign universities and research institutions to study the safety and effectiveness of key products so as to accumulate data and a theoretical basis for ushering its products into the mainstream western market.

As of June 2016, Tongrentag had opened 115 retail terminals, TCM clinics and health centers in 25 countries and regions. At the same time, it opened the largest Chinese medicine health care center, initiating a new model of health care development. Tongrentang medical practitioners around the world have won worldwide recognition and trust. The number of people who receive medical treatment in Tongrentang totals 30 million.

On October 10, 2015, Tongrentang's international cross-border e-commerce platform "Natural Search" was launched. This platform laid the foundation for recognition of Tongrentang on the Internet. "Natural Search" has established a tracing system for all products at home and abroad. Every single product is printed with QR code so that consumers can scan and check information about every aspect of the product from production to sales.

Tongrentang international took advantage of global health and hospital resources to enter the health field, integrating health monitoring, cloud computing, and mobile Internet technology so as to provide people with packaged solutions for preventative health measures, care, treatment, insurance and rehabilitation. The platform consists of four business sectors: health monitoring and consulting, cross-border health vertical e-business, cross-border electronic traditional Chinese medicine and financial insurance.

Sector 1: Health monitoring and consulting, designed to prevent diseases before they emerge. It is essential for health care services to protect people from diseases, and to monitor their health in order to increase medical care information, to cure more efficiently at a lower cost. Based on user testing data and integrating global medical resources, this sector provides users with health tonic, tracking management, and convenient, high-level individual health care consulting services.

Sector 2: Cross-border health vertical electronic business, introducing global quality health resources. Establishing China's first vertical cross-border electronic business platform which focuses on health, it has implemented direct local purchase without intermediate links, providing world-wide consumers with high quality professional health products and services.

Sector 3: Cross-border traditional Chinese medicine electronic business is taking Chinese medicine health services abroad. Based on traditional Chinese medicine, and with the aid of a cross-border electronic business platform, it integrates such high quality resources as traditional Chinese medicine and plant medicine at home and abroad. This important platform can be regarded as an overseas output channel for Chinese medicine, serving people throughout China and the world.

Sector 4: Financial insurance and blue ocean innovation. Based on users' health detection data, "traditional Chinese medicine health insurance" will break into the market, developing health insurance products for disease prevention and extending Internet liability insurance product innovation aimed at electronic business dealings.

The core of "Internet +" lies not in the "Internet", but in the "+". If we only reinforce traditional industries based on the Internet, we will not move forward. Only when we have a deep understanding of the Internet, can we really deepen the relationship between traditional industries and the Internet.

In the process of pushing traditional Chinese medicine to the world, in order to bring Tongrentang from mere public awareness to gaining consumer loyalty, Tongrentang will always put the interests of customers first in all aspects from production to after-sale services. It tries its best to be truly kind-hearted, help people to remain healthy. As a result, it provides consumers with trustworthy, high-quality products. Tongrentang's internationalization is in line with "where there are Chinese, there is Tongrentang", first choosing areas with large Chinese communities to open stores as a way into the market. This "nostalgia" land marketing has opened the door for Tongrentang into the international market. By cooperating with Hutchison Whampoa, Hong Kong, Tongrentang has integrated overseas research and development, sales terminals and production base, and insisted on adopting a brand path of "famous doctor + famous brand + famous medicine". The famous doctor not only has superb medical skills, but also has a profound understanding of Chinese medicine culture and the history of Tongrentang. Meanwhile, it strives to use local research institutes to develop new products suitable for local needs, so as to improve operational efficiency and the recognition of traditional Chinese medicines in the international market. The internationalization process of Tongrentang begins with an old brand that conveys the cultural charm of traditional Chinese medicine. It also incorporates Chinese traditional culture. The model is founded on Chinese circles. Only a small portion of Chinese medicine enters the mainstream of European and American market as health food.

In advancing the process of internationalization, Tongrentang has valuable experience, that is, "to give priority to a cure so as to bring along medicine". In other words, make the field of traditional Chinese medicine spur on Chinese drugs. These two are inseparable. Only when traditional Chinese medicine gets recognition from the world can Chinese drugs be accepted by international markets. Of course, cultures different from place to place, which makes it difficult for other regions to accept traditional Chinese medicine and Chinese drugs. Therefore, it is foundational to get patients to understand the theory of traditional Chinese medicine. Only in this way can Chinese traditional drugs penetrate the global market. Chinese drugs cannot be separated from traditional Chinese medicine. If it is, traditional Chinese medicine becomes like water without resource, and trees without roots. Therefore, the role in the international marketing of traditional Chinese medicine is apparent and indispensable. In addition to helping patients be restored to health, traditional Chinese medicine can spread Chinese culture. Strengthening the understanding of TCM theory in other regions is an imperceptible way to increase trust in traditional Chinese medicine and accept Chinese drugs.

Discussion Questions:

1. What are the driving forces for Tongrentang to enter the global market?

2. What are the barriers for Tongrentang to go globally?

3. How does Tongrentang comply with the trend of globalization? How does Tongrentang cope with anti-globalization protests?

2.

The Globalization of Yili

Yili Industrial Group Co. Ltd. , is located in Inner Mongolia. It is one of the leading enterprises in the dairy industry in China. Yili was the only dairy sponsor of the Beijing 2008 Olympic Games, and also, historically, the only Chinese food brand which ever sponsored Olympic Games. On May 25, 2009, Yili successfully became the only company to partner with World Expo 2010. Having met the Expo's standards, it was approved to supply dairy products to Shanghai's World Expo.

In the context of the integration and internationalization of the global dairy industry, the linking of high quality resources in the dairy industry is increasing. China's dairy industry has been growing with the world diary industry, leading to resonance and cooperation between China and the rest of the world. The internationalization of China's dairy industry covers at least three aspects: resources, standards, and research and development. In several ways, Yili is also constantly adapting in order to accelerate its progress. In the area of resources, Yili has established the world's largest integrated dairy production base in New Zealand. With regard to standards, Yili has attained strategic cooperation with such international quality institutions as SGS (Switzerland), LRQA (Lloyd's quality certification Co. , Ltd.) and Intertek (Britain). In research and development, Yili has jointly established research and development centers with well-known universities in Europe and Oceania.

In early July 2013, Yili joined with America's biggest milk company Dairy Farmers of America Inc (DFA), portraying their global ambitions. DFA is headquartered in the United States, in Kansas City, Missouri. It is that nation's largest milk company, with 18000 large farms in 48 states across the USA. It independently owns 21 large dairy production and processing bases in the United States, whose exporting markets cover Mexico, Europe, Central America, South America, Asia, the Middle East and the Pacific Rim. The day that the largest milk companies in the United States cooperated with Yili in China was a significant event in dairy industry cooperation between the two countries.

In the tide of globalization, Yili's process has three aspects: brand, technology and resources globalization.

In brand globalization, Yili Group's path to cooperation with foreign countries was skillful and displayed easy rhythm. In 2007, Yili Group exported 28.8 tons of butter to Egypt, implementing significant dairy exports from China for the first time. And it is worth mentioning that the butter was exported to Middle Eastern countries, where dairy production has a relatively long history. This was an important first step, testing the quality of Yili dairy. At the time, however, China lacked a dairy brand with a good reputation in the overseas dairy industry. After a first try in overseas market, Yili found it important to promote brand renown throughout the world. In 2008 and 2010, Yili successively stepped onto the world stage through the Beijing Olympic Games and Shanghai's World Expo, getting the attention of foreign consumers. At the end of 2010, Yili has carried out a comprehensive brand upgrade, establishing the vision of the enterprise development, "to become a first-class world health food group". Brand globalization strategy introduced Yili, to the world and subsequently more and more world-class partners joined with Yili. Since 2011, Yili launched a five-year comprehensive cooperative project with the U. S. Disney, which is not only one of the few cross-border co-operations for major brands in recent years, but also a clear signal of international prospects released by Yili's new brand image. Through greater brand awareness, Yili, a dairy company from China's Inner Mongolia, became known to consumers around the world in a short span of three years. This explosion of brand energy is rare in the current dairy industry global context, and it attracted a more heavyweight international partner: the DFA Company from the United

States.

In terms of the globalization of technology, Yili, aiming at its development, has made practical but feasible adjustments. As early as the 1990s, China's dairy industry began the application of international advanced production technology. Recently, Yili and other top Chinese dairy companies purchased advanced equipment from the international market, so in terms of production equipment there is no gap between China's dairy industry and that of other countries. In fact, China is even more advanced than some abroad. As for technology and management, Yili maintains communication and cooperation with its foreign counterparts. In the years when Yili studied and was introduced to international advanced technology, it made the effort to bring the domestic market in line with the advanced level found internationally. Now, globalization means that it is necessary to integrate technology into the global industrial chain, an unavoidable trend. The strategic cooperation between Yili and DFA includes pasture management services. DFA has the world's best milk control experience and the most scientifically advanced processing technology. Access to that technology will play a large part in advancing China's milk resource management. In addition, the DFA has a large number of modern pastures and rich pasture management experience, which can inform Yili's construction of modern and specialized pastures. The two-way partnership will give Yili the DFA's guidance in concepts of dairy farming as well as technical support. This will improve the dairy production and quality of Yili's meadow, and enhance the modernization of Yili.

Resource globalization gives Yili even greater advantages. Yili's long-term strategic procurement is a significant part of cooperation with DFA. It shows that Yili has always emphasized a global strategy—taking advantage of global resources. In terms of production of raw milk, Yili Group is the first enterprise to complete a blueprint for the national milk industry. In the 1990s, Yili began to design raw milk resources, and formed a network of production bases covering three first-rate milk resource areas: Hulun Buir, Silingol and Xinjiang Tianshan. It is the only dairy enterprise to control "the three first-rate milk bases" in China. Operating in a global market with global resources is a widespread trend for dairy businesses. In this sense, Yili is one step ahead of the pack. The DFA is one of the largest upstream raw material suppliers in the US dairy industry. The DFA has a huge advantage in the area of cheese, whey powder, large scale milk powder packaging and other products. For a very long time, DFA has been supplying Starbucks, Kraft, and many other well-known food companies with dairy raw materials. The marketing demand of dairy product has increased rapidly in China. However there is no enough raw milk to supply, especially the whey powder which is the very important resource to make milk powder, is based on import. Yili's cooperation with DFA may obtain a stable, low-cost supply of raw materials, which will help to further enhance the competitive advantage.

From the point of view of current overseas globalization strategy, Yili Group has followed the path of "making advantages more advantageous", continuously strengthening their own milk advantage, focusing to improve quality in a fundamental way, aiming at consolidating and controlling the upstream industry chain. China's current speed of development in the dairy industry is slowing down, which gives the large majority of Chinese enterprises a chance to improve their product quality. As an important step in Yili's internationalization strategy, cooperation with the DFA is a new beginning.

Discussion Questions:

1. What convenience factors promoted the globalization of Yili group?

2. What are the benefits of globalization for Yili groups? What are the disadvantages?

3. Is globalization a good thing or a bad one?

Part Ⅱ

International Business Environment

3.

Huawei: Overseas Markets Refuse Opportunism

Following the financial crisis and investigation by the U. S. Department of Commerce, Huawei still performed well in overseas markets, and reports of new successes kept pouring in. Huawei had 220. 2 billion yuan income in 2012 which was 8% up from the year before, using a fixed exchange rate, and net profit was 15. 4 billion yuan, up by 33% in year-on-year terms. Huawei products and solutions are being used in more than 150 countries, and serve 45 of the world's top 50 operators and a third of the global population.

In a sense, the global financial crisis created new opportunities for domestic manufacturers such as Huawei to expand their overseas market. Analysts pointed out that overseas enterprise asset prices have plunged due to the downturn in the market, which gave Chinese companies an opportunity to "go all out" for further development.

The rise of overseas markets greatly improved Huawei's market position. So far, the company is not only established in Asia, Africa and the Middle East but has also successfully entered the markets of several European countries. It is also gradually making breakthroughs into the world's high-end markets such as Japan and North America. In Africa emerging markets, Huawei has set up representative offices in more than 10 countries such as South Africa, Nigeria, and Kenya. In order to get closer to the customer, Huawei has established three new regional departments in Southern Africa, Eastern Africa and Western Africa to speed up the response to customers' needs and improve service quality. After nearly 10 years of market cultivation and hard work, Huawei has full access to most countries in the Southern Africa market and become the primary local communication equipment supplier for most of countries in Africa.

However, Huawei's performance is not satisfactory in the USA due to an intensive market which continues to have high completion barriers for new entrants. In the second half of 2007, in order to expand into the U. S. market by acquiring 3COM Corporation, Huawei sought to become a minority shareholder in the private capital operation firm Bain, but the deal eventually failed because it was not approved by the review of foreign investment in sensitive industries by the government. Then Huawei had to accept the suggestions from Committee on Foreign Investment in the U. S. to cancel the application plan of acquiring 3 Leaf in 2011. In October 2011, The Department of Commerce of the U. S. also impeded Huawei to bid the National Emergency Response Network System.

Huawei is one of the top providers in the global telecommunications industry with its high sales volume and overseas market shares on a variety of products. The quality of its products is recognised by the customers. Huawei overseas business has been growing and sales volume from overseas reached two third of its total sales revenue. But as a Chinese local high-tech company, it is time for Huawei to think about how to manifest its unique characteristics in the internationalisation process, how to promote the brand influence, and how to achieve genuine internationalisation.

In the past, Huawei's success in the international market was mainly based on the advantages of low cost and corresponding low price. However, competition in the international market, superior quality and competitive prices are not core strategies for the company because international rivals may have larger scale production and more flexible for price reduction. In fact, Huawei has also started to notice that a critical factor is to develop its own attributes and brand for the international market. For example, Huawei developed a number portability service for Hong Kong fixed-line operator Hutchison in 3 months, something an established brand European equipment supplier had not been able to complete in 6 months. Meanwhile, Huawei's delivery cost and efficiency began to give it a good reputation in the industry. Those strategies helped Huawei become a speed response brand image.

The global journey will not be achieved overnight. The market requires unremitting pioneering and patient cultivation. In the journey to globalization, Huawei is moving ahead according to the enterprise and the industry, it divided the globalization process into three stages: first, a trial and error stage, namely repeatedly trying different things until a breakthrough is attained. The breakthrough should be marked by participation in international bidding and should include winning the bidding rather than simply increasing sales. The second is the breakthrough phase, which is typified by increasing staff in markets with a large population and corresponding demand for telephones. After years of hard work, Huawei's sales reached more than 300 million yuan in 2001. The third phase is expanding the European and American markets and consists of two strategies: one is to develop the market outside of Europe and the U. S. after setting up a global sales network. The other is to expand the European and American markets.

Huawei carefully developed their entry model into the global market. They formulated corresponding strategies for the different needs of different regions in different periods. Huawei strategically chose the time to enter the international market with its cost leadership advantage at the beginning of 21st century when relatively low tariffs on communication equipment coexisted with tense competition in the domestic and international markets. At that time, international telecom tycoons were suffering from high R&D costs, and thus were forced to make strategic alliances with Huawei. In choosing their international market entry model, they established 12 research institutes around the globe, with a CMM system for research and development to serve and support the products develop by advanced international talents and technologies. In developing countries, they rely on a low price strategy to build an independent brand. In developed countries, it actively seeks strategic cooperation with international telecom tycoons on OEM business. In choosing their market, Huawei continues the strategy of ' encircling cities from rural areas ' in the domestic market. The first aim was Shenzhen's neighbour city—Hong Kong. S. A. R. Russia and Latin America were also Huawei's early target markets. They further focused on countries with underdeveloped telecom industries, and captured regional markets such as Southeast Asia, Middle East and Africa step by step. Meanwhile, they expanded to developed countries and infiltrated European and American markets.

Huawei also spares no efforts in terms of globalization strategic plans, striving for maximum efficiency at the lowest cost. They invest heavily in human resources and capital and have established 9 regional departments around the world with 90 representative offices and technical service centres. They have quietly set up more than 50 offices globally for research, development, production and sales with more than 4000 employees in overseas markets.

"Overseas markets refuse opportunism" stated by Ren Zhengfei, president of Huawei which has become their philosophy to extend international markets. Huawei has recently adopted a series of overseas expansion plans. They are making full preparation to actively respond to the challenges and opportunities of globalization, trying to overcome obstacles, while tightly grasping opportunities. Huawei has already earned its place through the competition in the overseas markets. Its internationalisation road will be more and more expansive with this good start.

Discussion Questions:

1. Analyse Huawei's globalization strategy in-depth from three aspects: background, driving forces and role positioning.

2. What were the problems Huawei encountered in the process of globalization? How did Huawei resolve those problems?

3. In the process of globalization, how did Huawei achieve its management level globally and capital operations globally?

4. How would the process of Huawei's globalization give experience and inspiration to Chinese manufacturing enterprises?

4.

The Localisation of KFC in China

In March 2010, KFC announced that eight of its restaurants in Shanghai would offer two rice products. If sales were sufficient, KFC would offer rice meals in its restaurants all over the country.

Diversified operation is a trend for fast-food restaurant chains in Asian markets, such as McCafe from McDonalds, rice meal at KFC, tea at Starbucks, etc. And there is no doubt that adaptation to Chinese culture and the consumption habit of Chinese customers in order to compete in Chinese market are the driving forces for diversification.

Kentucky Fried Chicken, is a famous chain of fast-food restaurants from the U. S.. It mainly serves fried chicken, hamburgers, French fries, soda and other western-style fast food. Since KFC opened its first restaurant in Qianmen, Beijing in 1987, it has opened over 5000 restaurants across all of the provinces, municipalities and autonomous regions of China. It has become the largest and fastest growing fast-food enterprise in China.

Since entering China, KFC has been committed to a localisation strategy to avoid being outside the culture. During Chinese New Year 2003, Colonel Sanders of KFC changed from the usual white suit, a classic image, and began to wear red Tang uniforms in 800 chain restaurants in 170 China cities. It was an important measure that helped KFC to become embedded in the way of Chinese dining. Newly-developed local products account for 20% of KFC global products, while traditional products account for 80%. However, the proportion of new products may have reached more than 40% in China. The nutritious breakfast alone is unprecedented throughout the world. But KFC restaurants in China improved exotic flavours to Chinese style. On January 23, 2008, KFC Beijing started selling fried dough sticks at breakfast time. Serving health food is the selling point that counters the weakness of Chinese traditional fried dough sticks. KFC kept the traditional shape and taste of fried dough sticks without adding alum. KFC spent more than one year studying and testing a new technique that replaces the traditional process without relying on the additive alum. Finally, it launched wholesome, alum-free deep-fried dough sticks which sell for three Yuan each. The new dough sticks would serve KFC as a long-term breakfast product. KFC "safe fried dough sticks" brought about the excellent match of "fancy porridge plus fried dough sticks". For creative consumers, KFC believes that the new match of "fried dough sticks + milk", "fried dough sticks + milk tea", or "fried dough sticks + coffee" could be worth a try.

KFC began to serve breakfast in some China cities in 2002, and launched two types of fancy breakfast cereals with Chinese characteristics in the same year: porridge (congee) with seafood and egg, and porridge (congee) with mushrooms and chicken. And KFC has been speeding up localisation in China. The head of product research and development for KFC said that they have long attached importance to the localisation of products. KFC cares about pairing a wide range of products with nutrition. To meet consumers demands, KFC's breakfast products are tailored with local characteristics. For example, in addition to porridge (congee) with seafood and egg, and porridge (congee) with mushrooms and chicken, the company offers Dragon Twister, Egg & Vegetable Soup, Preserved Egg & Lean Pork Congee, Sichuan Spicy Beef Roll, Dough Stick, Beef Congee, Bacon Mushroom Chicken Rice, and Spicy Chicken Rice.

Consumers have a different view on KFC localisation strategy. Customers were surveyed about KFC selling fried dough sticks, and the results indicated that 26.69% supported KFC, 56.04% did not care, while 17.28% of them thought KFC should keep to American style fast food. Obviously, cultural differences also bring challenges to product sales. Actually, multinational companies are tuned to discovering the business value of local culture, and the truth lies more in the fact that local residents ignore their own culture.

In fact, other western fast-food providers also adopt a localisation strategy to fit into Chinese culture. From food packages to restaurant decoration, Chinese style is integrated into the companies' strategies. For example, Starbucks sells Chinese tea and McDonalds presented red envelopes to customers from January 23 to February 19, 2008. Consumers who bought McDonald's Bonanza Gems Package or medium and/or large package received lucky red envelopes with 100% chance of winning. The awards included cash which was provided by the Bank of Communications, a "blessing pure gold mouse" provided by Chow Tai Fook, and a pendant marked with "ILOVEU". In order to fit with the habits of Chinese consumers, Papa John's introduced a tailor-made pizza shaped like a Chinese golden pancake, covered by an extra crust and sprinkled a layer of sesame seeds.

Discussion Questions:

1. Why does KFC sell rice meal, fried dough sticks in China? What are the cultural ethics behind the business strategy?

2. Why are western fast foods putting on Chinese style? What lessons can be learned by Chinese restaurants?

3. How would Chinese enterprises cope with cross-culture conflict and adapt cultural differences while they are internationalizing?

5.

International Mobilephone Giant in Business Ethics Morass in China

Since 2007, Apple sales boomed as it released the iPhone, iPad and a series of IT products with its fashion design and innovation technology. When Apple introduces new products, large numbers of fans who want to be the first to buy these products will queue overnight outside an Apple store in New York, London, Tokyo, or Shanghai. But, behind the beautiful and fashionable appearance, there is a dark side to the products: pollution, violation and poison. These problems are deeply hidden in its secretive supply chain and rarely exposed to the public. The workers suffer from toxic chemical exposure during the production process, while the company constantly sets new sales records. The workers suffer both physical and mental agony, and their labour rights and dignity are ignored. At the same time, the surrounding environment is polluted by waste water and gas. In 2010, twelve consecutive suicides occurred in the Foxconn company plant. Foxconn is one of Apple's largest suppliers. The loss of 10 lives is still a heartache. Because Apple rarely discloses details about its suppliers, public didn't get more than a brief statement issued by the company, saying that the company felt sorry that it had happened.

In fact, there is a lot of negative news about the Apple's contribution to social responsibility. Environmental groups reveal the pollution and poison of Chinese supply chain of the company in the report "The other side of Apple". Following that, Darwin Natural Knowledge Society, Friends of Nature, Friends of Science and Technology, Public Environment Research Centre and Nanjing Green Stone, these 5 environmental groups who found, after 7 months of research and survey, that 27 factories whom were suspected to be the suppliers of the giant have environmental problems. Ma Jun, the director of Public environmental research centre, said some Apple suppliers caused serious pollution, even serious damage, according to the survey. On the east of the Meiko factory in Wuhan, there is a white canal connecting the southern Taizi Lake, called "Milk River" by the local residents. Next to the third party environmental monitoring station, the water in drainage channels contains the heavy metals copper and nickel, which contaminate plants. The content of copper in southern Taizi Lake is higher 56-193 times higher than that in the middle reaches of the Yangtze River. Ma Jun said that environmental protection organizations have evidence that these companies are suppliers to Apple. It is called the suspected supplier because the company has never released the names of their suppliers. The company replied to the environmental protection organization charges by saying that "our long-term policy is not to disclose suppliers".

United Win Technology Limited, an important supplier of touch screens, exposed scandals and pushed the mobilephone giant into the teeth of the storm. In August 2008, workers were asked to replace alcohol with hexane to wipe the phone's screen. In the survey, the workers said that the volatilization rate of hexane is much faster than alcohol, so efficiency is improved. The effect of hexane was better and the rate of defects is greatly reduced. However, the miracle material is poisonous. Related studies show that hexane can lead to multiple peripheral neuropathy, numbness and other sensory abnormalities in the limbs, as well as sensory and motor disorders.

Supplier Code of Conduct of the company states that ensuring the staff of supply chain companies have safe working conditions is a priority. Nevertheless, in using toxic and hazardous chemical solvents, United Win Technology Limited broke the China Occupational Disease Prevention Law. It neither applied to the department concerned nor informed the staff and did not even provide effective protection to workers. According to some poisoned workers, representatives from the company visited the plant, but they had never been told that hexane is toxic and harmful or how to protect themselves. During the long and painful treatment of poisoned workers, no one communicate with them and no one visit anyone of them from the company.

Hardly has one wave subsided when another rises. In 2010, 12 employees of Foxconn jumped to their deaths which not only shocked the whole of China, but also forced society to reflect on how to give workers their due respect, rather than treat them as inhuman machine parts in the production line, working overtime to earn a poor salary.

It is reported that a Foxconn employee's salary sheet showed: Time: November 2009. Base salary: 900 yuan; Normal work time: 21.75 days, usually 60.50 hours of overtime, paid 469 yuan; On Saturdays 75 hours of overtime, paid 776 yuan; Total wages 2145 yuan. 60% of the employee's monthly income was earned through extra hours. 136 hours of overtime, 100 hours more than the maximum overtime hours stipulated by labour law! The Shenzhen Municipal Human Resources and Social Security Bureau surveyed a sample of 5044 Foxconn employees and found that 72.5% of employees worked overtime, averaging 28.01 hours of overtime per month. The poor salary leaves Apple's foundry employees facing a dilemma—there is no future without working overtime. But working overtime every day makes them miss out on the present. What's more, the limited overtime pay still won't let them see the future.

Another supplier, Dafu Computer (Changshu) Co., Ltd., which belongs to the Quanta Group, treated employees dehumanization and put Apple into business ethics morass in China. After that, a survey in Jiangsu Province, by Suzhou City Federation of trade unions confirmed that the company had forced female workers to unbuckle their belts, and strongly recommended that enterprises set up trade unions as required by the law in order to protect the rights and interests of staff.

Discussion Questions:

1. Apple has strict requirements for suppliers' social responsibility. If the supplier does not meet those requirements, is Apple really responsible for?

2. In this case, what are the ethical issues in business activities? Facing these issues, how did the company respond?

3. How should a company make the decision to select outsourcing suppliers regarding the origins of immoral?

6.

Implementation of Coal Import Contract of Aluminum Corporation of China Limited was Baffled

Mongolia is located between China and Russia. Mongolia's land area covers 156.65 square kilometers, most of which is desert and Gobi, so the natural environment is not so well. The size of its land is the 19th largest in the world, and it is also the second biggest land-locked country only smaller than Kazakhstan, with about 3 million population. In the 1990s, the democratic revolution was broken out in Mongolia, and the new constitution was published in 1992. The new constitution set the multi-party political system and the economic system was started the transition to a market economy.

The implementation of "the Belt and Road" initiative has added new energy to the economic development of countries en route. In the future, railways, highways, airline businesses, ports and other infrastructure construction will become the new breakthrough point for economic development. The infrastructure construction and equipment manufacturing will further propel the need of iron and steel, non-ferrous, building materials and other energy-intensive products, and then motivate the demand for coal, then promoting the development of international coal trading. However, on the process of bulk commodity coal international cooperation, the implementation of some coal contracts has been obstructed. There are also some cross-cultural integration and trade barriers problems.

On January 28, 2013, the International Trade Co., Ltd. of China Aluminum Corporation (Chinalco) confirmed that on January 11, 2013 Mongolia ETT Corporation (Erdenes Tavan Tolgoi LLC, ETT) took the initiative to scrap the contract, saying that it would no longer perform the agreement to supply Chinalco with coal, and that both sides would renegotiate "TT East Coal Long-term Trade Agreement" signed in July 2011. ETT demanded a higher price of coal, and a less supply. ETT is Mongolia's largest state-owned coal mining enterprises, located in Ulan Bator. According to the TT East Coal Long-term Trade Agreement, Chinalco provides a $350 million loan to TT, which repays the debt with a certain level of coal price.

Chinalco hopes that the new government of Mongolia and the new management of ETT make a close study of the contract. Once broken, Chinalco will resort to law. ETT unilaterally demanding to break the contract reflects the foreign investment environment of Mongolia turns to unfriendly direction. About 5000 Chinese companies have business in Mongolia, of which only around 50 could make the profit.

In August 2012, Mongolia formed a new government. Subsequently, ETT company management was replaced. This series of changes directly caused the implementation of "TT East Coal Long-term Trade Agreement" was obstructed. In October 2012, the delegation of Chinalco to Mongolia to meet ETT'S new CEO Yasser Basu, who immediately requested to pay Chinalco's advance payment ahead of time, and required negotiations for amending the contract. Yasser Basu's request was refused by Chinalco. On January 11, 2013, ETT stopped supplying coal to Chinalco. The reason was that the company was in financial distress, and was unable to that year's coal storage expenses. Response to the difficulties mentioned by ETT, Chianlco was willing to pay the storage charged temporarily. Chianlco is willing to help them get over the financial difficulties, and help ETT pay direct costs, but ETT gave only one response: change the contract. ETT also unilaterally negotiated about coal supply contracts with several companies, including China Shenhua. What ETT wants to do is to cooperate with Shenhua Group, which is the largest major coal company in China with its coal relevant infrastructure. It is also a large international company, whereas Chinalco has no relevant coal business at all.

The supply agreement between Chinalco and Mongolia EET company only accounted for less than 1% of the reserves of Tavan Tolgoi coal field. It is expected that the coal field can provide more than 1 billion tons of high-quality coking coal. But Mongolia has not yet determined whom the rights of developing other blocks belong to. During the 2011 process of inviting bids, which was suspended, China Shenhua Group, Peabody Energy Company of the United States and a Russia-Mongolia consortium participated in the bidding. Unless the new Mongolian government can prove that it welcomes foreign investors, and that it will not try to modify or approve the law to limit foreign investment in the coal mine share, foreign companies will truly participate in Mongolian resources development in a big way. But the reality is not optimistic, for the government of Mongolia is to curry favor with its impatient people, to maintain the fragile coalition government, so it is difficult to create a stable legal environment.

ETT mentioned that Chinalco is only using the opportunity that the Mongolian government is in urgent need of finance to win the deal. From the angle of international trade, it is hard to accept this remark. In response to this remark, Chinalco commented that ETT is indeed facing financial difficulties, but "TT East Coal Long-term Trade Agreement" was reached after nearly a year of negotiations, and the two governments approved this agreement. It is for the purpose of long-term cooperation that Chinalco immediately provided ETT with $350 million in advance even ETT did not have the financing conditions. So the supplying contract, on the one hand, was to meet the strategic transformation of the Chinalco investment demand; on the other hand it also met the need of the development of ETT on side of Mongolian government. It is a win-win business cooperation. Chinalco thinks that even at the time when the Mongolian coal prices are low, "TT East Coal Long-term Trade Agreement" is still profitable for the ETT, for the quality of the ETT coal is not very good. According to the agreed price signed by both parties, plus the expense of logistics, the cost is in line with the current international market commodity prices. Therefore, Chinalco has urged ETT to continue to perform the contract, otherwise it will recover the ETT "unlimited liability".

Since the second half of 2012, Mongolia energy mineral investment environment has been more and more unfavorable for foreign investors. Mongolia's latest legislation about foreign investment stipulates that Mongolian national capital must have 51% of strategic assets. This regulation led directly for Chinalco to abandon acquiring its Mongolia's south Gobi coal mine. Not only Chinalco was faced with unilateral breach of promise, another company Rio Tinto Group's copper and gold mine in Oyu Tolgoi, Mongolia, is also facing Mongolia's unilateral change of the contract.

Among China's neighboring countries, Mongolia has the worse investment environment. Many foreign investment projects are difficult to operate in Mongolia, or it is hardly to recoup the investment. Especially when a new government replace another, or when the management of a company has been changed. The cooperation investment agreement might be changed or canceled. Corruption in Mongolia is serious also result the cost of investment in Mongolia is hard to predict. It is worth noting that the trade order in the ports between China and Mongolia is chaotic. There are disorder competitions among Chinese enterprises. Because Chinese enterprises frequently force prices down among themselves, contracts are likely change. This factor can also bring risk to Chinalco's long-term contracts with ETT.

Chinalco has warned that once ETT breaks the contract, it will have serious legal consequences, and more importantly, it will have a negative impact on the international reputation of Mongolian companies, which will be obstacles for Mongolia to attract foreign capital for a long time.

The coal trade between China and Mongolia is an important content of the economic and trade cooperation between the two countries, so Chinese government attaches great importance to it. Under the promoting of Chinalco, after negotiating, ETT Company of Mongolia eventually agreed in April 2013 to continue to perform the contract, promising not to make any changes. Chinalco restored coal imports.

Discussion Questions:

1. What are the political and economic reasons that the implementation of coal import contract was obstructed?

2. What are the main reasons that the profit of Chinese enterprises was low from their investment in Mongolia?

3. What the major national differences should Chinese enterprise pay attention to when investing in foreign countries?

4. During foreign investment, how would Chinese enterprise resolve the difficulties and barriers caused by national differences?

7.

Geely's Acquisition of Volvo

Geely Holding Group Co. , Ltd. , founded in 1986, entered into motor industry in 1997. Geely has concentrated on motor manufacturing, innovation of technology and personnel training for many years. Its total assets is over 100 billion Yuan now. Geely now is one of the top 500 enterprises in China. It is also one of the top ten motor manufacturer, the national innovative enterprise, and national export base of passenger cars. Geely is the only private enterprise to manufacture passenger cars in motor industry in China. March 28, 2010, the acquiring agreement of Volvo was signed in Gothenburg, Sweden. Geely acquired 100% stock right of Volvo, including intellectual property right.

Volvo, a famous Swedish car brand, was founded in 1927 in Goteborg, Sweden. Volvo group is the world's leading manufacturer of commercial transport and construction equipment. Volvo group have sold its Volvo car business to the United States Ford motor company in 1999. Volvo is now divided into fertile car branch (Volvo Car Corporation) and Volvo Group (Volvo Group), Volvo was part of the car business of Volvo group, Volvo company was acquired in 2010 by Geely. Volvo has held by Geely after 2010.

However, in the later acquisition, during company integration, the company has emerged some problems due to difference in the history and education. There is a huge cultural difference between east and west in term of ideology, morality, binding and so on. Geely was established in China, it is mainly based on Confucianism Chinese culture, emphasize collectivism, mean and humble, interpersonal relationship. While the Volvo Group is the typicality of European culture, advocating personal heroism, pay attention to work and at the same time pursuit the quality of life, in strict accordance with the rules and regulations. There is relatively little difference of living standard in Sweden, from politicians to ordinary citizens, the wealth gap is not large, car is no longer seen as luxury, it is more of transportation mode. But in China, there is very respected right stratification system in ancient times, from the society to the school, honoring the teacher and respecting the older. This all showed the difference ideas between Chinese and Sweden in terms of the social hierarchy system.

At one point, China and Sweden have similar characteristics, that is the emphasis on teamwork, collective interest almost to the individual value, but at this point, the two countries are slightly different, that is to advocate Swedish collectivism value, not prominent individual value. But the Chinese people pay more attention to the interests of the individual to the collective interests, the highest point of interest is the national interest. Swedish is good at accepting the changes in life and work, rather than not to be good at planning, but with the Chinese people can be more different, uncertain things to accept and make changes, more optimistic and open. In contrast, the Chinese people in their work and life, more accustomed to the formal rules, all affairs in accordance with the rules and regulations to implement, will be able to take into account the variables are included in the mechanism, not accustomed to accept the unknown changes. Employees in China enjoy a comfortable environment with little change, while Swedish are more likely to accept changes in life and work or temporary deployment.

The gap between China and Sweden in culture has made it more difficult to integrate after Geely acquired Volvo. There are some big differences between two national staff in cultural background, behavioral standards and so on. All these have led to different behavioral characteristics in their work, including the delivery of work tasks, which can not only solve by the training and meeting, and it's a deep-rooted problem, but Geely has found a solution to this problem.

After the acquisition of Volvo, Geely was not anxious to emphasize the importance of its own brand, but learned from the failure due to the cultural differences in the merging process. Geely has restored the brand awareness and brand depth of the Volvo brand in the Chinese market. Geely was also aware of the importance of personnel integration in the process of cross-border mergers and acquisitions. In the financial and human aspects of mergers and acquisitions, Geely kept their culture to the utmost extent, including the continued use of its headquarters in Sweden and Billy's production base, while its management autonomy was relaxed to the maximum. At the same time to maximize the retention of the two sides, the company can also be effective for the two companies to separate the different cultures. Geely also effectively isolated the culture of the two companies. Geely and Volvo's brand positioning is different; the market level is also difficult to match. It would be blunder if these two brand integrated but still competing in the same market. Geely was very successful in separating two different car brand in the market in order to compete in different customer market.

Geely can absorb the good side and eliminate the bad part in the culture and management system of the each side. Geely understand that they and Volvo come from different cultural backgrounds, there are different views on the same thing. Geely often arrange personnel to travel abroad for mutual learning, they came to each other's countries to do scientific research, learn advanced technology and culture, to lay the foundation to train more talents. After the completion of mergers and acquisitions, using the Volvo brand enable Geely to hire professional managers, controllers in other global auto companies, the management team, which can bring advanced thought, has laid a solid foundation for the development of Volvo. Geely also formulate corresponding rules and regulations in the retention of Volvo corporate culture. Geely held talks with Volvo employees and management, negotiated with the company's new management system and daily sales incentive system, established the evaluation mechanism for the new Volvo employees.

Geely can look at the cultural differences with Volvo directly, and make timely adjustment of the company after the merger. After several years of mergers and acquisitions, Geely achieved the overall promote in sales, as well as brand value and awareness.

Discussion Questions:

1. What were the difficulties when integrating between two companies after Geely's acquisition of Volvo due to cultural differences?

2. What are the key factors for the successful acquiring of Volvo?

3. How did Geely minimize the risks caused by cultural differences after the acquisition?

8.

The Development of Economic and Trade Relationship between China and Russia under The BRICs Cooperation Mechanism

Due to the dramatic change of Russia's geopolitical situation in recent years, and the good strategic cooperation between Russia and other BRIC nations, Russia decided to choose BRICs cooperation mechanism, and put it as one of the foreign policy priorities. There are rich resources in Russia, and its economic development rely heavily on natural resources. It is more than a quarter of GDP gained from the raw materials or primary processing products on world markets, export structure is the resource depended. Raw materials direction on Economic of Russia is the important characteristics in the global economy. If the structural reforms wouldn't be realized, there must be certain economic risks of Russian economy under the circumstance of heavily reliant on the international raw materials market. After the Ukraine crisis, western sanctions made foreign investors reduced the enthusiasm to invest in Russia. Faced with such deadlock, Russia began to focus on the east on the basis of their own interests, more emphasis on economic exchanges and cooperation with the BRICs, to create the external international environment conducive to the development of their own.

At the same time, the "the Belt and Road" initiative, proposed by China, have made the economic cooperation of the main line running through central Asia countries and Russia, have closely connected China, Russia and other countries for economic development, which provides a good opportunity for Russia to hedge the negative impact of the external international environmental degradation, to enter the global economy once again, also accord Russia to seek new economic growth point of foreign cooperation, expand its depth and breadth on cooperation with China and other BRIC countries. Economic and trade cooperation is one of the core issues of the BRICs countries. The economic cooperation between China and Russia under the BRICs cooperation mechanism with respects to energy, cross-border e-commerce, monetary and financial cooperation.

On May 21, 2014, in the aspect of Sino-Russian energy cooperation and development, Chinese President Xi Jinping and Russian President Vladimir Putin have witnessed the signing of the Chinese and Russian governments "Sino-Russian Gas Cooperation Project Memorandum", the "China Russia Eastern Gas Purchase and Sales Contracts" between China Petroleum Corporation and the Russian Gas Corporation in Shanghai. According to the contract, from 2018, Russia would began the supply of gas through East pipeline, gas volume would then increased year by year and eventually reach 38 billion cubic meters per year, the total contract period is 30 years. In line with the Contract, the main gas source is Russia's Irkutsk region of Eastern Siberia Kovykta gas and Sakha Republic Cayan payment field construction, the Russian Gas Corporation is responsible for field development, gas processing plants and Russia's domestic pipeline construction. China Petroleum Corporation is responsible for the construction of gas pipeline and gas storage facilities in China.

The east line gas cooperation of Sino-Russian, is realized under the guidance and direct participation of Sino-Russian government in the long-term joint efforts of both sides, is another important achievement of comprehensive Sino-Russian energy partnership to strengthen and deepen the comprehensive strategic cooperative partnership, fully embodies the principle of mutual benefit and mutual trust. The two sides will work together to implement the relevant work to ensure the successful implementation of the project.

Sino-Russian gas cooperation will accelerate the development of oil and gas resources and the economic and social development in the Far East, to achieve export diversification. Russian gas export target market is mainly Chinese northeast, Beijing-Tianjin-Hebei and the Yangtze River Delta region, to meet the domestic energy consumption growth in China, improve the atmospheric environment, optimize energy use structure, promote diversification of energy imports and other needs, and to promote the development of related industries along the region.

About cross-border e-commerce between China and Russia, China has a mature e-commerce platform and strong financial resources, lager commodity production capacity, as well as the geopolitical proximity to Russia to expand the logistics and other favorable conditions. Russia has a population of 142 million, 80 million residents are using the Internet, of which 40 million people are online shopping users, the demand for a variety of consumer goods is larger. Russian consumers more mature and rational, even if the income level is limited, the product quality requirements is still relatively high, even the pursuit of price maximization, through cross-border platform, they can buy more high quality and inexpensive goods. In the context of the global economic slowdown, the rapid development of cross-border e-commerce trade between China and Russia, had an annual growth rate of 50%. According to the Russian Association of electronic trading platform, the cross-border e-commerce trade between China and Russia will reach $2.5 billion in 2016.

The rapid development of cross-border e-commerce trade between China and Russia also benefited from the relevant policies and measures of the two governments. The main measures of China: strengthen the cooperation of Sino-Russian between customs, postal and railway departments, set up the three party contact mechanism, support column transport international mail through Russia passenger trains and freight trains in Central Europe, transit for international mail to facilitate customs clearance. At the same time, increase the bilateral cooperation between banks and financial institutions, vigorously promote the RMB denominated settlement, effectively prevent the receipt and payment risk from import and export enterprise. The main measures of Russian: the Russian government provides the Russian Federal Customs entry package in a month to buy, the value of not more than 1000 euros, weighing less than 21 kilograms of goods with duty free. In addition, the two customs also constantly improve regulatory measures to improve customs clearance speed. These measures to a certain extent, improved the cross-border e-commerce environment, to ensure its efficient operation, also to promote the quality of daily necessities in China to enter the Russian market. To achieve effective integration of information resources through the development of electronic commerce, strengthen the exchange of information, the two sides fully understand the bilateral economic and trade related policies and regulations, efficient and accurate understanding of the market dynamics and market demand to capture each other.

At the same time, it shouldn't be ignored that the rapid development of Sino-Russian cross-border e-commerce also have problems, such as perfecting the relevant foreign-related laws and regulations system; exchange rate risk, the ruble devaluation led to a decline in the price competitiveness of China commodities, which affect the level of Chinese profitability; logistics, payment and clearance efficiency requires further improvement; the cross-border e-commerce talent is in short supply. We should pay attention to trade protection signals, Russia may raise taxes to protect local enterprises. In the future, the two sides should maintain a close cooperation and communication, and further promote trade facilitation, provide a broader space for the development of cross-border e-commerce.

In terms of monetary and financial cooperation, China and Russia have been committed to promote the reform of the international monetary and financial system. In recent years, under the background of the economic downturn in the United States and Europe, the BRIC countries have become an important force driving the development of the world economy, however, the BRIC countries are still at a low position in the international monetary and financial system, the lack of sufficient discourse power, the important goal for BRICs cooperation is to improve its position in the international monetary and financial system, to match the rapid growth of economic power and comprehensive national strength. In 2013, the development bank and foreign exchange reserves of the BRIC countries should be build, which is proposed by "Durban Declaration" in fifth BRICs Summit. The long-term financing and foreign direct investment in developing countries, especially in the capital market, are in short supply, so they are faced with the severe challenge of infrastructure construction, which has seriously hindered the growth of global aggregate demand. For the BRIC countries led by emerging market economies and other developing countries in infrastructure construction projects to raise funds to maintain the financial stability of the BRIC countries, creating a multipolar conducive to the economic development environment and the promotion of the global financial system is not far. On July 15, 2014, BRIC countries issued the "Fortaleza Declaration" announced the establishment of the BRICs Development Bank, the initial capital is $100 billion, equally funded by 5 founding members, headquartered in Shanghai, China. The establishment of the BRIC banks adumbrate that the cooperation between Russia and BRIC countries is transferred from "mainly focus on economic governance" to "the combination of both political and economic governance", an all-round coordination mechanism.

Thus, Russia take joining the BRICs as an opportunity, through expanding and deepening cooperation with China and other BRICs member states in the field of energy, economic and trade, monetary and finance, to promote economic development, expand global influence, promote the reform of the international monetary and financial system to safeguard national economic security etc.. Through extensive cooperation and exchanges between China and the BRIC countries, Russia will promote the process of modernization economic and enhance its position and role in the global economic system.

Discussion Questions:

1. What are the impacts of the Sino-Russian natural gas projects on the economy of China and Russia?

2. What are the problems of Sino-Russian cross-border e-commerce trade?

3. How to promote the reform of the international monetary and financial system through cooperation among BRIC countries?

Part Ⅲ

International Trade and Investment

9.

New International Division of Labour and Sino-US Trade Relationship

The aggregate economy of China and the U. S. ranks top two in the world. Especially since China joined the WTO, the volume of import and export trade between China and the U. S. has increased significantly. China and the U. S. has becoming one of the largest trade partners in the world. In 2015, the trade volume between China and the U. S. reached by $558. 39 billion and increased 0. 6% year on year.

Since reform and opening up, China's import and export trade has increased significantly. It has had a huge and far-reaching impact on China's international influence, promoted the development of the domestic economy, promoted the fine-tuning of industrial structure and scientific and technological progress. With the expansion of between China and the U. S. in the economics and trade exchanges, the imbalance of trade is continuing to expand. According to data from the U. S. Department of Commerce and the U. S. International Trade Commission, the U. S. trade has been in a deficit situation since 1993. China replaced Japan in having the largest deficit with the U. S. in 2003. The trade deficit between China and the U. S. was $143. 38 billion in 2009, which accounts for one third of the entire U. S. trade deficit and the trade deficit between China and the U. S. was $261. 4 billion in 2015.

Naturally, Chinese trade surplus with the U. S. is mainly due to the international division of labour, rather than the implementation of protectionism policy in China. Therefore, it is not appropriate to use the trade deficit as the only dimension to measure the volume of global sales and competitiveness of enterprises in the U. S. .

The problem of Sino-US economic and trade friction was prominent which mainly reflected in the trade imbalance. During the period 1984-1992 China has been in a deficit position. Since 1993, the situation has reversed and China has been in the surplus position. Since China joined the WTO, China's trade surplus with the U. S. has risen sharply. According to American statistics, the trade deficit between the U. S to China reached $83. 8 billion in 2000. The deficit of the U. S. trade with China surpassed that with Japan for the first time that year, when China became the largest source of trade deficit for the U. S. . The Sino-US trade deficit continues to expand, hindering the development of normal economic and trade relations between the two countries. The trade deficit also become the main reasons that the U. S. countervailed duties were imposed on Chinese products, requiring the appreciation of the Chinese Yuan and the protection of intellectual property rights. According to the Industrial Injury Investigation Bureau's statistics, by 2015, the U. S. had become one of the countries launching the most trade investigations into China. Looking at the development and change of this problem in recent years, political factors are far greater than economic factors, and it is becoming a focus of Sino-US relations. The situation in the U. S. has caused dissatisfaction and criticism from some special interest groups.

But the truth is that under the guise of economic globalization, international industrial transfer has become the main reason for the Sino-US trade surplus. In the early 1990s, China began to develop processing trade, creating the trade surplus in China. In order to reduce production costs and avoid trade friction with the U. S. , Japan, South Korea, other East Asian countries and some regions transferred their product assembly processes, which had had trade friction with the U. S. and the European Union to China. They have established a large number of enterprises in China. These foreign-funded enterprises import raw materials and semi-finished products from East Asia and other countries. After processing and assembly, these enterprises export to traditional American and European markets, relying on existing sales channels. In foreign trade, countries use " substantial change" as the principle criteria in determining the origin of imported goods, and the export of processed products was transferred from these countries and regions to China. Now the trade surplus between China and the U. S. is mainly due to shifting production from other East Asia countries and regions to China, and China has replaced existing East and Southeast Asia exports to the U. S.. Thus, the international industrial transfer has resulted in a trade surplus between China and the U. S. to a large degree. Internal adjustment of American industrial structure has produced atrophy in industries associated with exports and domestic consumption, with the lack of exports in the service sector putting it in the lead. Due to the shortage of investment in product innovation, lower efficiency, and higher labour costs, America no longer has a production advantage in the manufacture of consumer goods, and only can rely on large numbers of imports from China.

In addition, looking at the main commodity in the China trade surplus with the U. S. , it stems from the reasonable international division of labour, mainly because of two competitive advantages China played: the competitive advantage between industries and the competitive advantage of internal industries. The trade structure between China and the U. S. has determined the imbalance of bilateral trade. The U. S advantage is in capital technology intensive high-tech industry, and China's competitive advantage is mainly in labour intensive products. Because commodities from China to the U. S. include daily necessities with small demand elasticity, the impact of American economic growth on China's exports increased significantly and can effectively expand the China trade surplus with the U. S.. Commodities exported from the U. S. to China are mainly high-tech products, while high-tech products demand greater flexibility. With the high technology development of Japan, South Korea, and China, high-tech products are gradually replacing those of the U. S.. Therefore, with the economic growth, China has reduced its dependence on the U. S. imports, which also expands the trade surplus between China and the U. S.

Discussion Questions:

1. As the world's largest developing country, what are the unique competi-

tive advantages of China?

2. If international trade is the external performance measure of the international division of labour, how should we understand the international division of labour through the competitive advantage and factor endowment theory?

3. In the commitments that China joined the WTO on agriculture, financial, telecommunications and other sectors in services, and automotive sector in industries, China retains the necessary conditions for expansion of the market. Why?

10.

The PV Industry of China Cope with the Challenges of "Double Opposition" Investigation

Chinese photovoltaic industry has suffered repeated blows, not only that the EU's "anti-dumping" investigation may be accelerated, India as the emerging market intends to follow the footsteps of Europe and the U. S. to conduct an anti-dumping investigation into China photovoltaic products. In this situation, the Chinese PV industry how to react is becoming a matter of life and death.

As people worried about the fossil energy supply crisis, new energy sources, such as solar energy and wind power are sought after and regarded as the core of the third industrial revolution in the world. The EU and the U. S. have introduced a variety of initiatives to support the development of new energy and the European Union has become the world's largest PV market. But the U. S. subprime mortgage crisis and the European debt crisis broke out in succession the policy of government subsidies for photovoltaic market was sharply cut, and Europe's PV market volume is shrinking rapidly, so overcapacity issues have begun to emerge. In order to prevent the rapid development of Chinese PV companies seizing the international market, the U. S. and some European Union companies continue to apply for an anti-dumping investigation into China PV.

In October 2011, the U. S. solar cell manufacturer Solar World proceeded to launch a "double opposition" investigation into 75 Chinese companies, at the same time, the U. S. began to initiate an investigation. On 20th March, 2012, the U. S. Department of Commerce made a preliminary decision to levy the countervailing tax from 2. 9% to 4. 73% on China's solar cells. On 17th May, 2012, the U. S. Department of Commerce made the preliminary ruling on the import of photovoltaic products from China raises the high anti-dumping duties from 31. 14% to 249. 96%.

Just two months after the U. S. Commerce Department anti-dumping preliminary results were released, the German company Solar World submitted a formal petition to the European Union, making inquiries about anti-dumping on China photovoltaic enterprises. In June 2013, European Commission announced that European Union would levy the temporary countervailing tax of 11. 8% on solar panel and key devices produced from China, the countervailing tax would be raised to 47. 6% if China and Europe could not reach to a agreed solution before 6th August.

Indian photovoltaic battery manufacturers have repeatedly submitted anti-dumping complaints to the India chamber of Commerce. However, due to the problem of product scope definition, the India government has made a number of changes to the complaint.

By the containment of Europe and America traditional markets and India emerging markets, the liabilities of whole photovoltaic industry is getting worse and the industry is close to an existential predicament. The Ministry of Commerce and other relevant government departments already have acted to take measures to deal with the crisis. There are 4 polysilicon enterprises representing 80% of domestic polysilicon production capacity, Jiangsu Zhongneng Silicon Industry, Jiangxi LDK Photovoltaic Silicon Technology, Luoyang Silicon High Technology, and Chongqing Daquan New Energy proposed to the Ministry of Commerce of China that should impose a "double opposition" survey to EU polysilicon and the Ministry of Commerce has accepted the case maintaining that some of the support policies and measures of the U. S. renewable energy industry create trade barriers, and according to the provisions of the "foreign trade barrier investigation rule", the Ministry of Commerce shall take relevant measures to urge the U. S. to revoke any content that does not match the World Trade Organization Agreement giving Chinese renewable energy products fair treatment.

After the China Mechanical and Electrical Products Import and Export

Chamber organizations expressed their opposition, the New Energy Chamber of All-China Federation of Industry & Commerce released a statement in Beijing saying, "China's industrial and commercial sector is against the EU anti-dumping case regarding China's PV industry". The statement against the EU anti-dumping case calls for EU representatives to come to China as soon as possible for dialogue to resolve trade disputes. In addition, there are 33 PV companies participate the third meeting of China's photovoltaic technology standards committee in 2012 to discuss resolve the situation.

In 2011, China imported $764 million of polysilicon material from Germany, accounting for 20% of China's imported products and the value of silver pulp raw material imported from Germany PV reached $360 million. China procured a total of about 40 billion yuan in photovoltaic cell production equipment from foreign markets, of which Germany, Switzerland and other European countries accounted for 45%. If the EU imposes restrictions on Chinese photovoltaic products, direct damage comes from the importing of EU. When Prime Minister Merkel leads a delegation to visit China and attend the second round of talks, German Environment Minister Peter Altmaier will take the initiative to talk about the EU photovoltaic products trade remedy investigation. Prime Minister Merkel will not talk about corporate disputes, but will urge the two sides to create a fair competitive environment for the companies in their respective countries.

Discussion Questions:

1. Solar energy enterprise Solar World is regarded as the initiator in the encounter with trade barriers for China photovoltaic products. It has not only launched the U. S. and China PV double reverse investigation, but also has triggered a new round of prosecution in EU. Please investigate and research the background of this enterprise and the cause of this matter.

2. Since the U. S. Department of Commerce ruled that China photovoltaic products receive subsidies, China has faced a "double opposition" investigation from the European Union and India. Discuss whether the charge is reasonable,

whether the government of China gives the subsidies for this industry, and whether China photovoltaic enterprises are dumping their products.

3. Since the U. S. ruled that China photovoltaic products is subsidized and engaged in dumping, EU has put forward anti-dumping complaints to China photovoltaic products again. Once filed, this will be a new record in the number of anti-dumping cases in the history of the European Union. Please explain the reasons that China photovoltaic has been the recipient of the international block.

4. Facing a rise in international trade protectionism and pressure from all sides, how should China PV enterprises deal with this?

11.

The Development of Bilateral Trade between ASEAN and China

Since 1990s, the integration of regional economy has becoming gradually the trend of cooperation in world trade and regarded as the new driving force to promote economic development by majority countries. China as the largest developing country in the world, the economic strength already has considerable scale and has already been the world second biggest economy through forty years' reforming and opening, which has close economic and trade cooperation relationships with each country all over the world. It is very necessary to join the association of regional economic integration to protect the foreign interests of China and to promote the continuing and rapid development of foreign economy. China-ASEAN Free Trade Area (CAFTA) is the first association of regional economic integration which China joined, it includes 11 country members, nearly 2 billion populations and it is the free trade area which comprises most large population and the largest association of regional economic integration in the developing countries. CAFTA has been established officially in 2010 which marks the important step in the road of trade liberalization between China and ASEAN countries.

The trade between China and ASEAN has increased rapidly Since China-ASEAN Free Trade Area (CAFTA) was established in 2010. The bilateral trading volume reached \$472. 16 billion in 2015. Exports from China to ASEAN countries reached \$277. 47 billion with a year-on-year increase of 2. 0%, and exports from ASEAN countries totalled \$194. 68 billion with an decrease of 6. 5%. The Chinese surplus was \$82. 79 billion and it was the 1. 3 times of surplus in 2014 which it was \$63. 75 billion. The trade between China and ASEAN accounts for 11.9% of the total trade volume in Chinese foreign trade in 2015 and it raises 0.7% compared with 11.2% in 2014. Since 2011. ASEAN continues to remain the third largest trade partner position with China after EU and the U. S.. The proportion of both parties' trade accounting for the total amount of importing and exporting of China in corresponding period maintain at 10%, China keeps the first largest trade partner position with ASEAN.

In 2015, the top three trading partners of China among the ten ASEAN countries were Malaysia, Vietnam and Singapore, among them Malaysia's bilateral trading volume of $97.312 billion, decreased 4.6% of year-on-year, Vietnam's bilateral trading volume of $95.976 billion, increased 14.9% of year-on-year and Singapore's bilateral trading volume of $79.559 billion, decreased 0.1% of year-on-year.

CAFTA is the free trade area having the largest population in the world comprised of developing countries. CAFTA, EU (European Union) and NAFTA (North American Free Trade Area) are three regional economic cooperation zones in the world. The proposal for CAFTA was put forward during the China-ASEAN Leaders Conference which was convened in Singapore in November 2000. During the meeting, taking into account ASEAN's concern about the impact of ASEAN on China's entry into the WTO, China's Premier Zhu Rongji suggested carrying out a viability study on establishing a free trade area between China and ASEAN countries. A China-ASEAN economic cooperation panel was organised at the instructions of the leaders. Based on the study, the panel brought forward a proposal to build a close China-ASEAN economic partnership, including establishing CAFTA. In the fifth China-ASEAN Leaders Conference in Brunei on November 6, 2001, all sides reached a consensus to establish CAFTA in the upcoming decade. Premier Zhu Rongji and leaders of ten ASEAN countries signed "China-ASEAN Comprehensive Economic Cooperation Framework Agreement" at the sixth China-ASEAN Leaders Conference on November 4, 2002, and decided to establish CAFTA by 2010. This framework agreement was a milestone of the comprehensive economic cooperation between China and ASEAN and ushered in a brand new stage of bilateral economic & trade cooperation. The agreement stipulated that official negotiation to establish the free trade zone would begin in 2003 and be completed by June 2004. Bilateral tariff concession plans commenced officially in January 2005.

CAFTA was officially established on January 1, 2010. It benefits nearly 2 billion people in countries with a gross GDP of $6 trillion and trading volume of $0.45 trillion. CAFTA is a new endeavour for international economic cooperation, and will unquestionably enhance the meaning of regional economic cooperation. During exploratory talks, the best choices are made for China and ASEAN by referring to the successful experience of EU and NAFTA as well as APEC (Asia-Pacific Economic Cooperation) and adapting the features of regional economy in establishing of free trade area. Since CAFTA was established, both sides have implemented zero tariffs on over 90% of products. The average tariff levied by China to ASEAN countries dropped to 0.1% from 9.8%, and the average tariff by six long time members of ASEAN to China plummeted to 0.6% from 12.8%. The dramatic tariff drop facilitated effective development of bilateral trade.

Bilateral trade has increased significantly since CAFTA was officially established. Bilateral trade was below $80 billion in 2003, when leaders agreed to aim for $100 billion in 2005. Subsequently, bilateral trade actually exceeded $100 billion in 2004, one year earlier than plan. The next goal was to reach $200 billion bilaterally by 2010, but the reality was that the figure was reached in 2007, three years early. Bilateral trade volume set a new record in 2008 when the financial crisis occurred, but it was still maintained at over $200 billion in 2009. The tax reduction coming from the establishment of CAFTA in 2010 raised bilateral trade volume to a new level close to $300 billion. In 2011, bilateral trade volume was $362.33 billion, reaching a new record. The total included exports from China worth $169.86 billion with a year-on-year increase of 22.9%, and imports to China totalled $192.47 billion, increasing 24.7%. The top 4 sources of import to China among 10 ASEAN countries are Malaysia, Thailand, Indonesia and Singapore. The corresponding import volumes to China from these four were $62. 02 billion, $39. 04 billion, $31. 32 billion and $27. 76 billion respectively in 2011, increasing 23. 1%, 17. 6%, 50. 9% and 12. 9% respectively, and they made up a total of 83. 2% of China's imports from ASEAN.

Through longitudinal observation, the total amount of trade between China and ASEAN raises to $472. 16 billion in 2015 from $8. 4 billion in 1991 when both parties established dialogue partnership, and $54. 8 billion in 2002 when both parties singed the agreement of "Overall Economic Cooperation Framework". The average increasing rate is 18. 3%. The total amount of bilateral trade between China and ASEAN decreased slightly in 2015. The total amount of trade between China and ASEAN maintains rapid increasing in most time except Asia financial crisis in 1998, global financial crisis in 2008 and the severe economic situation of China which caused the negative growth in 2015. The trade deficit between China and ASEAN has been serious for many years and the trade deficit accounts for 15% in the total trade, in some specific year, the trade deficit between China and ASEAN even exceeds 20%. From 1996 to 2011, the trade deficit situation always exists between China and ASEAN and it has been changed until 2012. The amount of bilateral trade in 2012 is $400. 15 billion and exporting amount from China is $204. 25 billion, importing amount from ASEAN is $195. 89 billion and the trade surplus is $8. 5 billion which accounts for 2% among the total amount of bilateral trade. The trade surplus has been continuing to expand from 2013 and it is $44. 48 billion which accounts for 10% among the total amount of bilateral trade. Since 1991, China is in the position of trade deficit at the most time, especially the deficit has been reached $22. 69 billion in 2011. However, since 2012, China is in the position of trade surplus from deficit and the surplus has been created a new level of $82. 79 billion in 2015.

The economic and trade relations between China and ASEAN countries is ushering in favourable conditions for further development. The signing of free trade agreement swept away barriers in systems concerning trade and investment on both sides. In accordance with Chinese commitment regarding agreement, China has lowered tariffs dramatically, while reducing and cancelling non-tariff barriers. The further opening up of the Chinese market, especially its in the service and trade areas, will also offer a number of business opportunities for foreign investors including those in ASEAN countries. For now, ASEAN countries have together become the fifth largest trading partner of China in the last ten years, and the largest among China's partners in developing countries. Moreover, bilateral trade is increasing far more rapidly than with other major trading partners.

The "China-ASEAN Comprehensive Economic Cooperation Framework Agreement" signed by China and ASEAN was a milestone in China and ASEAN relation development. Bilateral economic & trade cooperation goals will be clearer and cooperation prospects are brighter since the establishment of CAFTA.

Discussion Questions:

1. Give a brief introduction to the development course of CAFTA and analyse its current status.
2. Illustrate the motivation of China and ASEAN to establish the free trade area.
3. Analyse the investment environment of enterprises in CAFTA.
4. Give a brief introduction of opportunities and challenges which Chinese enterprises face in CAFTA.

12.

Hongdou Group Investment in Cambodia SSEZ

The textile industry is a traditional pillar industry in China. With development of China's economy, the excess manufacturing capacity happens in the textile industry and it is facing more and more competition, there is also an urgent need to reduce costs and transfer the remaining production capacity. The Ministry of Commerce provided macro-guidance to investment in the construction of regional cooperation. Moreover, they supported the country and its industry, capital investment facilitation, overseas investment protection and so on. In this way, it provided convenience and concessions to a number of overseas investment enterprises.

Hongdou Group is the representative of the textile industry enterprises, headquartered in Wuxi, Jiangsu province. They believe that creating national brand is their duty, since it boasts excellent sales and ranks next-to-the-top hundred runners-up. It has become a large private-owned garment industry, a collection of scientific research and development, manufacturing, and global trade. In June 2015, World Brand Lab published the list of the 500 most valuable brands in China, with the red bean brand (?) in the top 100. In August 2016, Hongdou Group ranked 265th in the "2016 Chinese enterprise 500"

As early as 2007, Hongdou Group actively responded to the call of "Going Global" in the country. With the strong support of the Ministry of Commerce, the Ministry of Finance and other government ministries and the government departments of Wuxi, Jiangsu Province, several Wuxi enterprises and one Cambodian Enterprises made joint efforts to march into the SSEZ. Hongdou Group is solely responsible for the park management, so the Chinese management capacity is combined with the local workers: Chinese factory management staff has less than 30 people, with nearly 700 local employees.

In 2010, the Hongdou Group's International Apparel Garments settled in SSEZ. In 2016, Hongdou Group garment factory opened four production lines: two for trousers and two for suits. The monthly output is 30 thousand and 55 thousand respectively. The products obtained the certification of Spain, France, Italy and other countries, and the vast majority of customer orders come from Europe.

The Cambodia Sihanoukville Special Economic Zone (SSEZ) has been developed jointly by Jiangsu Taihu Lake Cambodia International Economic Cooperation Zone Investment Co., Ltd. and Cambodia International Investment and Development Group Co., Ltd. The total planning area is 11.13 square kilometers, with textile and garment, metal machinery, light industry and home appliances as the leading industry. Meanwhile export processing zones, business and trade district, living area are founded in one area. The first phase of the SAR has formed the construction including construction of 5.28 square kilometers. They built 85 factories, and set of offices, residential, catering and cultural entertainment buildings and other services in one integrated service center building. Moreover, Cambodia staff quarters, trade market, and life service area have also been built. In addition, the construction and development of SSEZ Special Administrative Region led to the development of the surrounding economies. Murderang, a town close to SSEZ, is booming rapidly. The original muddy roadshave have been turned into cement ones, and more and more new houseshave are rising up. More than 30 percent of the local population was employed in the town, and the income of the villagers in SSEZ greatly increased. At the same time, the development of SSEZ has also brought many opportunities to the villagers. Lots of them rented dormitories or opened small shops to broaden their income sources and become "the first people to get rich".

It is the requirement of era and enterprises development for Hongdou Group to open up overseas markets actively and make the cross countries investment. China's economic development has entered the new normal, and actively promoted international capacity cooperation. The economy expanded its development from the local to the cross-regional, and to foreign countries. It is conducive for private enterprises, to continuously upgrade technology, quality and service levels, enhancing core competitiveness. If enterprises want to be internationalized, they must try to get more cake in the international market. One product is not enough to expand abroad. Capital, brand, market, management, personnel etc. should also develop to get the level occupy international markets. This is the only way for enterprise internationalization.

Hongdou Group invests to build factory in Cambodia to obtain more cheap labor. China has a large population, and labor resources are abundant. However, with China's economic development and the spread of higher education, labor cost is increasing. While economic development in Cambodia's is still in the early stage, labor resources is abundant and compensation cost is low. Young population in Cambodia (10 to 35 years old) is more than half of the total population of 7.5 million, an annual growth rate of 2.7%, but also to Malaysia, South Korea and other labor delivery. It's labor force is in the field of agriculture, garment industry, service industry. In this way, the Hongdou Group in SSEZ can make full use of the local abundant and intensive labor, access to production costs on the advantage.

Hongdou Group transfers surplus production capacity and opens up the market by investing overseas. Textile and garment industry is a labor-intensive industry, the standardization of mass-scale production. Chinese market demand for clothing products become saturated, and the industry is in the product cycle mature stage. In recent years, China's labor costs and rising prices, have resulted in highercosts. Enterprises also need to open up to other markets, and transfer domestic surplus capacity. In addition, compared with Cambodia, China's textile and garment industry have technical advantages. This makes part of the entrepreneurs look for rich labor-intensive, broad market place further to reduce costs, enhance competitiveness and gain more profits.

Hongdou Group obtains benefits and advantages from many aspects. Labor costs in Cambodia is low, about 200 US dollars per person per month, equals to 1362 Yuan, far below the wage level in China. Enterprises can obtain benefits in tax. Cambodia gives a series of preferential tax policies, such as exempt from import and export tariffs, value-added tax. Hongdou Group's products in SSEZ can make use of the generalized system of preferences of European and American countries to sell to Europe and the United States, so as to have more cost advantages and a broader consumer market, thereby greatly enhancing the Hongdou Group's profit margins; as to the enterprises that entered SSEZ.

Hongdou Group will bring its textile and garment technology and equipment from China to Cambodia, continue to extend the life cycle of the industry, while making full use of a series of local tax incentives to increase production capacity, reduce costs and increase profits.

Discussion Questions:

1. What trade theories does Hongdou Group show in SSEZ?

2. What benefits can Cambodia have from Hongdou Group's production and construction in SSEZ?

3. What factors will affect Chinese enterprises continuing to enter SSEZ?

13.

China's Poultry Meat Export to the EU

Poultry industry, the earliest development and highest degree of industrialization and scale of China's livestock industry, possesses export price advantages. The EU is China's major business partner in poultry. But as early as 2002, the EU was building technical barriers of poultry products trade which sticks on the grounds of China exporting some of the animal-derived foods that contain residues harmful to human health, prohibiting the export of China's animal derived products to the EU, except casing and fish products captured in high seas and transported directly to the EU market. In 2004, Chinese cooked poultry products were subjected to the EU ban because of the avian flu issues. The closure of the EU export market was a heavy blow to China's poultry product industry, but also a major turning point into the new life. In order to return to the EU market with a brand-new image, the Chinese relevant authorities collected and translated a large number of the EU related laws, regulations and hygiene requirements for imported poultry products, processing serious guidance to export enterprises on poultry breeding, slaughtering, cooked processing and other links that strictly followed the EU regulatory requirements. In accordance with the EU requirements and guidance of inspection and quarantine, poultry export enterprises pumped money into establishing a whole process of standardization system and quality traceability system, and continuously improved the level of safety quality management. Eventually, in 2008, thanks to the cooperation of the government and enterprises, the EU member states approved the resumption of its imports of cooked poultry products from China.

China still faced some problems after the ban was lifted. One of the most notable things was the EU proposed to amend tariff for poultry products that was about goose liver or duck liver products, cooked chicken, cooked duck and other eight tax numbers and implemented a quota management. According to article 28, paragraph 1, GATT1994, if a member proposed to amend a concession, the member should negotiate with the following members about question of compensation: one is the member who has the INR and the other who has the principal supplying interest. In addition, the member will need to consult with any other members who have substantial benefits in the concession. The EU negotiated with major suppliers such as Brazil and Thailand in the light of imported product situation for the previous three years, but China was not in it because China was being closed by the EU. However, the result of negotiations is to allocate 96% low tariff quotas to Brazil and Thailand, China and other countries (regions) can only share the remaining 4% of the quota, the part of exceeding quota needs to pay high tariffs. Specific regulations were published and implemented in 2013, which were regarded as a thunderbolt for China. It's equivalent for the EU to make the use of quota management to implement the soft "closure" of China once again after the entry into force of the regulations. Because the tariff adjustment was too large, China's export price advantage of poultry meat did not exist, and some customers may no longer buy Chinese products.

This means that China's poultry products will be out of the market because Brazil and Thailand's products have more comparative advantage and the EU poultry market of China strenuously reopened will be lost once again. All the previous input and pay made by relevant businesses and government will be wasted. The decision of the EU not only undermines the export interest of related enterprises in China and hinders the development of domestic poultry industry, but also seriously affects the employment of Chinese industry practitioners. As the downstream suppliers of poultry industry are farmers, and Chinese enterprises are subject to the EU quotas, the reduction of export will mean to reduce the domestic downstream supplier's orders which will lead to farmers' having to give up the aquaculture industry and find other ways to make a living.

On April 8th, 2015, China proposed to submit the application of consultant with the EU to the WTO Secretariat, about the EU's taking tariff quota management measures on part of the poultry meat production, but the consultation failed. In order to safeguard China's normal trade interests with the WTO and meet the requirements of domestic poultry industry, through consulting with CFNA (China Chamber of Commerce of Import and Export of Food stuffs, Native Produce & Animal By-Products), China first proposed that an expert group be formed on the measures that the EU effects the tariff reduction of some poultry products (DS492), the application was decided on at the WTO Dispute Settlement Body's regular meeting on June 19, 2015. China has reasoned that exporters are facing the dilemma of high tax rates and the number of orders has drastically reduced, export sales have fallen sharply, also the market share has been severely reduced, and all of this is affected by the EU's revised tariff reductions for part of poultry products. In May 2015, China and the EU held consultations on the dispute but didn't reach a consensus, China proposed to the Dispute Settlement Body for the application of establishing an expert group later. The EU believes that China has no substantial supply of benefits based on the relevant import statistics and hasn't proved its interests as a large number of suppliers within 90 days. And the EU believes that its practice follows the proper procedure. In view of the fact that the EU had held consultations with China on the dispute in May 2015, the EU believes that China's proposal to set up an expert group was too early, so it did not approve the establishment of the expert group. Accordingly, WTO Dispute Settlement Body will postpone the establishment of expert group on the case. On 20 July, 2015, at the regular meeting of Dispute Settlement Body, the WTO made a decision on the establishment of expert group on the tariff reduction measures (DS492) about China's part of the poultry products affected by the EU. At this regular meeting of the Dispute Settlement Body, China proposed for the second time to set up a group of experts on the tariff reduction measures of some poultry products affected by the EU, China hopes the EU can adjust its controversial measures through the dispute settlement procedure. In this regard, the EU stated that its measures are in line with the provisions of the WTO Agreement and that it's prepared to defend the Panel's procedures. Brazil, Russia and the United States will participate as a third party in the case of the Group of Experts.

Discussion Questions:

1. What measures did the EU use to limit the import of poultry products from China? What was the reason for the EU to take these measures?
2. How did the EU use the tariff quota to softly "close China"?
3. Why can only China share 4% with other countries in the EU quota? Is this provision of the EU reasonable?

14.

Ant Financial Service Investment in Indian Paytm

Ant Financial Services Group, the parent company of AliPay, was officially established in October 2014. It completed the B round financing of USD 4.5 billion in April 2016, with estimated value USD 60 billion. Ant Financial Service has never concealed one of its three major strategies, its ambition to internationalize. CEO Eric expressed during the first FTCC Summit, projecting that in the next four years, 50% of Ant Financial Services users will be overseas, with domestic users comprising the other 50 percent. Over the upcoming nine years, Ant Financial Service could deliver services to 2 billion consumers around the globe. As a matter of fact, its internationalizing plan has sped up since 2015. As a new force within the Alibaba Group, its businesses provide extensive financial services, such as payment, wealth management, banking, insurance, loan, and credit investigation. Although its overseas business is currently not as popular as it is in China, Ant Financial Services frequently releases news of overseas acquisitions.

Ant Financial Services overseas plan is focused mainly in two directions. The first is to attract and encourage outbound Chinese tourists and overseas Chinese residents to use AliPay services while in Europe and Asia; the second is to promote participation in investment bank, insurance, and payment institution services.

In Asia, AliPay is developing cooperative agreements with enterprises in Thailand and Singapore; in Europe, AliPay has joined hands with German payment service provider Concardis and jewelry brand Wempe; As well, German payment service provider WireCard already has cooperative agreements with Ali-

Pay. The second focus of Ant Financial Services overseas plan is investment co-operation through insurance, in an attempt to build up standard and contextual insurance businesses through the Internet.

In 2016, Ant Financial Services extend business opportunities for AXA insurance products and services utilizing Alibaba's global E-commerce system through reaching an agreement of strategic partnership with Alibaba and AXA Group. Further investment direction is in companies related to AliPay. For example, on a technical level, Ant Financial Service invests in Singaporean mobile security and encryption technology V-Key in order to strengthen its product security.

In the Indian market, Ant Financial Service has begun considerable investment in Paytm, India's largest payment platform, and in its parent company One97 Communications. The full name of Paytm is "Pay through Mobile", and it is a consumer brand of One97 Communications, which is one of the largest mobile Internet companies in India. Paytm was merely a mobile prepayment website when it was established in 2010. In 2014, Paytm entered into the Indian Internet financial arena and promoted E-wallet. Moreover, Paytm now delivers E-commerce services to its customers. Paytm has acquired the first payment bank license in India, issued by Central Bank of India, allowing it to develop banking services such as payment, savings, remittance, transfer, etc. , while providing online financial services with lower rates for small- and medium-sized enterprises and low-income groups in India.

At the beginning of 2015, Ant Financial Service launched the first round of investment in Paytm, Ant Financial Service and Alibaba made the second round of investment in September 2015. Two rounds of investment and intensive exchanges and cooperation have enabled Paytm to become an official strategic partner of Ant Financial Services. Since then bilateral cooperation has moved to the fast track. Two rounds of investment discussed below enables Ant Financial Service to hold an advantageous position in Indian inclusive finance. Since Ant Financial Service became shareholder in Paytm, the number of Paytm users has grown to 150 million from just over 20 million within one year, and is now the 4th largest E-wallet in the world. Paytm is also known as the "Indian AliPay".

Further, a trans-development team consisting of at least 20 members from Ant Financial Services has flown to Noida, a satellite city of Delhi, where Paytm is headquartered, and is working with Paytm to improve its platform capability in an integrated way, from system architecture reconstruction and risk control systems building to data capability. The team's work with Paytm team focuses on all procedures involving technology, risk control, products, operations, and so on. Meanwhile, Paytm has also sent a number of staffs to Hangzhou, the headquarters of Ant Financial Services, to comprehensively study business content and corporate culture. For example, when Ant Financial Services launched its investment, the risk control architecture of Paytm had only just over 10 rules and became susceptible to Internet fraud. Further, its system could only bear 10-20 thousand trades every day. One year later, Paytm has developed architecture capable of bearing 100 million trades daily, up from 1 million; the risk ratio drops to one in ten thousand from the earlier level of several percent. In early 2015 when cooperation between Paytm and Ant Financial Services got started, Paytm user quantity was about twenty million, and the figure has increased by five times in only one year and a half. Now, Paytm boasts 140 million users, and its market share is over three times of all the rest of its rivals. Off-line contextual payments rapidly accounted for half of the daily average trading amount.

As for Ant Financial Services and Paytm, the two have intensive cooperation in terms of capital, underlying technology, business model, and corporate culture, and the synergy is projected to generate huge win-win results. In future the two plan to connect their online payments. In other words, users of AliPay may scan QR code of Paytm in India, and Paytm users may scan QR code of AliPay in China or even in the world. The total population of China and India is close to 40% of the global population, suggesting enormous opportunities.

Upgraded consumption by the poor in India will also show the colossal potential and need of such systems. For example, at present a half of Paytm users live in top 10 cities of India, and the other half is from tier-two and below cities and rural areas. According to the recent performance, the figure of users in tier-two and below cities and rural areas has increased dramatically, showing good growth.

At present Ant Financial Services has set up branches in six countries, namely the U. S. , Singapore, South Korea, the UK, Luxembourg and Australia. In Southeast and South Asia, it has acquired 20% shares of Thai payment company Ascend Money, launched investment in One97 Communications, the parent company of Paytm, and in Indian E-wallet Paytm, thus further promoting its internationalization process.

Internationalization is the inevitable choice for internet development in China. However, the path of internationalization is not as smooth as expected. Baidu's failure in Japan and the predicament of WeChat in Southeast Asia are both valuable lessons to learn from. On this long journey, and in addition to exploiting experience accumulated in domestic markets in China, Ant Financial Service is also exploring some new trajectories, such as bringing in Douglas Feagin, former senior partner of Goldman Sachs, to participate in strengthening its internationalization team building. However, confronted by complicated international markets and the uncertain policies of other countries, great tests are still in store for Ant Financial Service.

Discussion Questions:

1. What is the motivation for Ant Financial Services to expand abroad?

2. Why does Alibaba choose Southeast and South Asian countries as its investment priorities in its early expansion period?

3. Why does Alibaba choose to become a shareholder of local enterprises, instead of establishing sole proprietorship or adopting other ways to enter into foreign markets?

4. What advantages Alibaba has when it invests in Indian Paytm?

15.

Vegetables-for-Oil Plan between China and Thailand

In June 2008, China and Thailand governments inked the General Trade Framework Agreement for China-Thailand Vegetables-for-Oil. The program involves the Yunnan Xishuangbanna Petrochemical group, Yunnan Xinnong Science and Technology Company and Thailand National Oil Company. The purpose of this program is to export vegetables such as potatoes, tomatoes, snow peas, and so on, to trade and import the equivalent value of petroleum, tropical fruit and seafood products from Thailand. The creation of this program is suitable for the trading situation of Yunnan province and Southeast Asian countries and complies with the 'Bridgehead' strategies of the China-ASEAN Free Trade Area and national development in Yunnan province. According to the Agreement, China provides 300 thousand tonnes of vegetables with the total value of about $100 million to Thailand each year. In exchange, Thailand exports to China the same value of oil products, about 150 thousand to 200 thousand tonnes.

The project will not only help alleviate the problem of oil supply in Yunnan province, but also strengthen brand reputation, driving 100 thousand farmers to spur production of 150 thousand to 200 thousand Mu of vegetables, at 1000 yuan per MU. Additionally, the program will bring 80 thousand employment opportunities in vegetable planting and produce, and 7000 jobs in transportation, distribution, sales and services.

The demand for vegetables in Thailand is 14 thousand tons per day, about 5 million tons per year. However, the sales volume of Chinese Vegetables is only hundred tons per day on Bangkok market. The market share of Chinese vegetables in Thailand is small. Thailand has a subtropical climate which is conducive to growing certain vegetables, hence, the prospects in China-Thailand vegetable trade are broad.

During the implementation process, this program met many problems. There are two transportation models of the "vegetable-for-oil" plan: one is to transport the oil by Man-Kun Express from Thailand to Mokan port of China. and Xinnong Company distributes the oil to the Yunnan Vegetable Circulation Industry Association members and planting base, agricultural products transport households, and the rural areas by the cooperation with Sinopec of China. Another shipping model is shipping by tanker from Bangkok of Thailand to Zhanjiang of Guangdong, and then Xinnong company transports the finished oil to Yunnan.

To June of 2009, due to accessibility issues along the Man-Kun Expressway, the program was stopped. The transportation route from Kunming to Bangkok needs to go through four customs clearance procedures through three countries, and the length of time for customs clearance procedures, charges are not the same. More than 20 hours away travel, even if the driver shifts down, customs clearance requires at least two or three days, Due to the high cost, many companies would rather bypsaa.

The program was influenced further by the Thai political situation in 2010. Great changes within the Thai government further affected vegetable and oil exchange program.

In early 2010, the second year of the agreement, the program was implemented successfully by the effort of both sides. However, many problems needed to be solved in regards to road transportation, and at this point the program entered a new negotiation process. However, in 2010 the vegetable export was still 1.3 billion yuan, and 160 thousand tons of refined petroleum products were imported from Thailand.

There are land transportation and ocean shipping models for oil importing process of vegetables-for-oil plan. From the perspective of the Xinnong Company, even though the transportation capacity is huge, the method of shipping has many restrictions, such as expenditure, currency exchange and payment systems.

However, as of October 2012, relevant decision makers still suggested this method of shipping for the Vegetables-for-Oil program. Yunnan province attaches great attention to this program and the provincial departments have held several conferences and meetings to discuss problems. In November of 2012, two tankers with 250 tons transportation capacity took 22 days to arrive at the Guanlei Port of Jinghong.

In March 2013, the Association of Yunnan-Southeast Asia and South Asia Trade and Economic Cooperation and Development held a preparatory conference for Kunming-Bangkok economic corridor, discussing the "Vegetable-for-Oil" program. This conference has came to an agreement with Thai prime minister's office and the PTT Company. PTT signed an agreement for the sale of 1 million tons of refined oil products with Yunnan Lianmeng International Technology Company and the Xinnong Company, including 800 thousand tonnes of diesel and 200 thousand tons of gasoline. The production and supply of refined oil products supplied by Thailand was in accordance with standards provided by China, and was transported by ocean shipping and multi-transport model.

To ensure the implementation of the program, PTT established a special international logistics trade services team, and added 100 new Volvo tankers, while the Chinese company bought 100 high standard refrigerated vegetable trucks.

As of June 2014, China had purchased 40 thousand tons diesel oil from Thailand, approximately half the amount called for in the "Vegetables-for-Oil" plan by the Ministry of Commerce. The program achieved some progress, as according to the market price, 1 ton of export vegetables is equal to the value of nearly 1.5 tons of diesel oil.

This program has significance for both countries, but marked only a few achievements in the past eight years. Due to limitations in the institution, system, management, industry development, and the drawbacks of traditional trading methods, the trading of agricultural products in large-volume still have not achieved expectations. Due to these factors, plus corruption in the trading process itself, this program has been shelved.

Discussion Questions:

1. What is the trading method of "Vegetable-for-Oil"? What are the features of this method?

2. Why has the program been stopped many times, and with such little achievement?

3. In looking at the experience of trying to implement this program, please discuss the business ethics in this case study.

16.

GMS Cross-Border E-Commerce Enterprise Alliance Platform

Sub-regional economic cooperation appeared in the late 1980s and early 1990s, as an expression of integration in economic globalization and regional economic policy. In 1992, under the leadership of the Asian Development Bank (ADB), 6 countries within the Lancang-Mekong River region-namely China, Laos, Myanmar, Thailand, Cambodia and Vietnam jointly launched the Greater Mekong Sub-region Economic Cooperation (GMS), to strengthen economic contact between countries and promote the coordinated development of Sub-regional economic society to achieve regional common prosperity. The Greater Mekong sub-region is rich in biodiversity, agricultural, water, mineral, land, and human resources, and holds many tourism development possibilities. The region's advantages are quite obvious and both resources and markets highly complementary. The Greater Mekong sub-region overflows with huge trade and investment opportunities, and has great potential for development.

Since the beginning of its cooperation with the Lancang-Mekong sub-regional group in 1990s, China has attached great importance to this regional relationship. GMS economic cooperation has been a priority in the construction of the China-ASEAN Free Trade Area. GMS economic integration plays an important role in promoting and catalyzing economic integration between China and ASEAN. Since the beginning of the Greater Mekong sub-regional economic cooperation, the sub-regional economic cooperation between China and Southeast Asian countries has been deepening and expanding: the field and areas of cooperation have been amplified, cooperative mechanisms have been improved, and the degree of coordination has intensified. After more than 20 years of development, the results of cooperation in all GMS countries have been fruitful. It not only has bettered prospects for the countries involved, but also has made positive contributions to peace and development in Asia and in the world at large.

However, within the context of the information age, traditional trade patterns can not completely meet the requirements of economic development. At this time, as a new business model for continued globalization, openness and efficiency, e-commerce is an effective means for enhancing the economic strength of the country and allocating advantageous resources. As the world's most dynamic e-commerce country, China now has more than 200 thousand e-commerce enterprises, including 5000 enterprises with high reputation. In 2015 cross-border e-commerce transactions reached 5. 2 trillion yuan, with more than 250 thousand enterprises carrying out cross-border e-commerce trade. With the development of overseas online shopping on the rise, cross-border electronic business platforms have also accelerated planning at home and abroad. Premier Li Keqiang has made it clear that using the cross-border e-commerce "Internet plus foreign trade" model to facilitate import and export business and to achieve optimal output, will continue lead to the development of domestic shops and factories, and help to create more employment opportunities. Cross-border electronic commerce is now the leading way to connect domestic factories with foreign markets. Therefore, cross-border e-commerce supply systems will be an important tool for industrial restructuring and market development. It is not only the Chinese government which supports and encourages this, the Greater Mekong sub-region countries' governments as a whole are also very concerned about development and cooperation in cross-border e-commerce. As such, they are actively exploring new models of regional cooperation in cross-border e-commerce platform construction, researching and formulating measures for infrastructure construction, legal frameworks, transaction and payment systems, logistics and transportation facilities, human resource training and network security measures. Sub-regional cooperation in cross-border e-commerce, integration of network information resources, promotion of the flow of information sharing, and the acceleration of construction of cross-border e-commerce platforms for public service are matters of mutual benefit to all countries in the region.

At the GMS National Leader Summit in December 2014, Premier Li Keqiang proposed the establishment of the "GMS Cooperation in Cross-Border E-Commerce Platform". With the support of GMS national governments and the Asian Development Bank (ADB), the "7th GMS Economic Corridor Forum" held in Kunming published a Ministerial Joint Statement approving the implementation of a GMS Cross-Border E-Commerce Cooperation Platform Framework Document, and confirmed the setting up of the "GMS Cross-Border E-Commerce Cooperation Platform Contact Center" in China (Yunnan) at the Lancang-Mekong River Subregional Economic and Trade Development Center.

The Enterprise Alliance is a branch of GMS Cross-Border E-Commerce Cooperation Platform Contact Center. GMS member countries have recommended that e-commerce promotion agencies, trade promotion agencies and e-commerce enterprises, on a voluntary basis, and in conjunction with the Enterprise Alliance, establish more closely linked non-governmental, non-profit regional and international cooperative organizations, for the promotion of development of GMS international cross-border e-commerce, and the sharing of the subregional consumption market. Under the guidance and with the support of International Department of Chinese Ministry of Commerce, other Member States' Government GMS Electronic Commerce Departments, Yunnan Provincial Department of Commerce and the GMS Cross-Border E-Commerce Cooperation Platform Contact Center, the Enterprise Alliance carries out the work of reporting on the progress of cooperation to the appropriate GMS state government departments.

The principle of Enterprise Alliance is: "Build, Share, Share, Win". Firstly, Enterprise Alliance will establish, in 7 languages, the GMS Cross-Border E-Commerce Trading Platform, the GMS Cross-Border E-Commerce Talent Training Platform, and the GMS Cross-Border E-Commerce Virtual Incubator Platform to provide a full range of cross-border e-commerce services for GMS enterprises, as well as hold an annual GMS Cross-Border E-Commerce Dialogue to promote the development of regional e-commerce. This will effectively improve the level of GMS e-commerce cooperation and application.

Secondly, the Alliance promotes the sharing of GMS markets and the Chinese market, which is the world's largest e-commerce retail market. E-commerce is the best way for GMS companies, especially SMEs, to enter the vast Chinese market, the world's largest e-commerce trading market. GMS countries which are member states in the ASEAN Free Trade Area, have shown rapid growth in economy and have had good economic reciprocity with China in the recent years. As the Enterprise Alliance has online and off-line business cooperation resources in each country, it is a good way for Chinese companies to enter the GMS market.

In addition, the GMS Cross-Border E-Commerce Trading Platform can translate the contents and product information of GMS electronic commerce website companies into multiple international languages, such as Chinese, English, French, Arabic and so on automatically, to promote global B2B e-commerce, and to promote GMS companies development within the global e-commerce market.

Finally, as an important platform for GMS regional development and economic growth, the GMS Cross-Border E-Commerce Trading Platform effectively promotes the economic and trade development of the Greater Mekong sub-region.

Discussion Questions:

1. What is the opportunities and challenges brought by cooperation of GMS?

2. In what aspects does the enterprises alliances of GMS Cross-Border E-Commerce cooperation Platform has positive role?

3. How does the enterprises alliances of GMS Cross-Border E-Commerce cooperation Platform improve the economic and trade cooperation in GMS?

Part Ⅳ

International Finance

17.

The Hedging Strategy of Tongling Nonferrous Metals Group

Established in June 1952, Tongling Nonferrous Metals Group was an extra large state-owned enterprise integrating copper metal mining, dressing, smelting, and processing as well as production, operation and processing. Now it is one of 300 large groups with state key support, and it enjoys developmental priority in Anhui Province. In 2012, the company took the lead to become the first in Anhui Province with sales income over 100 billion yuan, its total volume of import & export trades has been ranked in first place nationwide in the copper industry for 14 years in a row, and output of its main product, cathode copper, is in the 5th place among copper refining enterprises in the world. In 2015, the copper produced by Tongling Nonferrous Metals totaled 1. 31 million tons.

In China copper is scarce and most cathode copper concentrate processed is imported from foreign countries every year. Generally, the pricing system applied for copper concentrate imported from abroad is according to international practice. The pricing here means that the buyer and seller only talk about quantity without prices involved, and the price is subject to the market price of a given day or period on the London Metal Exchange, implying that there are many uncertain factors from the signing date of the copper concentrate contract to receipt of material. In order to avoid impact from raw material and copper market price fluctuations and spot market credit risks, Tongling Nonferrous has developed a domestic futures hedging business, operating since 1992. As direct hedging on international markets are not possible and hedging efficiency of imported raw materials is difficult to optimize, the company applied for an overseas futures hedging operation and received approval from the state in April 2003.

In 2004, targeting the increasing copper prices on markets, the enterprise conducted hedge selling overseas, as the futures copper price went up when the hedge closed, and so the enterprise suffered futures losses. However, it reaped profits on spot markets, exceeding hedging by USD 6.4 million, so eventually the spot sale profits made up for the loss on futures market. Based on the futures operation, the enterprise avoided market price risks, locked costs of raw materials, and realized expected profits. In 2004, the enterprise realized remarkable profit growth totaling to 550 million yuan, 530 million yuan more than the previous year.

Tongling Nonferrous has its own risk-owning operational model and methods. Firstly, it employs prudent operation principles and procedures. Tongling Nonferrous futures trading is limited to hedging only of its dominant product, cathode copper. The main practice is standard entry and reinforced internal control. After the state completes futures market rectification standards, and after obtaining futures trade qualification, Tongling Nonferrous set up its special account for futures in the designated bank. It chooses four overseas futures brokerage agencies with different strong points as its overseas futures hedging business agents. Meanwhile, Tongling Nonferrous authorizes its four wholly-owned subsidiaries to engage in copper hedging business in the name of the group, formulates strictly detailed management methods and operation regulations, and expressly stipulates the implementation of steady operational hedging principles. Secondly, the company must be trustworthy and control the flow of funds. On one hand, it strictly observes futures credit guarantees. Margin systems are implemented on futures market, and in the case of Tongling Nonferrous, its overseas futures brokerage agencies provide the line of credit for trading on its behalf, and control its overseas futures trading fund within its line of credit. On the other hand, it puts the foreign exchange fund limits under effective control. As per national regulations, overseas futures trading remittance funds are specially settled and managed by the opening bank authorized by the Exchange Office, and annual risk exposure management is applied for futures trading.

With the deepening of the financial reform, Tongling Nonferrous has employed new hedging instruments to avoid risks. On February 6, 2015, Interbank Market Liquidation Co., Ltd. was officially established in the Shanghai Free Trade Zone. On the same day, Bank of China developed a cooperative agreement with Shanghai Tongguan Trade Development Co., Ltd., a subsidiary of Shanghai Tongling, and did the first copper premium swap trade in Shanghai Free Trade Zone, and provided agency clearing services for the enterprise.

On January 8, 2015, People's Bank of China officially approved Shanghai Clearing House for development of a copper premium swap business. The copper premium swap business uses Yangshan Copper Premium Index as the underlying standard for cross-border Renminbi pricing, clearing and settlement of bulk commodities and financial derivatives. The deal is made with the help of the brokerage company, and CCP Clearing services are provided by Shanghai Clearing House. Copper premium swap services not only meet hedging needs of Tongling Nonferrous, but also attract extensive participation of overseas enterprises.

Once copper premium swap services in the Free Trade Zone came officially online in February 2015, Shanghai Clearing House joined hands with Shanghai Nonferrous Network again to promote CUS products. CUS is a copper derivative outside of the free trade zone within China, and it is a swap contract targeting the overhead prices of domestically traded copper. The premium and discount result is that copper enterprises, no matter the traders or upstream or downstream enterprises, have no way to guarantee 100% price hedging. After Shanghai Clearing House promotes CUS, the premium and discount may be bridged over, and hedging is 100% seamlessly connected and without risk. In addition to the model of employing full pricing, premiums and discounts, CUS makes prices more flexible and controllable for participants. Swap is similar to futures, but the two have core differences, because CUS must have one index provider. CUS has No. 1 cathode copper index released by Shanghai Nonferrous Network as the target index for Renminbi pricing, clearing and settlement. As for the method of settlement, CUS employs cash settlement, and the final settlement price is subject to the spot goods price of domestic cathode copper released by Shanghai Nonferrous Network on the agreed expiration date. According to the pricing method used, CUS overhead copper price is the futures benchmark price, plus premiums and discounts of spot goods.

Developing copper financial derivatives, such as copper premium swap and Renminbi cathode copper swap, provides more effective hedging instruments for Tongling Nonferrous, so that the company is able to avoid price fluctuation risks and reap more profits. Apart from this, copper financial derivatives also make some contributions to the transition of enterprises.

Discussion Questions:

1. What are the risks faced by Tongling Nonferrous in International markets?
2. How does Tongling Nonferrous avoid risks? How does it implement policy specifically?
3. What are new hedging instruments developed by Tongling Nonferrous? What's its significance?

18.

Youku and Dangdang Listed in the U. S.

On December 8, 2010, the video service platform Youku. com and e-commerce company Dangdang. com listed on the New York Stock Exchange (NYSE). On that day, Youku closed with a robust growth trend, up by 161. 25%, bringing its market value to USD 3. 4 billion. It is the most successful of Internet enterprises, and a milestone for Internet industry development in China. However, it is merely a successful phase, and in future Youku and Dangdang will face more operational pressures and will be under more stringent supervision after they become public companies.

Youku is the leading video sharing platform in China. In 2007, Youku raised the notion of "videographers everywhere" and welcomed "everyone to be a videographer". It started the popular video making culture, and has already become a base for Internet videographers. Headquartered in Beijing, Dangdang is jointly invested and founded by the famous domestic publishing company Kewen Company, the U. S. Tiger Fund, the U. S. IDG Group, Luxembourg Cambridge Holding Group, and Asia Venture Capital Fund, among others. Starting online in November 1999, Dangdang sells books and audio-visual products as well as other commodities, such as small electrical home appliances, toys, and online game cards. Now Dangdang is the largest Chinese online book and audio-visual product mall globally.

The reason why Youku chooses to go public on the NYSE is that the NYSE is a global quality listing platform, there is historic significance for Youku to go public with a number of world-class media companies and group corporations, and listing on the NYSE can increase brand value. It is crucial that American investors accept Chinese Internet concepts, but a more important reason for Internet companies to go public overseas are: firstly domestic listing has higher costs, a tedious listing process and rigorous supervision; secondly, there is a technical threshold, i. e. there is a rigid requirement for profits of listed companies in China.

Dangdang made profit in 2009, while Youku has not realized any profit before its listing, only reducing its losses. According to relevant standards of China SMEs board and Growth Enterprise Market, neither company is qualified for listing in China. However, there are more reasons for listing in the U. S. NYSE has four modes for listing, and enterprises meeting any one of the mode requirements could go public. For example, although Youku did not make profits, it can choose the mode without profit items, but emphasizes its large business scale and market share to investors. The American stock market focuses on the prospects of enterprises who don't have profitability at the present but need significant funds. It indicates that a mature stock market is estimating future profitability of enterprises and focusing on their development.

The Chinese stock market has compulsory requirement for company's profitability before its listing and it implements an audit system instead of a registration system. The audit mechanism implements rigorous standards and is lack of transparency. In terms of time, it only takes nine months for enterprises to go public in the U. S. , but it at least takes two years from preparation to completion in China. The Chinese market cannot satisfy the needs of the company that wants quick financing. The strict audit for refinancing of enterprises on Chinese stock market is equal to another IPO, and there are not such requirements abroad, so for Internet enterprises that need a large amount of funding, there is no doubt that it is a better choice to get financing in the U. S. where the Chinese Internet concept is widely accepted.

After Youku and Dangdang's listing in the U. S. , it shows the world that Chinese Internet companies can adapt to a foreign environment and it is also a sign that Chinese Internet enterprises are becoming mature and implementing higher standards. Inevitably investors will see giant Chinese Internet markets behind these enterprises. It is reported that the number of Chinese netizens has already exceeded 400 million before the two companies' listing and the number has reached 632 million in June, 2014. Youku has benefited from Chinese Internet development.

Later, however, Youku and Dangdang will be confronted with more severe industrial competition. Several other video companies, such as 56. com, CorePlayer, 6. cn, have also expressed to the media their desire to list. And Dangdang has also been rapidly challenged by Jingdong and Amazon. Li Guoqing, CEO of Dangdang who is immersed in the joy of listing, declares they are ready "to cope with all price wars at any time".

The Chinese copyright environment is increasingly strict, and video service platform need funds to build good video content libraries with their own copyrights. Youku is bound to face pressure from traditional platforms, large platforms and traditional broadcasting stations in future. For example, CCTV will enjoy advantages in building video content library with copyrights. Another example is that 85% of Dandang's profit is from books, so its approach is too singular; and that digital books will have a larger impact on the sale of paper books in future. Besides, after going public in the U. S. , Youku and Dangdang will face stricter supervision. False or untimely information disclosure will result in prosecution from investors and punishment from the Securities Regulatory Commission in the U. S. , and even management personnel of the company may be subject to criminal investigation in the U. S. Therefore, to weigh the gains and loss of going public in the U. S. , it is necessary to examine internal resources endowment, and enterprises should keep their cool in deciding if listing in the U. S. is the best choice for themselves, and that it is unreasonable to just look the at positive side of others' experiences.

Discussion Questions:

1. Youku and Dangdang are the famous video platform and E-commerce platform in China respectively. Why did they choose to list in the U. S. ?

2. What opportunities and challenges will Youku and Dangdang encounter after listing in the U. S. ?

3. The two companies raises funds on global capital markets. Please give a brief introduction of the related European monetary market and global bonds market.

19.

Alibaba Group Listed in the U. S.

Alibaba Group was founded in Hangzhou, China in 1999. After nearly 20 years of development, Alibaba has become a world well-known Chinese Internet brand in China, and its ecosystem penetrates and covers all trades and professions. The main business and affiliated companies include Taobao, Tmall, Juhuasuan, Ali Cloud, Ali Mother, Alibaba International Trading Market, Ant Financial, Rookie Network, and so on. Alibaba believes that small businesses could gain favorable competitive advantages in domestic and global markets through the innovation and expansion of its technology in a fair environment created by the Internet.

After years of preparation, Alibaba was successfully listed on the New York Stock Exchange on 19th September, 2014 (stock code: BABA). By setting the IPO price at 68 dollars per share, Alibaba planned to raise 320 million shares. In order to meet the strong demands of investors, Ali made its underwriters of initial public offering known to the public, including Goldman Sachs, JP Morgan Chase, Citibank, Morgan Stanley, and so on. The exercise of over-allotment options made the financing volumes the largest IPO in history, reaching 25 billion dollars. Since Ali began to trade on the NYSE, the stock price has continued to soar as expected, with the highest price reaching 120 dollars per share. Alibaba successfully surpassed Facebook as the second largest company, second only to Google. In the following six months, investors made high estimations of Alibaba's evaluation.

Back in October 1999, led by Goldman Sachs, fund companies, including Transpac Capital Investor AB of Sweden and Technology Development Fund of

Singapore, jointly invested 5 million dollars in Alibaba.

In 2000, Alibaba began a second round of financing amounting to 25 million dollars, with funds coming from Softbank (20 million dollars) and five venture capital companies including Fidelity International, Transpac Capital, TDF, and Investor AB of Sweden. In the second round of financing, Softbank group expressed its desire to invest 30 million dollars in order to own 30% stake at Alibaba, but was rejected.

In February 2004, Alibaba completed the third round of financing that raised 82 million dollars from venture capital companies. Softbank invested 60 million dollars among them. Ma Yun and his team were still Alibaba's largest shareholders, accounting for 47% of the shares, with the second largest shareholder being Softbank (20%), the third being Fidelity (18%), and finally with several other shareholders (15%).

In August 2005, Yahoo exchanged 1 billion dollars and Yahoo's total assets in China (fully diluted) for 39% of Alibaba Group common stock, receiving 35% of the voting rights. After the deal was completed, Yahoo became the largest shareholder in the Alibaba Group and received one of the four seats in its board of directors. Ma Yun and the holding executives lost their status as major shareholders, with the proportion of these shareholders decreasing to 31.7%. After Yahoo took shares in Alibaba, venture capitalists (such as Fidelity Fund, etc.) exited its investment in a large scale. Other venture capitalists basically withdrew when the Alibaba Group B2C business was listed, and Ali Group entered into the era of "three pillars" -Ma Yun, Yahoo, Softbank. Before the B2B business went public in 2007, Ali's shareholding ratio was as follows: Yahoo accounted for 43%, Softbank 29.3%, management and staff 27.7%. In May 2012, Ali repurchased the 20% of the stake held by Yahoo with 7.1 billion dollars. Ali Group announced that the group would repurchase the half of the shares held by Yahoo. At the same time, Ali Group announced it would launch an IPO when the Group had the right to repurchase the remaining 50% of the shares held by Yahoo.

On November 6, 2007, Alibaba Network Co. , a B2B e-commerce trade platform owned by Alibaba was listed on the Main Board of the Hong Kong Stock Exchange (code 01688. HK). The issuing price was HK $13. 5, with an opening price of HK $30. With a value of HK $199. 6 billion, Alibaba became China's first company worth more than 20 billion dollars.

Alibaba Group and Alibaba Network Co. , Ltd. declared jointly on February 21, 2012, that Alibaba Group gave a buyout offer to Alibaba Network Co. , Ltd. , and planned to buy back shares at HK $13. 5 per share. Alibaba Network Co. , Ltd. (01688. HK) was delisted officially from the Hong Kong Stock Exchange, and privatization was achieved in June 20, 2012. According to the Alibaba Group, the privatization aimed to achieve a transformation in business strategy and to create opportunities for small and medium investors to earn more profits. However, some observers argued that Alibaba Group was preparing for a share repurchase from Yahoo, and its ultimate aim was to gain back control and to have the whole group listed. The delisting price of Alibaba Group, HK $13. 5, was basically at the same level as its issue price. If the inflation rate is 10%, HK $13. 5 is equal to HK $20 at present. Alibaba Group borrowed money without interest, and earned HK $6. 5 pershare. Excluding the dividend, it still earned HK $6. The delisting ensured the maximization of profits for both Yahoo and Softbank, but directly hurt the benefits of many small investors in Hong Kong.

In July 2013, the CEO of Alibaba Group, Lu Zhaoxi, admitted to preparing for listing, then the market followed the news saying that it had prepared for listing in Hong Kong in September. In August 2013, it was reported that Alibaba Group Co. , proposed being listed in a partner system with the Hong Kong Stock Exchange. In the beginning of September, the HKEX, for the benefit of investors, refused the approval of Alibaba. On March 16, 2014, Alibaba announced its plan of listing in the U. S. On June 26, it decided to apply for listing on the New York Stock Exchange, with the stock trading code "BABA". On September 19, Alibaba was officially traded on NYSE. With the issue price of $68/ADS, the amount of its financing exceeded VISA, and thus refreshed the record of the highest amount of IPO in the U. S.. On the first trading day, Alibaba opened at 92. 70 dollars, 36. 32% higher than the issue price, and its total market value amounted to 228. 5 billion dollars.

Discussion Questions:

1. Why did Alibaba go public in the U. S. market?
2. How will it affect the Chinese market after Alibaba's listing in the U. S. ?
3. Compare and analyze the market value of Alibaba and Tencent.

20.

Infrastructure Construction of Philippines with the Help of the Asian Infrastructure Investment Bank

As financial crises have taken place frequently around the world since the 1990s, and are extremely damaging to regional economies and even the global economy, the international financial order is experiencing a major challenge, and is now in a reform and restructuring stage. Especially the 2008 global financial crisis makes the financial market undergo a new round of violent fluctuations, prove the vulnerability of global economic recovery, give salience to the necessity of strengthening the global economy and monetary policy coordination, and further promote global economic governance reform and rebuilding the international financial order.

The modern global financial governance system originated from the Bretton Woods System and dominated by developed countries like the U. S. and the EU nations. After its evolution over five decades, the system has increasingly revealed its inherent defects and shortcomings. Firstly, the system cannot sufficiently reflect economic strength growth of countries, especially failing to reflect the emerging economy realities in a timely manner, and the voices of developing countries is seriously not heard. Secondly, to a large extent, the frequent global financial crises are because of the unstable US dollar and the neo-liberalism advocated by the "Washington Consensus". The lack of rights of speech causes developing countries difficult to keep the currency and exchange rate stable.

The opening ceremony for the Asian Infrastructure Investment Bank (AIIB) & the founding conference of Board of Directors and Board of Directors was held in Beijing on January 16, 2016, marking the official launch of AIIB. Ushering in a new era of regional multilateral financial cooperation, the mission of AIIB is to provide financing support for Asian infrastructure construction, promote regional interconnectivity, facilitate regional economic development, and drive global economic growth.

AIIB is an useful supplement to the present international financial system, multilateral development organizations and the international development agenda, and also an opportunity for China to take the initiative to take part in beneficial global economic governance. The focus of AIIB is to promote infrastructure interconnectivity and regional economic integration, and is dedicated to sustainable development of Asian economies.

As a new regional international financial institution, the reason AIIB draws attention is not only its functions and influence (focusing on regional infrastructure interconnectivity and regional economic integration), but also that the global restructuring of the global economic landscape within the existing international financial order is unreasonable. The establishment of AIIB attracts the global attention and participation, which reflects the lasting evolution of the existing international economic order and the historic transition of the international economic pattern.

Some Philippine authoritative experts have noted that development is the most important task facing the Philippines currently, and backwards infrastructure and limited financing channels have already become the vulnerabilities that hamper its economic development. According to "2016—2017 Global Competitiveness Report" released by World Economic Forum, the infrastructure level of the Philippines is ranked 95th in the world and according to an International Monetary Fund study, the key infrastructure service level of the Philippines is ranked in last place among ASEAN countries. Air traffic jam, urban transportation jam and public transportation difficulties in Manila were not properly addressed, with nearly 500 thousand people squeezing into trial transit cars with designed capacity 350 thousand persons, and the International Air Transport Association urging Philippine government time and again to prepare a new international airport development plan as soon as possible to no avail.

For this reason, the Philippines signed AIIB agreement at the end of 2015, joined AIIB as a founding state, and made capital contributions of $196 million in stages; President Duterte approved this agreement on October 19, 2016; on December 5, the senate passed resolution No. 241 with a majority of 20 votes. It is generally accepted in its political and economic circles that AIIB is of in promoting sustainable economic growth and economic-social development in Asia, and can help improve the region's capability to cope with future financial crises and other external blows. Meanwhile, as a member state of AIIB, the Philippines will now facilitate its infrastructure construction, and reshape the situation to realize high-speed economic growth.

Thanks to the demonstrated effects of the first programs of AIIB, the Duterte administration plans to start "the golden era of infrastructure construction" in the Philippines, and it is estimated that the total investment will be 8 trillion pesos (about $160 billion) during the term, including building the Mindanao railway, cross-sea bridges, addressing water supply concerns, and so on. Duterte told the media that as a founding state of AIIB, the Philippines hopes to obtain more financing, and Chinese companies and capital are welcomed and encouraged to get involved in Philippine infrastructure construction. The Philippines Treasury Department Director Roberto said the other day that the Philippines will submit loan applications for two projects, namely bus rapid transit and Manila flood control systems, and it hopes to be granted $300 ~ 500 million loans in 2017.

Asian infrastructure investment market potential is inviting, but the risks are also severe. Phenomena like extremely unstable political society, defective laws, frequent changes in government policies, poor credit, etc. are quite universal in the majority of Asian countries in need of infrastructure investment. As for AIIB, how to control fund security risks will be a very arduous operational challenge. AIIB is expected to highlight risks and potential challenges in financing businesses during actual operation, and keep a policy of "slow instead of rush" when choosing investment projects. It should draw lessons from the inadequate development investment supply of traditional development institutions resulting from harsh loan conditions and performance grading mechanisms, meet the needs of development investment of developing countries based on investment availability, and guarantee effective global development aid; moreover, it should also stick to sustainable development principles, give consideration to economic rationality and socially sensitive issues involving environment and labor, etc., blend sustainable development concepts when necessary, and comprehensively consider all issues and make prudent choices regarding investment projects.

Discussion Questions:

1. How Phillipine uses AIIB to conduct its infrastructure construction?
2. What problems urgently need to be addressed by AIIB?
3. As a member of the international financial community, how should AIIB take part in the regional financial governance process?

21.

The World Bank and International Development Aiding

In January, 2013, Myanmar and the World Bank declared that Myanmar has paid off its historic debts to the World Bank and Asian Development Bank. Both sides will start with new cooperation to accelerate reforms. The World Bank Group has been involved comprehensively and positively to provide funds and technical assistance to formulate development programs and extend benefits to all Burmese people. The World Bank Group is in discussion with the Burmese government to decide priorities for development. On January 22, 2013, the Executive Board of the World Bank approved Myammar re-engagement and reform support credit worth $440 million. The credit will support the government in implementing important reform measures, strengthening macroeconomic stability, improving financial fiscal management, and the investment environment, etc. The funds will also help the government to resolve foreign currency needs, including repayment of bridge loans to pay off debts provided by the Japan Bank for International Cooperation.

The World Bank was established in December 1945 and began operation in June 1946, becoming a special agency of the UN in November 1947. Its members must be member states of the IMF (International Monetary Fund), but member states of IMF are not necessarily part of the World Bank. Since it was founded in 1945, the World Bank has already developed into a group of five closely linked development agencies from a single institute. Its mission has evolved to closely coordinate with other member agencies through its subsidiary, the International Development Association (IDA), to promote poverty reduction in the world by promoting post-war reconstruction and development through the International

Bank for Reconstruction and Development (IBRD). Other member organisations of the World Bank include International Finance Corporation (IFC), Multilateral Investment Guarantee Agency (MIGA) and International Centre for Settlement of Investment Disputes (ICSID).

Since its inception, the World Bank mainly provided funds to western European countries to restore their economies damaged by war. However, after 1948, European countries began to rely on the "Marshall Plan" of the U. S. to recover their post-war economies, because the U. S. provided loans directly to them to rebuild their economy according to "Marshall Plan". Subsequently, the World Bank underwent its first mission transition. The World Bank shifted its focus to "economic development", i. e. offering long- and middle-term loans and investment for developing countries so as to promote their economic and social development. In the 1950s, the World Bank put its emphasis on public programs, especially power plant projects, road construction and other transportation investments. In the 1960s, the World Bank began to provide significant funds to support agriculture, education, population control and urban development.

When the World Bank was founded in 1945, countries suffering from poverty and economies destroyed by war could not attract private capital, so the World Bank provided low interest loans to high-risk customers with poor credit ratings. However, after the post-war construction finished, private capital makes public development assistance look pale. The world is changing, so is the World Bank. Now the mission of the World Bank is to "build a world free of poverty".

Obviously the World Bank is not merely a bank. It is mainly responsible for economic recovery and development, and provides long-term and middle-term loans to member states for their economic development. However, the World bank is not only a banking institution that includes loans and grants. It also function to promote growth and help with poverty reduction in the open international system. It helps countries to build longer term development initiatives through loans, expertise and experience.

The President of the World Bank, Jim Yong Kim, thinks that the World

Bank offers wise investment in infrastructure and institutional building in a financially sound and sustainable way by working cooperatively with countries. Through international financial companies and multilateral investment guarantee organisations, the World Bank supports private sector in playing the role of catalyst, since nearly 90% of jobs in the world are in the private sector. By tapping into the experience of shareholder countries, the World Bank is able to develop solutions for transnational issues. In order to promote confidence for decision-making among investors, enterprises and residents, the World Bank actively promotes public financial transparency and strengthens governance. Public trust is valuable assets for government, and in order to cope with the vulnerable global economy, people should first be convinced that the economic systems and policies are able to bring more sustainable, fair and inclusive economic growth.

The World Bank is dedicated to delivering services to customers, especially to developing countries, rather than being involved in the outdated practice of structural adjustment policies. The World Bank has changed its approach as it seeks solutions, rather than to spread laws and rules. If the best solutions cannot be worked into a customer's political and economic context, the World Bank will not help customers to solve their problems.

Jim Yong Kim says that as a global development agency, the World Bank is urgently needed to help cope with risks which threaten global growth anywhere, anytime. All countries benefit from a robust global economy, but if the global economy is sluggish, all countries will become vulnerable. European countries take necessary measures to restore stability, and their actions will influence growth of worldwide regions. In recent years, the World Bank sees itself as a solution seeker, and developing countries are its customers. The World Bank delivers services to public and private sectors of developing countries. If the best solutions cannot be adapted to a customer's political and economic context, the World Bank is not able to help customers to solve their problems. The World Bank expands its capital through innovative channel financing instruments. It not only resolves global issues with its funds, but also works the "responsible stakeholders" concept into its loan flows. Just as Jim Yong Kim said, as a global development agency, the World Bank will build itself to be an organisation which effectively responds to the needs of different customers and donors through cooperative efforts with old and new partners, and provides more powerful solutions to support sustainable development and help governments to shoulder more responsibility for their people. An institution that puts empirical solutions on the top of ideology; A harness and attract the best talent mechanism; A mechanism to expand voice of developing countries; A reference to the people we serve the professional knowledge and experience of the organization.

Discussion Questions:

1. How did the international monetary system evolve? In what historical context did World Bank emerge? What is its mission?

2. What is the difference between Wold Bank and the commercial banks?

3. Who are the customers of the World Bank? Since 2007, how has the World Bank delivered service to customers in order to realise its mission?

4. Why do we need the World Bank when after war construction has completed?

Part Ⅴ

The Strategy and Structure of International Business

22.

International Strategy of Wanda Group

Wanda Group was founded in 1988, with the formation of four major industrial groups, business, culture, network technology, financial sections. It owns assets of 634 billion yuan in 2015 with 290. 1 billion yuan income. Wanda is the largest commercial real estate company and the largest five-star hotel owner. What's more, Wanda Cultural Group is the largest cultural enterprise in China and the largest cinema operator in the world. Wanda Network Technology Group focuses on the integration of online and offline business and creates a new generation of network model. Wanda Financial Group is committed to the traditional financial business.

Now the slogan of Wanda is "Internationalized Wanda of a Century Enterprise". Wanda's slogan is gradually updated. At the beginning, its slogan was "Be honest man, Do smart work." Around 2003, Wanda had improved corporate culture and modified the slogan, "Working together to create wealth, for the benefits of society" when it began to profit. Later on, the scale of the company becomes bigger and for the third time plans to elaborate the slogan— "Internationalized Wanda of a Century Enterprise". Internationalized Wanda means international and a century enterprise implies lasting. Also, Wanda must be international to achieve the grand goal.

Especially private enterprise need internationalization for internationalization can mitigate the risks. Enterprise's internationalization means reducing business risks. No matter how well a country's economy performs, there is still a period of adjustment for its economy. However, it is a very low probability that a great depression and a major adjustment happen simultaneously within the world economy. Chinese government also encourages its companies to allocate resources globally, and utilize the global market. In addition, Wanda needs to rely on internationalization, mergers and acquisitions to make it to a larger scale. According to the study of the world's top five hundred enterprises, Wanda found no one is entirely dependent on their own growth and development. None of them have ever had a merger before entering the world's top 500 wealth list.

Wanda put forward next five-year goal of a new strategy in 2016. That is by 2020 to achieve "2211". It means corporate assets more than $200 billion, corporate market value more than $200 billion, more than $100 billion of income, net profit $10 billion, and more than 30% of income from overseas. There are two kinds of international business enterprises. The one is to manufacture products in the country, and then sell around the world, which can only be considered internationalization of products. The other is to make investment in one or two countries. However, this kind of enterprise accounted for a small proportion of the total businesses, for management methods, talent structure and corporate culture have not reached the level of multinational enterprise. Therefore, the real multinational companies not only require large scale, which means at least tens of billions of dollars, but also achieve at least 30% income from overseas.

It is because Wanda has a large corporate vision that it has continued to maintain rapid growth. By 2015, its revenue, assets and profits will increase by 20% in 2014 on year-on-year basis. For Wanda, this is the first time falling below 30% in the past few years. Prior to this, Wanda maintains more than 30% growth in the past few years. With the major adjustment of the global economy, China's economy continued to slow down, Wanda's development rate also dropped a little, but still maintains a rapid growth rate, which is a guarantee for Wanda to eventually become a first-class multinational company.

Wanda Group's international strategic approach to mergers and acquisitions, are supplemented by investment. From the British Industrial Revolution to the present, the world markets, in particular, some of the major market areas, are basically occupied by the first entry enterprise. Because the world markets, especially some of the major market areas, are basically carved up to in the past few years at the beginning from the British industrial revolution to the present. Now Wanda wants to invest in sports industry, however, a variety of international brand sports tournament ownership and broadcast rights are owned by famous family companies or multinational companies. Wanda participates in it only relying on acquisitions.

Wanda's internationalization focuses on "right buying". Wanda has two standards, on the one hand, Wanda is associated with existing industries. Wanda International approach is to enter the existing industry. Whether it is real estate, culture, sports or tourism, anyway, Wanda is now engaged in the industry. The benefits of doing it are to make Wanda have a certain accumulation of knowledge and talent pool, to understand the specific situation of the industry. Wanda, on the other hand, whether it is cross-border mergers and acquisitions or investment projects, requires these services can be transplanted into China market, to get faster development in China.

As Wanda's mergers and acquisitions of the world's largest triathlon company, WTC in U. S. in 2015, it took less than six months to introduce the triathlon to Xiamen, Hefei in China. The sport used to be a blind spot in China, and, currently, the number of people in the country is so poor that only about 200 people are working on it. Wanda promotes the sport in China, at least hundreds of thousands of people to participate, because China enters a healthy era, the era of national running, which has a huge space for development. However, WTC is difficult to maintain rapid growth abroad, only with a little growth percentage. Only in China can it get faster growth rate.

In addition, Wanda's internationalization emphasizes using local talents. In 2012, when Wanda merged with AMC, the U. S. government had some restrictions on the acquisition of this type of company because it was a movie terminal channel.

Wang Jianlin, Chairman of Wanda, when he visited the Ambassador Locke in United States asked him to write a letter of recommendation for Wanda to the

U. S. government. Mr. Locke asked whether Wanda was going to send the Chinese nationals to manage the business in the United States? Mr. Wang Jianlin said it would not, for if after the acquisition company management all gone, in fact, it means that mergers and acquisitions failed. The final Wanda M & A AMC was approved by the U. S. government. Wanda acquired AMC, only set up a liaison. Wanda M & A object, its original shareholders are mostly large multinational companies. The best way for M & A business is to retain the original management and make it work better.

Wanda Group tries to retain the original management team as much as possible, no matter which country the mergers, acquisitions and investment happens. Wanda makes full use of the local talents, stimulating their enthusiasm instead of sending Chinese expatriates.

Wanda's international progress starts from 2012 and lasts for four years now, with Wanda investment in more than 10 countries around the world, and the investment amount more than $15 billion, of which $10 billion was invested in the United States. Wanda invests £1. 2 billion in the UK with more than 2600 employees. The recent acquisition of $3. 5 billion in January 2016, the legendary American film company, is China's largest overseas acquisition of cultural enterprises.

Although internationalization of Wanda is not so long, the paces are rapid, and progress is relatively smooth. From the dialectical point of view, Wanda transnational development implies no failure means closer to failure, so Wanda internationalization process does not rule out the fall in the future. But Wanda stands for a principle, as long as there is no subversive risk, they must do this thing. In fact, being brave to take the first step can make it feel that the internationalization is not so difficult.

Discussion Questions:

1. Wanda gets into the international market mainly on M & A, do you think Wanda Group can enter market in other ways, why?

2. During recent years, Wanda continues to broaden the international market, and invests in various industries, what do you think of it?

3. What problems are Wanda encountered in the implementation of the international strategy, how to solve them?

4. What is the enlightenment of Wanda Group's internationalization to Chinese Enterprises' "Going Out"?

23.

Internationalization Strategy of BYD New Energy Vehicles

BYD Company Limited, a high-tech private enterprise, was founded in 1995 with its headquarter in Shenzhen City, Guangdong Province, China. Originally, BYD was engaged in the production and sale of batteries and was listed on the main board of the Hong Kong Stock Exchange in July 2002. In 2003, by acquiring Xi'an Qinchuan automobile limited liability company, BYD officially entered the field of automobile manufacturing and sales, and started the journey to becoming a national independent brand automobile. At present, BYD has advantages in vehicle manufacturing, mold development, vehicle development, etc., along with three industrial clusters: IT, New energy and automobile manufacture. BYD's industrial plan gradually improved, and has quickly become the most innovative new Chinese brand. BYD is currently the only Chinese enterprise that has mastered large-scale productive technology for lithium iron phosphate batteries for vehicle, and is in a leading position in the world. This battery has the advantages of long service life, low cost and good safety performance. With its superb strategic cost management capability, BYD has a certain cost advantage and market share continues to improve. BYD has built nine production bases in Shanghai, Beijing, Guangdong among other places, and has set up offices or branches in India, South Korea, Japan, Europe and the United States, Hong Kong S. A. R., and Chinese Taiwan, with the total number of employees nearly 200 thousand.

BYD's overall internationalization strategy, including capital internationalization, international quality management systems, and localization of manufacturing and sales, innovative technology and social responsibility, fills gaps in the market in Europe and other developed countries. Unlike most Chinese enterprises, BYD sees the future development trends in the world. This forward-looking vision has allowed it to take the lead in the research and development of new energy vehicles and promotion at home and abroad. BYD electric cars have changed the business model of the past for Chinese car enterprises, skipping the traditional target markets such as Asia, Africa and Latin America, and pushing into California, Frankfurt, Tel Aviv, and so on.

BYD's K9 new energy vehicle is the first independently researched and designed electric bus, it has gradually moved into the international market, and has been through trial operations in Europe, North America, South America, Asia and other overseas countries and regions. BYD's new energy internationalization strategy is clear. In 2014, BYD took electric cars to California, so that the discerning American consumers could experience new energy electric vehicles. Further, California's auto emission regulations are the most stringent in the U. S. , and California has the highest environmental standards. In April, 2014, having passed inspection by the relevant inspection and quarantine departments, three BYD K9 pure electric buses were successfully exported to the United states. There are now 10 pure electric buses, having been exported to the United States in batches, which California's Stanford University uses as dedicated shuttle buses. In the United States, the concept of environmental protection has been deeply rooted in the hearts of the people, and it provides a good foundation for the continuing promotion of electric vehicles. It is one of the reasons for the BYD electric car entering the North American market. From the point of demonstration to final implementation and use, BYD reached its goal of producing and providing a "Green Dream" vehicle.

BYD confirmly follows the development path for electric vehicles. Following the BYD K9, BYD plans to launch a medium-sized bus which is step down from the K9 bus. The bus is a new entry-level bus, intended to compete with similar level models on the market, such as the TOYOTA Coaster. BYD does not only apply green technology in its vehicles, but also attempts to solve environmental problems and address economic recovery of cities by promoting electric urban transport schemes. This is BYD's strategic plan in the new energy market.

With the accelerated pace of internationalization, backed by the force of domestic markets, BYD is getting on the fast track, and extending outwards into foreign markets. As early as 2013, BYD received official permission from the EU, giving it the right to sell electric buses in all EU member states. The EU issued Whole Vehicle Type-Approval (WVTA). This means BYD can sell electric buses in all EU Member States, without the need to obtain individual countries' independent approval. BYD considers Europe as its pure electric bus sales target market, its electric buses are already driving in the streets of the United Kingdom, France and Holland.

In June 2016, BYD signed a strategic cooperation agreement with Electricite De France, one of the world's largest power producers. In October, BYD announced spending 20 million Euros to set up Europe's first new energy electric vehicle production base in Hungary, and is expected to formally put it into operation in 2017. The initial product is zero emission electric buses and trucks, with an annual output of up to 400 vehicles. At the same time, it will establish a European R & D center. The Hungarian government attaches great importance to the development of electric vehicles, and actively supports BYD in its investment in and building of factories, providing about \$3.4 million in subsidies. Through the production of electric vehicles, Hungary hopes to promote the development of related domestic industries and local employment, which will further contribute to the implementation of the "Paris Agreement".

The economics of scale brought about by the expansion of the market make the efficiency of automobile manufacturing increase and the unit cost lower. BYD's experience in product design, process design, automation, production organization and other aspects will gradually accumulate, through the continuous improvement of management methods, and improving the efficiency of staff. BYD has advanced experience in the production of rechargeable batteries and components, and the ability to further research and develop innovative tech, while practical operations are constantly improving.

The technical constraints of new energy vehicles are energy storage capacity and battery life. With the launch of BYD's pure electric vehicle E6, new energy vehicle battery technology has been further improved. BYD has realized technological innovation, effectively reduced the cost of the enterprise, and maintained the competitive advantage. Compared to other companies, BYD's core technology can reduce the technical constraints of developed countries, reduce patent costs, and can reduce production costs through continuous research and innovation.

BYD's use of new energy vehicles technology, as well as the opportunity for transformation and upgrading of the internationalization strategy will deep further. The electric automobile wave has intensified all over the world. So far, BYD pure electric vehicles are in use in more than two hundred cities across six states, including London, Los Angeles, New York, Kyoto, and so on. BYD will not only do more large-scale promotion of its new energy vehicles around the world, but also become more systematic in product design, supply chain systems, and in matters of production. BYD must integrate with the world's resources, and really push Chinese technology in foreign markets. BYD's big challenge is that, the upgrading of technology must be accompanied by the concurrent development of products, services, and brand systems.

Discussion Questions:

1. Why does BYD's internationalization strategy change the target market positioning of Chinese car enterprises? How does it advance smoothly in the United States?

2. What are the advantages for BYD in the European market?

3. How did BYD cope with cost pressures? What are the strategic advantages?

4. Which international strategy does BYD pursue? Can this strategy be sustained? If not, what choice should be made?

24.

Localisation Strategy of Nestle in China

On October 18, 2012, the world food magnate Nestle Group released a performance report for the third quarter of 2012 in China. Nestle's sales achieved 67.6 billion Swiss francs during the first three quarters, which reflected 11% sales growth. According to Nestle's data, the company achieved double-digit growth in emerging markets in the first three quarters, while achieving an organic growth of 2.4% despite the overall economic shrinkage in developed markets. Nestle's sales in China totalled 2.5 billion Swiss francs last year, and are projected to more than doubled. With a background of continuing financial crisis, Nestle's performance in China is really surprising. The extraordinary performance of Nestle is based on its overall localisation strategy.

Nestle, which has headquarters in Lake Geneva, Switzerland, is the world's largest food manufacturer. Nestle, which has a history of more than 150 years, was created by Swiss Henri Nestle in 1867. It originally started with the production of baby food. As one of the world's largest food manufacturers, Nestle has done business in China since 1984. It operates 22 factories in China with more than 14000 employees and more than 7 billion yuan in investment. Hefenstedi, who has been in charge of the business in China since 2006 and has seen an explosive growth in the Chinese market said that the performance of Nestle in China has been exciting, and its position has become more and more important.

Today, Nestle is implementing comprehensive localisation strategies on raw material supply, product production, business management, human resources, and marketing. In more and more places, people are willing to concede that Nestle is a Chinese company. Recently, president Bauer said that since entered the

Chinese market, the company has been breathing the same air, owning the same fate, experiencing the same high-speed development in China, has witnessed the global economic crisis, and in that time the company has become a member of the Chinese family.

Data shows that 98% of Nestle products sold in China are locally produced with the highest international quality standards. Milk products and ice cream are the core businesses of Nestle, and account for 18% of total sales around the world. Since 1987, when the company entered China, it has established diary processing plants in Heilongjiang, Shandong, and Inner Mongolia. Instant coffee is regarded as the first product of Nestle in the Chinese market and has captures 80% of the market share. It also plants coffee beans in Yunnan and purchases over 5000 tons of coffee beans from Yunnan annually. Local production and manufacturing not only help Nestle integrate quickly in China, but also to control raw material costs, as well as produce economies of scale.

The financial management of Nestle China is practicing localisation, believing that with a different financial environment in each country, applying a unified financial management model will leave the company unsuited to the local environment, therefore, localisation is as important a strategy as respecting China's laws and regulations, in such ares as tax law, economic law, financial accounting, auditing and other systems. At present, 20 of Nestle China's 22 factories are managed by local Chinese managers, and all chief engineers and regional sales managers are local staff. Hefenstedi stated that the high level local financial management time is composed of many experienced internal financial staff members. When deciding on major development strategies, he respect the local team's comments and suggestions. In line with Nestle training culture, Hefenstedi sends Chinese staff to Nestle headquarters every year, and training programs have helped many people to meet the standards of high-level financial staff.

In addition, Nestle has adopted a localisation of products strategy to meet the needs of Chinese consumers. At the end of 2001, Nestle established a research and development centre in Shanghai for dehydrated food and nutritious food research to satisfy the need of Chinese consumers. In the design and production of products, Nestle is mainly guided by Chinese consumers' tastes. The taste of coffee sold in China is different from the U. S. market or the French market, but closer to the Chinese people's taste. Nestle launched four flavours of ice cream named "banana", "blue bear toot", "pudding ice cream" and "lychee ice", designed for Chinese teenagers.

In order to meet the tastes of Chinese consumers, Nestle walked into an unfamiliar field and noticed that health tea has great market potential in China, so Nestle invested heavily with Coca-Cola to enter the healthy beverage market, including a variety of tea and herbal products. The president of Nestle China, Dike, pointed out that nothing is more localised than food and beverages, and that the most popular flavour milk product in China is peanut flavour, followed by walnut flavour. These products would not popular be in other countries.

Discussion Questions:

1. What has been the development process of Nestle? How is Nestle's global expansion strategy being implemented?

2. Why does Nestle implement localisation strategy in foreign markets? What localisation strategies does Nestle have? Are those strategies successful?

3. What inspiration could Chinese companies get from Nestle's localisation experience as they enter foreign markets? How can Chinese companies learn from them?

25.

The Evolution of ZTE's Global Organization Framework

ZTE is the leading global provider of integrated communications solutions. The company provides innovative technology and product solutions for telecom operators and business customers in more than 160 countries and regions. Founded in 1985, listed in Hong Kong and Shenzhen, ZTE is China's best-known listed communications equipment company. ZTE started it international strategy in 1995, and has 18 global R&D institutions, spread through the United States, France, Sweden, India, China and other places. There are nearly 30 thousand R&D personnel focused on industry technology innovation. In 2012, ZTE won the largest number of international patent applications in the global industry. There are 107 branches, 9 global delivery centers, 15 training centers, 45 local customer support centers, 10 thousand customer service personnel all over the world, with 3000 external partners to serve customers worldwide.

ZTE is a well-known communications equipment manufacturing enterprise, including wireless products (CDMA, GSM, 3G, WiMAX etc.), network products (xDSL, NGN, Photo-communication, etc.), data products (Router, Ethernet switches etc.) and mobile phone services (CDMA, GSM, PHS and 3G etc.). Its products cover wireless, core network, access, hosting, business, terminals, cloud computing, services and other fields. Its customers are domestic and foreign telecom operators.

In 1995, ZTE began to explore overseas markets. In May 1996, ZTE formally established an international department. The ZTE mainly adopted the typical linear function system. In the primary stages of entrepreneurship and development of various enterprises, it required an organizational structure that could play a leading role in corporate planning, collaboration and integration. At the same time, we need to take the specific characteristics of the various functional areas into account, as the linear functional organization structure is a type of organizational structure which is widely used by many enterprises in China and around the world. Under the leadership of the president, the vice president (or Deputy General Manager) responsibility system has categories: market systems, R&D and manufacturing production systems, financial systems, personnel management systems and integrated management systems. Marketing and R&D manufacturing are the two core business systems, directly managed by two deputy general managers.

In 1998, ZTE launched the business department system. The company set up a Network division, mobile division, Department division, CDMA division, mobile phone division, and the KANGXUN company (responsible for procurement); at the same time, ZTE set up several marketing departments, including the first marketing division, second marketing division, third marketing division and later, added two further marketing divisions. There are 6 function centers at the headquarters: quality control, IT, marketing, personnel, financial, and the office of the president. Each department is a virtual profit center with no independent property rights and personnel rights. From the beginning of 1999, ZTE sent a small group of employees to the telecommunication markets of less developed countries and began to expand. ZTE searched directly for customers through their overseas departments, and proceeded to move forward with this independent international strategy.

From the beginning of 2004, ZTE began to build its product management team, and established a cross-department team for product development, in order to solve the problem of cooperation between different divisions. But the business department had no direct marketing or supply chain department, and so the implementation was unsatisfactory. In accordance with the product division method of management, a product division has no ability to provide overall solutions, and as the communication barrier between the divisions was large, it affected the speed of overall response to customer needs.

In the beginning of 2005, ZTE entered a breakthrough period. During this period, ZTE carried out localization strategies through the establishment of organizations, such as research institutes, offices or overseas expansion departments, and hiring local talent; at the same time, ZTE actively expanded its overseas market, searched for quality customers, and strengthened the comprehensive and in-depth cooperation of global operators, establishing the MTO and other institutions. ZTE made an adjustment in the marketing divisions of the organizational structure, and sent domestic marketing employees abroad, expanding overseas markets. At the same time, in order to better serve customer and increase market management, the company implemented its market management platform overseas, establishing 14 overseas offices.

Since the second half of 2006, ZTE quietly made a major adjustment to its business department, establishing a system that is based on function, such as research and development, logistics, marketing and sales, and introduced a matrix management model. By comparison, HUAWEI, ZTE's competitor, introduced a matrix management model as early as 1999.

Matrix management coordinates all the functions of the system resources, breaking down barriers between the functions of the system, and uses cross- functional project teams. This type of system solves customer problems under the unified management of a project manager, and has become a preferred management model in large and medium sized high tech enterprises. Matrix management combines vertical functions with horizontal operations, hence to respond customers' demands rapidly.

At ZTE, the departmental, data, CDMA, network and mobile divisions of the original organizational structure have disappeared, replaced by the marketing, sales, research and development, and logistics systems. The mobile phone division did not participate in the adjustment, but has still been retained in the organization. Each function, in fact, is a department within various minor enterprises, and these systems can contain up to tens of thousands of people and can encompass many more complex functions. This function-based system, the matrix management model, has been adopted in product development and is a highly integrated solution for communication between structures within the company. After adjustment, ZTE had established an organizational structure characterized by this functional system, and clearly defined responsibilities within the system as a whole.

ZTE implemented matrix management in its business department. Due to the decentralization of decision-making power, enthusiasm and flexibility within the division was greatly improved, the specific product market and customer management tasks were undertaken by business department, and the headquarters was able to focus on strategic planning and coordination management. The flexibility of matrix management, which takes product management as its main line, can remedy disadvantages where system resources are difficult to share and coordinate. Matrix groups tend to be more flexible and collaborative than fixed product departments or divisions.

In May 2011, ZTE adjusted its organizational structure, in order to adapt to the changing situation of the industry, enabling it to win more market share. Part of this was used to adjust sales systems; as such, ZTE has been publicizing technical support and expanding it marketing divisions and number of sales consultant. At the same time, ZTE sent architecture engineers, the core employees for research systems, to high-end markets overseas, establishing cloud computing divisions, including global network sales systems and has since been able to better meet the needs of users and clients.

Since 2012, ZTE has attempted to further change the organization, and implement project organization operations.

Firstly, traditional organization involves a departmental or divisional system, whereas in a project-oriented organization, the project or the task is the unit, rather than the department.

Secondly, within traditional organizations, goals are driven by the authority of the position, but in a project-oriented organization, it is entirely driven by the project. In a project-oriented organization, all grassroots cadres should follow the directions of the project manager.

ZTE project management is divided into various strata, namely departmental, domain, company, and top levels. According to the characteristics of a given project, it is also further divided into project, project group, and project portfolio. The company's core business, marketing or R & D can be fit into the project, according to the project management method to set by project objectives, criteria and resource allocation, resulting in a better allocation of resources.

Discussion Questions:

1. Why is ZTE's business department effective?
2. Lastly, why problems can appear using this form of business department?
3. Why did ZTE implement a matrix management model?

26.

The Dilemma for Chery Entering into Overseas Markets

Chery Automobile Co. , Ltd. was founded on 8 January, 1997. It is a state-owned joint stock enterprise invested jointly by 5 investment companies from Wuhu city and Anhui province. In 2016, Chery's sales volume has reached 704. 7 thousand cars, which is an unprecedented 28% year-on-year growth rate. Its export has reached 88081 cars, which constitute 28% of the Chinese car export. Chery is listed No. 1 Car Export Company 14 years succesion.

Chey's product has covered more than 80 countries and regions in the world and has reported an export volume of 1. 2 million cars in sum. It established 14 production bases overseas and 2000 distribution dealers and service networks. Chery is also the first domestic vehicle manufacturer to export car manufacturing technology and CKD parts. The company has 13 thousand employees, including more than 5 thousand research and development staff, and nearly 210 foreign experts and management staff.

Chery desired to entire the international market since it is founded. The Middle East, South-East Asia, Africa and other developing countries are priorities, and with plans to then reach out to Russia, and slowly enter south eastern Europe and Latin America. Chery has built 15 factories in Russia, the Ukraine, Iran, Egypt, Malaysia, Indonesia, Uruguay and other countries and regions, and formed the local alliance to expand to the local maket. Its oversea sales network includes five car markets, which are Asia, Europe, Africa and South America and North America.

On December 16, 2004, Chery and Visionary Vehicles reached an agreement after eight months of negotiations. In the agreement, Chery contributes technology, plant and equipment with a total value of \$300 million, Visionary invested \$200 million in cash to jointly set up a research and development production base. Visionary owns the rights to distribute five new models of Chery car in North America (the U. S. , Canada, and Mexico), build a sales team with international standards, set up 250 car sales outlets, and sell 1 million vehicles in five years beginning in 2007.

Although the U. S. is the world's largest car market, it also has the strictest market standards. The sophisticated design of 5 models of car exported by Chery were required to be improved in accordance with market demands and safety performance requirements. Visionary announced on February 8, 2005 that the company has hired former Chief of R&D at Mitsubishi, Dennis Gore, to be the Chief Engineer and Executive Vice-President of R&D for the North American company. Gore worked for Mitsubishi company in North America from 1998 to 2005, Prior to this, he served as research and development executive at Honda North America and Nissan North America Inc. , and has experience in R&D and improvement of techniques, as well as rich experience in adapting to the American market. This experience will undoubtedly pave the way for Chery to enter the U. S.

Despite Chery is ambitions to enter the U. S. market, the road to development is full of hardship. GM sued Chery in 2004 to claim that the English trademark of Chery is similar Chevy by Chevrolet, it was hurting the prospects to enter the U. S. Market. At the end of April, GM entrusted a lawyer to write a letter to Chery' US dealer-Visionary Vehicles. In the letter, GM mentioned that the name Chery is too close to Chevy, and Chery cannot use the trademark to register, sell, agent and run any other business activities. Beside the trademark, GM filed a lawsuit to Chery with other three "reasons": first, Chery passed the crash test by cheating; second, Chery copied the appearance of Matiz; and the accessories of Chery can be substituted by Chevy. This trademark battle was only the fuse, the main concern of GM was that Chery through copying low cost strategy from Japanese companies to capture the market share. A major new paper of the U. S. reviewed: "Chinese car is expending at breakneck speed, and Chery is an adventurous ‘tiger’ from Chinese automobile industry. ”

The risk of failure exists for those companies who want to expand to foreign markets, such as the failure of First Auto Work – Xiali. While people worrying about Chery' exploration in the U. S. market, Visionary Vehicles announced at Beijing Motor Show in 2006 that it terminated the partnership with Chery, and interrupted the negotiations on establishing a joint venture to design, manufacture and sell automobiles. According to Chery the break-up was because it has not received money from Visionary Vehicles, but Brooklyn said that Chery cannot satisfy the quality and safety standards in the U. S. .

Discussion Questions:

1. Analyze Chery's internationalization strategy.

2. What are the reasons that lead to Chery's failure in the U. S. market?

3. What are the markets that Chery make its success in? Can those success experience copied to the other market?

27.

Transnational Entry Strategy of Nissan

In September, 2012, the sales of Nissan in China fell by 35.3% in September over previous year sales and Dongfeng Nissan's car sales fell sharply by 44.2%. On October 18, 2012, Nissan announced that they would provide full compensation to Nissan cars which were produced in China and damaged in the protest against the Japanese government's illegal purchase of Diaoyu island. Nissan's compensatory measures aimed to ease the burden on car owners and resume car sales in China.

In 1914, Nissan, a company formerly known as Kaishinsha, and renamed to Nissan in 1934, it was founded by Kenjiro Den and others. As Japan's second largest car company and one of the world's top ten car companies, Nissan has numerous car brands. Nissan is headquartered in Tokyo with nearly 130 thousand employees.

From the late 1950s, Nissan began developing an export-oriented strategy because of limited domestic market. In 1958, its exports were less than 3000 units, increasing to 45 thousand by 1963. In 1996, Nissan expanded exports by implementing adaptable management strategies which were coordinated with different market environments. In 1960, Nissan started a company in the U. S. for importing and selling cars, trucks and parts. In 1965, it expanded the company to Canada for selling cars and trucks. Nissan then shifted its export patterns into overseas production. From 1980, Nissan began to build truck factories in the U. S. followed by car factories. At the same time, Nissan's local production strategy in Europe was launched. In 1983, the Spanish Nissan began to produce the Nissan Patrol.

In 1990s, due to the slowdown in the international market as well as the quality of its products, Nissan experienced 7 years of consecutive losses. In 1999, the company lost more than 5 billion dollars. On May 28, 1999, French Renault became the company's largest shareholder by purchasing a 36.8% stake from Nissan for 5.4 billion dollars and formed the Renault-Nissan strategic alliance. Renault also implemented a bold reform by cutting the number of suppliers in half, the number reduced from 1300 to about 600. Purchase costs decreased 20% and sales costs and management costs decreased 20%. The company reduced 21 thousand workers and closed 5 plants within 3 years. A direct result of the closing of the factories was to improve productivity, and the operating profits of the company achieved 2.7 billion dollars in 2000.

Renault, Nissan and Daimler, the three auto giants, signed an agreement in Brussels on April 7, 2010 to form an alliance. The agreement showed that Daimler and Renault each hold a 3.1% of stake of Nissan. After that, Renault would exchange 1.55% of its shares for Nissan's 2% shares. With the alliance, Daimler believed that the competition in the small car market was fierce, and hence the car manufacturers needed to reduce costs effectively. Joint development of vehicle models, R & D, and the sharing of power system technology would save billions of euros.

Nissan adjusted their strategy according to the Chinese environment. In the 1970s, Nissan entered China with direct export of the Duke car. With the advancement of reform and opening up, Nissan set up offices in Beijing in 1985. In 1986, Nissan authorized the transfer of ATLAS technology to China's FAW. In the 1990s, the automobile market in China blossomed. Nissan began to implement a localization strategy by managing subsidiaries. In 1993 Zhengzhou Nissan Co., Ltd. was established, and in 1994 Nissan Motor (China) Co., Ltd. was established in Hong Kong primarily to engage in car imports. In 21st century, Nissan has tried various strategies to win market share. In September 2002, Nissan and Dongfeng Motor Corp formed a strategic alliance and established a comprehensive strategic cooperative relationship. In April 2003, Nissan and Dongfeng Motor Corporation (China) set up a joint venture, and in February 2004, a wholly owned subsidiary, Nissan (Chinese) Investment Co., Ltd. was established. In 2010, Nissan electric vehicle made a public appearance at the Beijing International Auto Show.

Discussion Questions:

1. Why did Nissan compensate for the damages?
2. What was Nissan's strategy for entering the European and the U. S. markets?
3. Why did Nissan expand into the Chinese market? How did Nissan adjust its strategies in the process of entering the Chinese market?

Part Ⅵ

International Business Operations

28.

Marketing Strategy of L'Oreal in China

The sales of L'Oreal in China reached 14. 96 billion yuan in 2015, an increase of 4. 6% over last year. It increased over 22% counting by Euros. The company has had seals growth in China for 19 consecutive years, another milestone for the company after it became a member of sales of "1 billion-Euro club" in 2010.

L'Oreal was established in 1907 and is now the biggest cosmetic company in the world. Its headquarters are based in Paris, France, and it is included in *Fortune* Global 500 and *Fortune* World's 50 Most Admired Companies. Besides selling cosmetic products around the world, the company is sells luxury products and does research on skin disease as well. 2016 showed that total global sales were 25. 84 billion Euros, year-on-year sales grew 2. 3%. Comparable sales on year-on-year increase 4. 7%. Chinese market is growing faster than other markets. The continuous growth has increased L'Oreal's market share in China and further consolidated China as one of L'Oreal's world top three markets.

L'Oreal's achievements were the result of outstanding sale strategies as it adopted a value-orientated pricing method, and selected brand segmentation strategies by price and product grade. This is mainly reflected in L'Oreal's Pyramid brand structure. Additionally, the company adopted promotion channels including high-grade fashion magazines, advertisement signboards on the street, TV and Internet. Different products are assigned various advertising strategies which allow the company to focus on different target customers. Advertisements are required to present the features of products, for example, HR is the top brand, Paris-L'Oreal is the common brand, Maybelline is the fashion brand, Mininurs is a compatible public image, etc.. Images of these brands are presented in advertisements received by the consumers.

Besides building strong brand images, the company also uses slogans to enhance the image of products. Some of their product slogans are 'Because You're Worth It' and 'Maybe She's Born with it. Maybe it's Maybelline'. These slogans are powerful and impressive which increases the effectiveness of the advertisements. Moreover, L'Oreal uses celebrity endorsement for its products lines, influencing consumer buying behaviours through celebrity promotion. Giles Weir, a senior executive at L'Oreal once said, "now that exports are out of date you have to be local, you must be strong as the local first-class company with an international image and strategy." Thus, the company combines internationalisation and localisation, and incorporates Chinese culture to emphasise the global image for international brands like Maybelline. The company uses new technology with acquired local brands such as Yue-Sai to build a new image on the foundation of local culture.

Over-advertising sometimes arouse the consumer's antipathy and the resistance, thus, adopting more public communication model will have unexpected results. No doubt, L'Oreal has had success in using these models. The company sponsored the China area screening competition for Elite Mode Look in 1998 and 1999 to encourage Chinese women to show the unique oriental charm. They also held 'Beauty Nights' in Chinese universities and colleges from 2000 to 2002 to encourage students to understand the inner beauty and sharp appearance. In the event, the chief makeup artist of Maybelline made personal image for female college students which caused a stir.

The company also holds public benefit activities in cooperation with trusted hosting organizations to expand brand effects. Such as, set "L'Oreal-UNESCO World Young Women Scientists Award" and "L'Oreal-UNESCO World Young Women Scientists scholarship" with UNESCO (United Nations Educational, Scientific, and Cultural Organization). Through these programmes to enhances the reputation of the company.

Furthermore, the company grabs public attention through contributing to social focus. For example, during the SARS epidemic, L'Oreal donated packages of skincare products to medical staff in Shanghai worth a total value of 1 million Yuan on International Nurses Day.

At last, the company improves the visibility of its products through participating in competitions like the third session of "China Brand Competition" which hosted by the State Administration for Industry and Commerce and the State Trademark Bureau, L'Oreal won China's top 10 famous trademark in 2002. "Maybelline" one brand of L'Oreal Group's won the "The Most Market Competitive Lipstick Brand in 2000" and "The Most Popular Lipstick Brand in 2002" with its lipstick sales in Chinese market. Through positive public communication strategy, L'Oreal successfully puts its products in view of people 24 hours a day which deepens the impression of its brands and goodwill.

Discussion Questions:

1. What factors caused good sales performance for L'Oreal?

2. What are the different sales strategies L'Oreal used in China? How effective are they?

3. What kinds of relationship should be established between L'Oreal and Chinese local corporate?

29.

Neusoft Guiding Embedded Software Outsourcing of China

As China's largest embedded software provider, Neusoft, along with other Chinese software companies, is facing new development opportunities brought about by the boom in embedded software.

There is great development potential for embedded software development in China. The support from the Chinese government for embedded software industry play a significant role in its rapid development. As well, advanced infrastructure, communication and information facilities provide the availability and preferential policies necessary for the expansion of the IT services industry. Software embedded systems technology can be widely applied to various fields of national economy, and the formation of multi-disciplinary, cross-platform and integrative systems in various fields.

These opportunities generate further software products and services business. Software has become an integral part of many devices: communications equipment, household appliances, automobiles, medical equipment, etc. As all these products are made in China and require software components which are also made in China, Neusoft stands to become the primary provider of such software nationally, as well as internationally. Currently, the development of the embedded software outsourcing business is rapid in China, especially from Japanese companies who are outsourcing in China. Products include mobile phones, electrical appliances, automotive electronics, semiconductors, and so on, and these form the basis of cooperation for Japan's electronics manufacturing industry and the software industry in China. This is an outstanding development environment for the embedded software industry, and creates new opportunities and challenges for Chinese software enterprises.

Neusoft Group provides IT solutions to services companies globally and is committed to promoting social development and creating new opportunities for people through the innovation of information technology. The company was founded in 1991, and it has nearly 20 thousand employees. There are eight regional headquarters in China, ten software research and development bases, 16 software development and technical support centers, and it has set up marketing and service networks in more than 60 cities. It has built subsidiaries in the United States, Japan, Europe, Middle East and South America through which the company provides industry and product engineering solutions and related software products, platforms and services internationally.

Neusoft's initial business was not domestic but based in foreign markets, providing software development outsourcing for foreign companies, and thus gradually expanding. Utilizing the experience of its international marketing service and training capabilities, the company leads the competition in the domestic market. At the same time, based on the stability of this local market, Neusoft is upgrading its strategic orientation from internationalization to globalization.

2011 marked the 20th anniversary of the founding of Neusoft. At this critical moment, Neusoft established a global, diversified business model based on the Internet and knowledge-driven assets for the implementation of its strategic business growth model and improvement of operational programs. After four years, through improved technology, and business model innovation and transformation, Neusoft successfully constructed a cloud-based medical health industry system, which covers medical institutions, hospitals, enterprises, communities, families and individuals, for the benefit the people. Neusoft is seeking competitive sustainability, to increase profits and accelerate the process of internationalization towards globalization, while expanding the business's scale.

Intelligent equipment is the future development direction of manufacturing, which need support by embedded software. Developing embedded software is an advantage of Neusoft Group. Neusoft is actively preparing to face the market opportunities of embedded software outsourcing. Therefore, according to 3 to 5 years strategic planning principles, the company trains its talent to better accommodate different directions in the development of future business. Similarly, it carries out the building and training of backbone staff and management teams.

As relates to technology, the company has established and improved mobile phone embedded software systems and staff capacity models. Using mainstream mobile phone software platforms (Symbian, Linux, Windows Mobile, Qualcomm, Android, etc.), it builds Neusoft on the core technical abilities of mobile phone software at all levels and for each software module.

As relates to management process, the company promotes a quality management system based on Capability Maturity Model for Software, while at the same time, has established information security management systems according to the ISO27001 standard.

After years' efforts, Neusoft has established cooperative relations with various well-known international mobile phone manufacturers, for participation in research and development of mobile phone products for operators from China, as well as Japan, Europe and the United States. Technical aspects cover the research and development of mobile phone software platforms, application and testing at all levels, and building a technical team of thousands of professionals. Neusoft plans to build a professional mobile phone software research and development team with 2000 to 3000 people, to become a first-class international mobile phone embedded software service provider.

The embedded software provider has the close relationship with the customer who requires a particular technology and experience. Moreover, the process within the cooperation model itself is crucial. After years cooperated, Neusoft has adapted characteristics of those industries and product developing, especially in car audio, having collaborated with Alpine for more than a decade. Successful experiences rely on comprehensive development processes, quality assurance systems, cost advantages, high-quality development, and good service attitudes.

More importantly, Neusoft has the concept of seeking common ground while reserving differences, complementing each other, growing together and winning together. the new cooperation model by Neusoft and Alpine can be seen TWO COMPANIES, ONE SYSTEM.

With its strength of experience and innovative technology, Neusoft wins the trust of customers and builds balanced cooperative processes for both parties. Neusoft QCDs have obtained customer recognition and continue to create value for customers. Neusoft also takes pride in its software conception, design and development with Alpine, which, having won many international prizes, has built visibility and brand competitiveness for both Neusoft and Alpine. Neusoft looks to cooperate with Japanese customers in this manner as well, with both parties looking for future cooperation "without borders", to jointly promote product competitiveness on the global market, to mutual benefit and win-win results.

Neusoft's software outsourcing services are mainly in two areas: application software and embedded software. Embedded software is the focus of the future development within the business. As the world's manufacturing workshop, it is necessary to expand the depth of the product design and software development in China. Neusoft has carried out early preparation in this area.

However, compared with European and American markets, the Japanese market is still "a small piece of the pie". IT outsourcing services in North America and Europe accounted for 75% of the global market, and will continue growth at an annual rate of 60% which is almost twice the Japanese market. At present, due to research and development costs at home, human resources costs and market expansion, European and American countries continue to move research, development and software outsourcing business to China.

In the past, the "Made in China" brand was a miracle, and while this miracle changed China, it also affected the world. In the future, China will become a country with huge potential in the field of service outsourcing. Neusoft is China's largest outsourcing service provider, and will certainly seize the opportunity to cause embedded software outsourcing to become the new engine for driving future development.

Discussion Questions:

1. What are the strengths of Neusoft's strategies to support it becoming the biggest outsourcing provider in Japan?

2. What are the benefits in providing outsourcing service for Neusoft?

3. Compare advantages and disadvantages between self-development and outsourcing in software industry.

30.

International Research and Development Strategy of Changan Automobile

Changan Automobile joined the global market is an inevitable choice as it is one of China's innovative independent enterprises. Changan Automobile spends 5% of profits on research and development every year. Changan Automobile has developed rapidly due to its large R&D expenditure and has become the first auto company to sell 1 million passenger vehicles annually within 9 years.

Changan Automobile makes good use of global resources by using a strategy of collaborative development. It has established R&D centers in America, Europe and Asia and has introduced advanced collaborative concepts based on the PDM global collaboration platform used by large manufacturing enterprises to realize online collaborative R&D 24 hours a day, all over the world. Changan Automobile had already mastered the following intelligent drive core technical skills: full speed adaptive cruise, lane keeping and automatic parking. In particular, structured road unmanned technology has been through substantive technical verification, and Changan has taken a solid step towards the rapid development of intelligent driving technology in 2016. Automatic driving will be a reality by 2025.

Changan Auto's global R&D system is distributed between centers in Chongqing, Shanghai, Beijing, Turin, Italy, Yokohama, Japan, Birmingham, UK and Detroit, USA. This has helped to form a solidly growing development pattern of from both inside China and globally. The global R&D system in each of the five countries and nine cities divides emphasis and division of labor by function, and forms a cooperative engagement system. The European design center located in Turin is mainly responsible for the research of car body development, modeling research and automotive trim. The Design center in Japan is committed to engineering design, model building and import and export trade business. The R&D center in the UK focuses on engines and gearboxes. The American R&D center specializes in the most core and difficult element-chassis.

The first overseas Changan Auto R&D center was founded in Turin, Italy in September, 2003, and is mainly responsible for auto modeling and feasibility analysis. By May 8, 2006, Changan Auto Europe design Center Limited Liability Company was officially registered, and mainly makes use of local talent in automobile design and R&D, with a focus on adopting local automobile design concepts and technology, modeling research, car body development and automotive trim for Changan Auto in Europe. It also cooperates with related companies and schools to establish training foundations to foster technical talent for Changan Auto.

The European design center possesses auto layout, creative design, digital design, and soft and hard grease model post-processing skills, covering the whole process of automobile modeling and design and contains, among other facilities, six model manufacturing platforms, a woodworking room and a paint room. From 2006 to 2012, Changan Auto in Europe cumulatively completed more than 800 creative design projects, and 23 car load development programs above S4 level. In particular, from 2010 to 2012, it undertook a total of 11 products projects and 4 concept vehicle projects.

April 17, 2008, Changan Auto officially opened its Japanese design center in the Yokohama north port area in Kanagawa county. This center primarily involves the development of interior and exterior automotive trim and contains an engineering modeling and engineering department. The main business scope includes automotive interior and exterior styling design, general layout and feasibility study, engineering design, model making, prototype production, engineering and production support and consulting, etc. The purpose in establishing this Japanese design center is to take advantage of the experience and technical means of the Japanese automobile industry, to improve the design abilities of Changan Auto and to foster a pool of top level R&D talent with international design concepts.

In June 2010, Changan Auto officially founded its UK R&D center in the Nottingham Science and Technology park, and then set up office in Fenn End and MIRA Tech Park. These three sites focus on advanced engine power research and development. R&D center moved into Birmingham in 2015. Birmingham not only is in a beneficial geographical location and has convenient transportation networks, and also it is the UK's main automobile industry center, home to many world famous automobile companies, attracting a large amount of professional automobile research and manufacturing talent.

Birmingham is nicknamed the British Detroit and the automobile industry in the UK is famous for research and development in engines and gear boxes Nissan, Toyota and Ford have all set up R&D centers in the UK. By establishing its engine research center in the UK, Changan Auto can rapidly gain product system knowledge and R&D abilities provided by overseas engineering teams. As such, it can help Changan Auto decrease the disparity of R&D abilities between and other first class global automobile companies. Finally, it fosters talent in China by enabling Changan Auto to learn from the experience and knowledge of others.

The average working age of engineers in the UK R&D center is above 25 years and there are more than 10% engineers holding a PhD. Most of them have working experience in famous automobile companies including Jaguar, Land Rover, Ford, BMW, Rolls-Royce and Bentley. There are 150 staff total in UK R&D center and 90% of the staff comes from overseas, while there is about 1000 staff members working with the power research and development team in China. The UK R&D center and China team have different divisions of work and focus. Whereas the China R&D center is responsible for basic research and development, the UK R&D center is responsible for higher level improvement. Under this management system, Changan fosters teamwork through advanced technical and creative ability, to attain the localization of professional talent.

In January 2011, American R&D center of Changan Auto was founded in the city of automobile in Detroit. So far, the global research and development structure with 5 countries and 9 cities and each has own focus has been completed after overseas R&D center in Italy, Japan and the UK.

The American Changan Auto R&D center specializes in the most core and difficult part of automobile technology-research and development of chassis, including the research of chassis performance turning skills, chassis engineered design, chassis technology research and chassis manufacture craft work. The American R&D center is the foundation for the intelligent pilot development of Changan Auto and located in the largest city in Michigan, USA – Detroit. In the field of intelligent development, Changan Auto has more breakout opportunities by relying on the American R&D center and reaps the benefit of R&D abilities and membership benefits with MTC global alliances. Changan Auto's intelligent automobile has been in the leading position in automobile industry, from its 2000 kilometer-long self-driving distance to the mass production of adaptive cruise control, automatic emergency braking, BLIS, and blind area monitoring systems. In particular, the mass production of self-driving vehicle systems is continually 2 years ahead of other automobile companies.

There are two main tasks for the intelligent work team in American R&D center of Changan Auto. One is researching safety drive assistance and self-driving technologies, the other is the researching of vehicles based on V2X. Before the Beijing automobile exhibition 2016, Changan Auto's self-driving automobile made an unprecedented feat for any Chinese self-driving car filed, by completing a 2000 kilometers distance from Chongqing to Beijing without sustaining any damage. Self-driving technology is still far away from practical production due to the issues of production cost and law, however, Changan Auto's American R&D center plans to mass produce level 3 self-driving technologies by 2020. At this stage, the main task is to realize the mass production of automatic cruise control and automatic parking systems.

Discussion Questions:

1. What is the effect of establishing overseas Changan R&D centers?
2. How to band Changan's overseas R&D and corporate sustainable develop-

ment together?

3. What are the constraint factors in building Changan's global linkage research and development network?

31.

International Human Resources Management Practice in Tencent

Tencent is a famous internet company in China. The issue price of Tencent's share was HK $3. 7 in 2004 and it has risen to more than HK $400 in November 2013, the increase has been exceeding more than one hundred times. In April 2017, Tecent's market value reached $279 billion, became the world's tenth largest market capitalization company.

Three major business indicators—the gross income, gross margin and annual profits have maintained two digit number increases every year since listed in 2004. Among globally listed companies, the long term financial statement is second only to Amazon. The excellent performance of Tencent reveals the success of human resources management in Tencent, being people-oriented from the beginning, boasting a highly focused organizational culture, high levels of tolerance and the spirit of cooperation.

At present, there are more than 24 thousand employees working at Tencent. Among them, 30% hold Masters or higher level degrees and 60% are technical staff. Their global human resources management strategy has been implemented in both middle and senior level management and Tencent encourages outstanding talent with practical experience from America and Europe to join. The average age of employees is 29 years old and the male to female ratio is 3 to 1. Tencent selects talent with Masters, PhD and post PhD in specific technologies and skills from around the globe. The human resources management at Tencent neither relies on rules and regulations, nor policies, but, rather, on organizational culture. Organizational culture originally comes from consensus and norm-forming within the company for long periods time and it leads to common behavior. There are many mobile, elite professionals from Google, Facebook, Oracle, Microsoft and Samsung, investment banks, consulting firms and media who work with Tencent every year. Tencent has created an open, equal and respectful organizational culture to foster diversified talent with different cultural backgrounds and work experiences. The charm of this organizational culture is in its becoming an effective method to solve issues of personality difference and culture integration.

The staff remuneration in Tencent is highly recognized among domestic IT companies. The overall remuneration has been divided into motivation compensation, and welfare. Motivation compensation covers regular plans, service rewards, performance bonuses and long term incentives for specific jobs. Welfare includes legal benefits – five social insurance and one housing fund, as well as commercial insurance and all kinds of paid vacation. The housing plan deserve particular attention among welfare schemes at Tencent. Tencent decided to set up a housing plan for qualified employees to offer interest free loans for down payments when they purchase their first house in order to help the employees who grow up with company together to settle down and start businesses. The Employee Assistance Program provided by Tencent is a significant innovation in the IT industry. It arranges for psychological counseling online 24 hours to provide consultation and relax the mental pressures of employees face to face. At the same time, Tencent invites two high level professional doctors from a traditional Chinese medical hospital to serve employees on a biweekly. These approaches not only guarantee the mental health of employees, but also greatly improves effectiveness and efficiency. As a talent-oriented company, the caring approach for employees is very detailed. For example, Tencent arranges free shuttles for employees in Shenzhen, Shanghai, Chengdu and Beijing, including more than 260 routes in order to reduce the commuting time of employees. More than 2 million people used the shuttles in 2010. The rational construction and rich content of remuneration and welfare programs account for Tencent being the leading company in the domestic IT industry.

With the listing of Tencent, the start the road towards international operations and diversified layout begins by making a series of acquisitions on both domestic and foreign markets. On December 18, 2015, Tencent, as the major stock holder, acquired all remaining shares of American company RIOT to make it a wholly owned subsidiary under Tencent. The human resources management system placed upon RIOT, which is a typical American company, has distinctive features and allows smooth transition and is worthy of being considered by other companies in IT industry. The method used by Tencent respects cultural differences. As a design-oriented company, Tencent authorizes the complete autonomy of independent management to RIOT and implements European and American compensation motivation systems rather than domestic models. Tencent created a comfortable, free and creative working environment for foreign employees and implemented the organizational culture concept at RIOT. For instance, it places customer experience first, focuses on team-building, and remaining curious. It allows foreign subsidiaries to maintain the planned development track of the home company along with the organizational culture and management philosophy.

RIOT offers highly competitive salaries for employees including four types of allowances: a medical insurance plan, a subsidized vision insurance plan, a dental insurance plan, and a retirement benefit plan, as well as many management programs, such as flexible work timing. RIOT has full service buffet restaurant which offers subsidized meals and coffee bars, office kitchens stocked with free cereals, fresh fruit, snacks, tea and fresh ground coffee; RIOT also provide reasonable accommodation for the disabled employees. All of these examples show attention to detail in regards to employee benefits, and also demonstrate a high degree of international tolerance in Tencent management style.

Another big change is to attach great importance to the value of the company's employees, as shown by the RIOT EDU program, which provides employees with further opportunity to learn and grow. Tencent highly recommend this program as Tencent firmly believes that it is worthy to invest in the educational training of employees and that future return will be doubled. RIOT's performance climbed steadily after Tencent became a shareholder, with the turnover close to a billion dollars by the end of 2013. That is quite considerable for a game design company.

Through the cases of both acquisition by Tencent and human resources management, it can be seen how important cultural tolerance and trust between overseas subsidiaries and the home company is in multinational corporate environment, especially high-tech enterprises. The aspiration for improvement is an inexhaustible driving force for becoming successful in the human resources and compensation management.

Discussion Questions:

1. What is the purpose of the human resources management method in Tencent?

2. What policy type is allocated to employees at Tencent? What are the details?

3. What attitude on human resources management does Tencent take in overseas subsidiary RIOT? Does it have optimum effect?

4. What valuable experiences can learn from the Tencent's transnational management method, as applied at RIOT?

32.

International Human Resources Management Strategy in TCL

TCL Corporation was founded in 1981 and is a consumer electronic enterprise with global economics of scale. There are three listed companies under TCL: TCL group, TCL Multimedia and TCL Communication Technology. The global revenue of TCL in 2011 was 60. 834 billion yuan and total staff exceeds 60 thousand people.

With the rapid development of economic globalization and regional integration, core competence has become the focus of competition between enterprises. At the same time, Human Resources Management is becoming a key factor to build core competence for enterprises. TCL has had massive development in overseas markets and, as a result, more highly qualified and adaptive staff are needed in TCL will. At present, 17% of TCL employees are non-Chinese and this proportion will increase in the next 3 to 5 years. Therefore, TCL is facing the challenge of talent selection and training which is totally different than in the past. TCL's vision for development requires staff with not only outstanding technical expertise and management skills, but also being self-motivated, self-learning, adaptable, having good communication abilities and a team work spirit.

In order to improve the quality of management in TCL, and to match the requirements of the international HR strategy, TCL embraces internal promotion and external introduction with equal stress on both. One the one hand, current managerial employees at different levels study to improve their operation abilities for international enterprises, and some employees are selected to work in overseas enterprises or study in world-class business schools. On the other hand, TCL recruits senior management personnel with international operations background and research and development talents to fill key positions. At the same time, TCL also looks for people with expertise and experience in foreign enterprices who have good future potential to build a reserve team of international staff to foster and train.

In June 2012, TCL organized a press conference named "Achievement Dream to Build World Class Enterprise with International Competition in Guangzhou". At the conference TCL announced its international talent introduction plan for 2013, with plans to recruit 2200 new employees in the electronic, information, communication, machinery, marketing, and accounting and HRM fields. The recruitment target is middle and senior managers with working experience in well-known companies at home and abroad, including general managers of business department research centres, and general managers in charge of sales in overseas regions. Recruitment has been in New York, Silicon Valley, the Pearl River Delta, around Bohai Gulf area and the Yangtze River Delta. Senior positions accounted for nearly 40% of the recruitment, R&D talent nearly 70%, TCL Thomson project and TCL mobile communications talent demand accounted for 60%.

As a transnational group, TCL was challenged by HRM internalization. At present, the HRM system of TCL is divided into three levels: headquarters, business departments and attached companies. The HRM model in different business departments is quite different. Some of them have a matrix model, meaning there is an HR centre in one business department which horizontally connects business departments and vertically connects attached companies. The HR centre sends a specialist who is managed by both the line manager and HR centre. TCL also has a linear function system where there one HR department for each department, and corresponding HR departments for attached companies. There are nearly 100 HR managers at this level and each has a different management approach, although there is a large HR staff complement, the HRM operation is simple.

TCL expanded into South and East Asia, South America, the Middle East, Africa, Oceania and Russia, it utilised managerial approaches to suit local circumstances and selected overseas employees in order to improve the initiative and flexibility of subsidiaries to adapt to the changing market environment. Firstly, TCL headquarters created an HRM programme framework which has been refined and implemented by branches and subsidiaries. Local managers are responsible for deciding and training host country nationals according to the specific circumstances in the host country, in order to help them to integrate into TCL. Meanwhile, local companies and TCL managers developed their own compensation and welfare policies and work hours according to the legal requirements, customs and life style in host countries, developing appraisal criteria and appraising actual performance in accordance with local work habits. HRM headquarters often sent mangers to work and supervise different branches and subsidiaries to ensure coordination and to maintain high operational efficiency in the HRM department between subsidiaries and group headquarters.

TCL strives to overcome the cultural differences in transnational HRM, and values multicultural immigration to "respect knowledge, emphasize abilities, encourage creativity, tolerate failure, foster professional integrity, teamwork, inclusive culture, and casting a wide net" for talent growth. This organizational culture benefits employees from different cultural backgrounds to work cooperatively and effectively to establish a strong competitive edge when TCL enters global markets.

TTE is a transnational corporation formed by the merger of TCL and Thompson, which boasts 1200 research and development employees all over the world. No matter what country they come from, all of them are members of TTE and they accomplish their tasks and are responsible for related tasks in different positions. When TTE sets its compensation standards, HR departments integrate many factors such as international markets, domestic markets and the current situation at TCL and Thompson to ensure that employees obtain fair compensation in different countries and global work sites. Meanwhile, TTE also provides a bonus and financial incentives to Chinese employees who work abroad, to motivate them to overcome all kinds of difficulties in a new environment.

Discussion Questions:

1. Why does TCL emphasize the role of human resources in the process of promoting internalization?

2. What kind of policy does TCL have to allocate human resources? What are the advantages and difficulties?

3. How does TCL reduce the rate of expatriate failure?

4. What are characteristics of TCL employees's compensation operations?

33.

Chinese Listed Company in Overseas Market Facing Going Short Risks

On April 11, 2011, the American market short seller, Muddy Waters, released a report about strong selling on DuoYuan Global Water Inc. (DGW). As a result, the share price of DGW crashed.

The report by Muddy Waters indicated that there were some problems, the valuation of land assets was too high, the figures for construction were incompatible in the two reports. The CFO of DGW lacked working experience in China and the distribution network was non-existent. Muddy Waters indicated that the annual income of DGW would not exceed 800 thousand US dollars, far different from the original income announcement of—154. 4 million US dollars when DGW was listed in the U. S.. This is the conventional methodology adopted by Muddy Waters—to conduct an investigation into the differences between two sets of financial statements of a company reporting in China and in America. The audit report was provided by a local accounting firm in Langfang named Zhong Tianjian Accounting Firm.

In fact, DGW is not the first company facing shortsell attack by foreign companies because of different accounting standards. On June 20, 2012, overseas short institution – Citron released a report that said Evergrande Real Estate had used false information and bribery to cover up insolvency. Stock of Evergrande Real Estate slumped 11% on June 21 after Citron delivered this report. On the same day, the market shrinkage of Evergrande Real Estate was 7. 626 billion Hong Kong dollars and it continued to drop another 3. 53% on June 22.

On June 2, 2011, Muddy Waters released a short report to indicate that Sino-Forest had made up fictitious assets and revenue. After two days, the share price of Sino-Forest crashed more than 80% with market evaporation of 5 billion US dollars. Sino-Forest has been suspended pending an investigation.

On February 4, 2011, Muddy Waters released a research report focusing on China Media Express and queried whether CCME had exaggerated profitability intentionally, indicating that the earnings data submitted by CCME to the Industrial and Commercial Bureau did not correspond with the financial statement data submitted to the U. S. Securities and Exchange Commission (SEC). In the end, CCME was delisted.

On June 29, 2010, Muddy Waters released a research report for Orient Paper Inc. on its website and suggested that there were misstatements in financial statements of Orient Paper. For instance, asset valuation has been exaggerated 10 times and the revenue in 2009 has been exaggerated 40 times. The effect of this report is obvious and the share price of Orient Paper crashed, dropping 13% overnight and in the next 6 weeks it continued to slump 32%.

Prior to that, on July 19, 2001, Nasdaq said that Netease Inc. did not submit annual statement in form 20-F to Nasdaq and US SEC, and Netease was suspended due to stringent Nasdaq regulation No. 4310(c)(14).

Investigations showed that Chinese companies had frequently been subject to short selling due to the differences between China and American accounting standards, in addition to some financial issues. Some Chinese corporations forge bank statements, fabricate non-existing loans, forge assets and sales contracts, or forge inventory lists in order to maximize value added tax cheating, etc..

Although accounting firms realize that there are differences between China and American accounting standards, they still cannot replicate American financial statements. Chinese accounting standards are formulated based on international accounting standards, and the U. S. accounting standards differ in some details. The main difference between Chinese and American accounting standards are disclosure of borrowing cost using capitalization or expense, the method of amortization of intangible assets, related party identification, revenue recognition methods and some other detailed items. For instance, there is a definite difference of recognizing revenue at the time of issuing the invoice or at arrival as offshore cargo. American accounting standards are more cautious on fair market value than international accounting standards which results there being a possibility to seek loopholes in the different standards. The U. S. accounting standards are gradually drawing close to international accounting standards, meaning they are also gradually becoming closer to Chinese accounting standards.

Some Chinese financial experts believe that Chinese accounting standards do not need special improvement, rather it is vital that they be implemented strictly and correctly. In the U. S. , a common auditing process used by the big four accounting firms or other firms appointed by the Public Company Accounting Oversight Board (PCAOB). When an IPO audit is assigned to a designated company, the firm will delegate a partner or senior manager to come to China and work with the brother office, which provides the main auditing team. When the fee for the audit is quite small, the auditing process is simply completed by the domestic firm and the financial statement will be delivered after the American firm examines them. If the American firm has no Chinese partner firm, it is common to cooperate with a Chinese accounting firm. Chinese accountants are very professional, but there are some differences in robustness between Chinese and American accounting standards.

Chinese accountants are too flexible on some specific issues, for instance, the length of account aging to provision for bad debts. Auditing firms do not demand a provision for bad debts if the audited company offer evidences to prove the money can be recovered. A few accountants agree that forging is obvious and frequent in the process of revenue recognition. In theory, the chain of inquiry that can break a lie exists, but even conscientious accountants can't easily detect them.

In July 2010, the PCAOB and SEC jointly released an official warning statement that it should be cautious in handling financial statements produced by Chinese domestic firms. The problem is that the investigation into these forged cases is hamstrung because the SEC has no right to subpoena any company in China. But, after the third Sino-America strategy and economy dialogue, both China and the U. S agree that an auditing cracking down on piracy will be a priority. The SEC has similar attitude about auditing cooperation through transnational corporations to narrow the grey area. But there are some people who think that companies will go to other countries rather than the U. S. due to increasingly stringent control environment.

Discussion Questions:

1. Why are Chinese Listed companies frequently attacked by foreign investigation firms? Why are Chinese enterprises often involved in financial reports forging scandals?

2. What are main differences in international accounting standards? What are the implications for Chinese overseas listed companies?

3. How should the difference in accounting standards between China and foreign counties be handled for enterprises listed abroad?

34.

Overseas Financing Strategy of Haier

In the heat of special purchases for Spring Festival, Haier continues to dominate the refrigerator market with a 14.8% global market share. The latest analytical report released by the Consumer Research Centre on the internet shows that Haier has become the number one refrigerator brand in internet searches attracting attention from 34.0% of users, putting it at the top of the list.

Haier Group was founded in 1984, in Qingdao, and it has become the largest white appliances group in the world through technology R&D, lean management, capital operation, merger holdings and internationalisation strategies. Haier Group has established 29 manufacturing bases, 8 comprehensive research and development centres and 19 overseas trading companies around the world, and employees number more than 80 thousand with customers all over the world.

In 2006, Haier Group entered into their fourth strategic development innovation stage—Globalization of brand stage, after the 'famous brand' stage, diversification stage and internationalization stage. Haier Group has followed a series of strategies including backdoor listing and swap financing in order to offer solid capital backing for this strategy.

In order to guarantee capital flow and expand development scale, Haier took some intentional actions including listing and seeking international strategic cooperation in the early part of 21st century. Because of the vastness of Haier Group assets, and complicated and harsh rules for domestic capital operation, they hope to acquire a company in the Hong Kong capital market to do a reverse takeover of group assets to enter the international capital market by backdoor listing. However, the whole implementation process included three steps to follow for Haier's backdoor listing.

The first step is the backdoor. Haier chose a listed company named Zhongjian Digital, owned by a Hong Kong businessman Mai Shaotang, as backdoor target, with its main business being baby hygiene products. As the initial step of the backdoor, Zhongjian Telecommunication, as the major shareholder of Haier Group and Zhongjian Digital, joined with Pegasus Hong Kong and Pegasus Qingdao company whose main business is production and sale of mobile phones. Pegasus Qingdao is owned by Zhongjian Telecommunication and Haier Investment with a 51% share controlled by Haier. Pegasus Hong Kong is owned jointly by the Hong Kong Fu Tung Company and Zhongjian Telecommunication, with a 49% share held by Fu Tung Company.

The second step is capital injection. By the end of 2001, Zhongjian Digital purchased all the shares of Pegasus Hong Kong held by Zhongjian Telecommunication and Fu Tung company separately, and then in August 2002, Zhongjian Digital purchased 15. 50% of the shares of Pegasus Qingdao from Haier Group. The equity of Zhongjian Digital became the payment cost for all transaction. As a result, the ratio of shares held by Haier Investment in Zhongjian Digital rose to 29. 94% and Zhongjian Digital was renamed Haier Zhongjian on January 23, 2002. The entire baby hygiene product business was peeled off from Haier Zhongjian in March, 2003, the only remaining business is production and sale of mobile telephones.

The third step is renaming. Haier's backdoor listing plan needs to speed up because under a new regulation released by Hong Kong Stock Exchange—backdoor listing will be regarded as an IPO from March 31, 2003. Haier plans to pour capital from white appliances and the remainding 35. 50% share of Pegasus Qingdao into Haier Zhongjian in June 2003. At the same time, the cost of Haier Zhongjian will be 1. 453 billion Hong Kong dollars, with new share, convertible debt an extra 50 million Hong Kong dollars. But this plan is still regarded by the Hong Kong Stock Exchange as an IPO and was delayed. Finally on January 28, 2005, the final capital injection step was completed, Haier Group president Yang

Mianmian became the chairman of Haier Zhongjian and Haier Zhongjian has been renamed Haier Electronics Group Company Limited.

Haier entered the international capital market successfully through a backdoor listing in Hong Kong S. A. R. and Haier has qualified capital support, and improved internationalization of financial management, especially with internal control, risk management, accounting standards, information disclosure and auditing being geared to international standards. The listing of Haier abroad not only gives Haier brand influence in the international product market, but also gives Haier good credit in the international capital market. Haier puts swap financing on the schedule after completing the backdoor listing.

Haier continues to open up new overseas market with product exporting, overseas local production and looking for merger and acquisition opportunites with overseas enterprises. Fisher & Paykel Appliances in New Zealand announced in May 2009 that it would issue shares and that Haier Group would take a 20% share. The company said it would raise at least 189 million New Zealand dollars, including 46 million New Zealand dollars by issuing its first allotment of shares to Haier Group. In addition, Fisher & Paykel will raise 12 million New Zealand dollars from Haier to ensure that a 20% share will be held by Haier. It means that Haier needs to raise 58 million New Zealand dollars to hold these share in Fisher & Paykel, but direct fund raising in New Zealand is restricted by the local government and national laws and policies. At the same time, Haier's credit rating will be a key point, so direct fund raising in New Zealand is not beneficial to Haier.

In May 2009, one New Zealand dollar was worth 4. 6 yuan. At this time, if a New Zealand company needs to raise 266. 80 million yuan to invest in China, it will be restricted by the law and regulations of Chinese governments and banks. That not only increases the fund raising cost, but also decreases the effectiveness of fund raising. Thus, it is an opportunity for Haier to make the currency swap with this New Zealand company to solve both parties' problems. The annual interest rate will be different because the two companies have differing credit ratings in their respective countries. Haier could attain a 5 year loan in RMB with 6.5% fixed annual interest rate in the Chinese market. But financing in New Zealand dollars would have an 8.2% fixed annual interest rate in the New Zealand market due to their low popularity and credit rating in the New Zealand market.

The currency swap has been divided into three steps. The first step was the initial principal exchange. Haier Group borrowed 266.80 million yuan in the Chinese market and Fisher & Paykel borrowed 58 million New Zealand dollars in New Zealand market. The two companies swapped the capital borrowed in their own countries. The second step was to arrange interest payment terms. Haier Group paid the required interest to Fisher & Paykel at the end of every year, and the New Zealand company paid the required interest to Haier Group, then these two companies paid the interest to the lenders in their respective countries. The third step was the mature principal swapping. At the end of fifth year, Haier Group paid 58.8 million New Zealand dollars to Fisher & Paykel and Fisher & Paykel paid 266.80 million yuan to Haier Group, then they returned this borrowed money to their own lenders. Haier and Fisher & Paykel Appliances have successfully raised funds through a currency swap to avoid local market constrains and currency risks.

Discussion Questions:

1. Analyse the advantages and disadvantages of listing Haier abroad. What problems does the transnational corporation need to consider when they raise funds in the global capital market?

2. Analyse how swap financing helps Haier to avoid currency risk?

3. List the types of foreign exchange risk encountered by transnational corporations, and analyse Haier's foreign exchange management model.

35.

Risk Management of International Business in CHANGHONG

Sichuan CHANGHONG Electronic Holding Group Go. , Ltd. was founded in 1958, and covers the multi-variate expansion of military, color TV and electronic information industries. It has been become a comprehensive transnational group by integrating consumer electronics and research and development of core devices, pushing forward to be a provider of information appliance content and service with global competitiveness.

The brand value of CHANGHONG in 2016 amounted to 120. 896 billion yuan and it ranks No. six in the Top 100 in the electronics industry in China. It is also No. 152 in Top 500 Chinese enterprises and No. 64 in the Top 500 of Chinese manufacturing companies. There are 4 listed companies under CHANGHONG group, including Sichuan CHANGHONG, MEILING Appliance, HuaYi Compression and CHANGHONG Jiahua.

CHANGHONG has been built to be a respected enterprise in the world by insisting on customer-centered, and market-oriented, by strengthening technical innovation, compressing internal management, and fostering core technical skills. It includes IC design, software design, industry design, converter technique and reliability engineering, and builds technical innovation platforms for consumer electronics, implementing intelligent strategies and improving its comprehensive competitive abilities.

In order to better meet the challenges of complex and volatile market conditions, it has developed its own countermeasures: combining high and low strategies. This means its high end market focuses on technology and low end market focuses on quality. CHANGHONG actively joins its global competition in the international market by using effective strategies and keeping an eye on world markets while determining victory and success in the domestic market. By 2016, CHANGHONG products were exported to Europe and America, Southeast Asia, the Middle East, Russia and Australia, with foreign exchange earnings remaining at 100% increments. CHANGHONG has already realized the transition from products export to technique and capital export.

In the early stage of international development, there was big mistake in the international financial management of CHANGHONG. In 2001, CHANGHONG started to do business with APEX. There was a crunch in payment collection that year and there only 41.84 million US dollars for accounts receivable at the end of that year. At a business summit in 2002, CHANGHONG sold 610 million US dollars in product to APEX, but collected back only 190 million US dollars and the accounts receivable outstanding was 462 million US dollars. The amount of business between CHANGHONG and APEX occupied 54% of CHANGHONG's whole year in color TV sales and it was 91.41% of overseas sales. In 2003, the sales amount decreased and collected amount increased, with CHANGHONG sales of 424 million US dollars to APEX, collecting back only 349 million US dollars, with the accounts receivable rising to 4451 million yuan. The amount of business between CHANGHONG and APEX occupied 33% of CHANGHONG's whole year color TV sales and 70% of its overseas sales. In 2004, CHANGHONG basically completed business with APEX and only sold 35.59 million US dollars products to APEX, at the same time, collecting the receivable accounts back 109 million US dollars. The accounts receivable was 463 million US dollars over the four years' business, with CHANGHONG sales of 1113 million US dollars to APEX and collecting back 649 million US dollars over the previous 4 years. The bad debt rate between CHANGHONG and APEX was 28.21% after 4 year's cooperation with APEX. As a result, there was a lawsuit between CHANGHONG and APEX for the 463 million US dollars accounts receivable due. It was possible for CHANGHONG to take back 150 million US dollars and the rest of accounts receivable were impossible to retrieve.

CHANGHONG learned a lesson from this bad debt incident and started to make rigorous policies and strengthen credit management for customers in international trade. It was necessary for CHANGHONG to make credit investigations of partner companies and establish a client credibility management policy, and regulate the daily management and credit policy of accounts receivable when cooperating with foreign companies. CHANGHONG built and improved its financial systems, improved current financial accounting systems, accounting standards, and internal control policy, regulating the approach and process of collecting the accounts receivable and choosing qualified factoring companies.

A factoring company is a finance company and there are extremely strict processes for the risk control in financial enterprises. There are still issues due to the complicated processes, though it is common for international trade to be engaged in by factoring company. For instance, companies need to submit an application stating product model and amounts first, then the insurance will be accepted only after the factoring company completes making the risk review for the insured goods. The speed of business is thus restricted by the reviewing process when there is multiple batches and models, or a large number of products. In addition, the factoring fee is another issue. The factoring fee is divided into two types—accepted insurance fees and unaccepted insurance fees, the latter allows enterprise to collect goods money, with the cost of this fee relatively low (3.5‰) as there is no guarantee remittance agreement. CHANGHONG usually takes the latter because of the consideration of cost due to the low profit margin in appliances. When products are sold in large amounts, there are some sales amounts that can not be put into the factoring account, and so CHANGHONG pays more attention on this situation. The ownership of products belongs to CHANGHONG before transferring to foreign company, though the goods have been sent to foreign countries. The factoring company is responsible for allocating sales money that 10% goes to overseas partner company and 90% goes to CHANGHONG after good has been sold by foreign company and sales money has been put into the factoring account.

Besides above policy, CHANGHONG has improved its governing structure, established effective internal checks and balances, restricts and supervises reviewing systems, and has builds strict accounting systems in the regular management of the company. CHANGHONG also makes related policy to avoid mistakes in international trade, focusing on the shareholders at management level. As the Chief Financial Officer of company, it is the responsibility of the CFO to advice strongly to senior management level immediately to stop delivering products to an enterprise when the sales money cannot be collected back, at the same time, makes ready to raise the accrued charges for the bad debt by arranging internally for urgent recall, or by entrusting an account company agent to do the recovery. At last, lawsuit must be used for recovery if the previous approaches can not collect back the sale money.

Discussion Questions:

1. What is the importance of accounts receivable in the business operation of enterprises?

2. What is the reason to cause the accounts receivable incident to be produced?

3. What kind of strategy does CHANGHONG take for dealing with overseas business after the APEX incident to guard against risks?

References

[1] Si Jianping. (2015) Internationalization Strategy of Traditional Chinese Medicine in Context of Large Health. *China Journal of Chinese Medicine*, (5): 678 – 680.

[2] Liu Wei-jun and Wang Ji-bin. (2013) Analysis on Export Structure of Chinese Materia Medica during 2005 – 2012. *Drugs & Clinic*, (4): 608 – 611.

[3] Weng Lihong and Lin Danhong. (2012) Strategic Analysis on the Intellectual Property Rights of Beijing Tong Ren Tang. *Journal of Fujian University of TCM*, (6): 52 – 54.

[4] Song Yingjie and Xu Huaifu. (2011) An Analysis of the Current Situation of China's Traditional Chinese Medicine Products' Foreign Trade. *Modern Business Trade Industry*, (1): 99 – 100.

[5] Wu Yaru. (2009) Review the Development of China's Time-honored Brand Through the Development of Tongrentang. *Review of Economic Research*, (37): 18 – 25.

[6] Li Jiang. (2010) *Research on Technological Catching-up of China's Diary Industry under Globalization.* Master Dissertation of Beijing University of Chemical Technology.

[7] Zhan Wenqian. (2012) *The Research on Strategy of Brand Internationalization for Chinese Dairy Corporation.* Master Dissertation of Ocean University of China.

[8] Jiao Yue. (2013) *Research on the Growth Strategy of Erie Group's Overseas Business.* Master Dissertation of Inner Mongolia University.

[9] Zhang Jianqiu. (2014) Exploring the Development of China's Dairy

Industry in the Tide of Globalization. *China Dairy*, (9): 6 – 7.

[10] Feng Liang (2014). Logical Relationship between Yili's High Efficiency Growth and Mode Innovation. Dairy and Human, 237 (6): 42 – 49.

[11] Xiao Yi. (2016) The Trend of International Trade Development under Economic Globalization and China's Countermeasures, (1): 128 – 130.

[12] Nie Yingli, Du Xinyu, Wang Mengmeng, etc. (2016) Year-end Inventory: A Review of the Big Events of China Dairy Industry in 2015. *China Dairy*, (1): 2 – 17.

[13] He Maochun, Zheng Weiwei. (2016) International Division of Labor System: China, Globalization and Future World. *People's Forum-academic Front*, (9): 6 – 13.

[14] Yu Jinyao and Hong Qingming. (2016) On the Standardization of Time in the Course of Globalization, *Social Sciences in China*. (7): 164 – 188 + 209.

[15] Liu Ming. (2010) *A Study on the Cultural Differences between China and Western Countries in Intercultural Business Negotiation*. Master Dissertation of Changchun University of Technology.

[16] Wu Qiaofang. (2012) The Impact of Cultural Factors on Business Activities. *Guang Ming Daily*, Vol. 12 – 09 (007).

[17] Chen Qi. (2013) The Practice, Effect and Reform Suggestions of International Business Negotiation-Based on the Thinking of International Business Training. *Market Forum*, (1): 102 – 103 + 109.

[18] Feng Tao. (2013) Study on the Cross-Cultural Differences and International Business Negotiation. *Journal of Harbin University of Commerce*, (1): 73 – 76.

[19] Liu Yuanyuan. (2006) *Research on Cross-cultural Integration after M & A*. Master Dissertation of University of International Business and Economics.

[20] Yi Rongrong. People Net. http://gongyi.people.com.cn/GB/191247/214653/13977894.html, 2011.02.22

[21] Friends of Nature, Institute of Public & Environmental Affairs, The

Green Beagle Institute, Another Side of Apple. http: //114.215.104.68:89 / Upload /201609021115599647.pdf. 2011.1.20

[22] Shi Haitao, Yu Feng. (2011) A Case Study of Geely's Acquisition of Volvo. *Modern Business*, (8): 250 - 251.

[23] Zhang Yanyan, Zhou Xingying. (2012) Cross-cultural Management Analysis of Geely's Acquisition of Volvo Case. *Economic Research Guide*, (8): 28 - 29.

[24] Ma Jiabin and Wu Ting. (2012) A Feasibility Study of Chinese Auto Companies' Overseas M&A—Based on the Analysis of Geely Buying Volvo. *Modern Property Management*, (12): 75 - 77.

[25] Li Dan. (2014) *Research On The Cross Cultural Management of China Enterprises Transnational Mergers And Acquisitions.* Master Dissertation of Guangxi University.

[26] Zhang Guojun. (2013) An Analysis of the Cooperative Significance of "BRICS Countries" from the Perspective of International Political Economy. *Business*, (14): 145 - 146.

[27] Georgy Toloraya and Xie Zhou. (2014) The Russian View on BRICS Strategy. *Russian literature and art*, (1): 123 - 129.

[28] Hao Yubiao, Tian Chunsheng. (2014) Sino-Russian Energy Cooperation: Progress, Motivation and Influence. *Northeast Asia Forum*, (5): 71 - 82 + 128.

[29] Zhang Bo. (2014) *The Research on the Development of Sino-Russian Energy Trade.* Master Dissertation of Northeast Normal University.

[30] Li Xing, Cheng Zhijie. (2015) China, Russia and India—Asia-Europe BRICs Countries are Key Forces to Promote the Silk Road Economic Belt Construction. *The Journal of Humanities*, (1): 28 - 35.

[31] Chen Yuan. (2015) Deepening Sino-Russian Economic and Trade Cooperation and Building the Cornerstone of the Relations between the Two Countries. *Management World*, (1): 2 - 6.

[32] Jia Zhongzheng, Ren Lin. (2015) A Study on the Economic Con-

nection between Russia and "BRICs Countries". *Russian Studies*, (5): 138 - 159.

[33] Zhu Jiejin. (2016) BRICs Bank, Competitive Multilateralism and Global Economic Governance Reform. *Journal of International Relations*, (5): 101 - 112 + 155 - 156.

[34] Li Jianlan. (2015) *The Role of Sino-Us Trade Imbalances*. Shanxi University of Finance & Economics.

[35] Zheng Yunxin. (2015) A Summary of the Studies on the Causes of China-US Trade Friction. *Journal of Xi'an University of Architecture & Technology, Social Science Edition*, (1): 37 - 41.

[36] Qiao Pingping. (2016) An Analysis of the Current Situation, Causes and Countermeasures of Sino-US Trade Imbalance. *Economic Relations and Trade*, (5): 34 - 37.

[37] Huang Da. (2016) *The Study of The Trade and Investment Effects of China-Asean Free Trade Area*. Nanjing University of Finance and Economics.

[38] Li Meilian and Li Hong. (2016) A Quantitative Analysis on Goods Trade of China-ASEAN in 2015 and Its Prediction in 2016. *Around Southeast Asia*, (2): 3 - 7.

[39] Huang Zhiming and Yang Yueyuan. (2016) Opportunities and Challenges of China-ASEAN Trade Development in the Belt and Road Initiative. *Coastal Enterprises And Science & Technology*, (2): 3 - 5.

[40] Zhou Haihong. (2015) Red Beans Group: to Build the Cambodia Sihanoukville Special Economy Zone (SSEZ) the Belt and Road Initiative cooperation and win-win model. *China Today*, (4): 88 - 89.

[41] Chang Ju and Wen Hua. (2015) Cambodia Sihanoukville Special Economy Zone (SSEZ): Create a New Model of "Maritime Silk Road". *China Today*, (3): 88 - 89.

[42] Zhou Haijiang. (2015) Cambodia Sihanoukville Special Economy Zone (SSEZ) "the Belt and Road Initiative" on the Responsibility of Enterprise Model. *Global Market Information Guide*, (11): 13 - 13.

[43] Liu Lin. (2014) The Construction Mode of China's Overseas Economic and Trade Zone – A Case Study Based on the West Hong Kong Special Administrative Region. *Manager's Journal*, (35): 162 – 163.

[44] Dong Yan. (2015) How did the "Cambodia Sihanoukville Special Economy Zone (SSEZ)" in Cambodia be Made? . *China Report*, (5): 32 – 33.

[45] Yu Jinghao. (2014) To Build the Cambodia Sihanoukville Special Economy Zone (SSEZ) into Cambodia's "Shenzhen". *People's Daily*, 07 – 14 (002).

[46] Yu Yichun. (2015) Cambodia Sihanoukville Special Economy Zone (SSEZ), Demonstration Park on the Belt and Road Initiative. *People's Daily*, 10 – 11 (003).

[47] Luo Rong. "China trade relief information network". http://www.cacs.gov.cn/cacs/newcommon/details.aspxnavid = C07&articleid = 131207

[48] Luo Rong. "China trade relief information network". http://www.cacs.gov.cn/cacs/newcommon/details.aspx.articleId = 129514

[49] China reports. "sina finance". http://finance.sina.com.cn/world/gjjj/20090120/15475782804.shtml

[50] Dong Xueqing, Xu Jianming. "Xinhuanet". http://news.xinhuanet.com/fortune/2008-09/03/content_9764144.htm

[51] "Popular daily. Xinhua". http://www.sd.xinhuanet.com/cj/2013-03/28/c_115187244.htm

[52] "People's Daily". http://world.people.com.cn/n/2015/0409/c1002-26819232.html

[53] "Green wheat fields. Flush finance". http://news.10jqka.com.cn/20150410/c571671785.shtml

[54] Tao Li. (2016) Ant Financial Unites Zhengda Group Copying Thailand Version of Alipay. 21*st Century Business Herald*, 11 – 02 (016).

[55] Bao Hui and Han Ruiyun. (2016) President of Ant Financial: How Difficult is It from "Globalization" to "Ahead of the World"? 21*st Century Business Herald*, 05 – 09 (009).

[56] Liao Yifan. (2015) Ant Financial How to Shape the Financial Architecture for Alibaba. *Manager*, (3): 90 – 91.

[57] Tao Li. (2016) Covet the India Market, Ant Financial Internationalization Pathfinder. *21st Century Business Herald*, 04 – 14 (016).

[58] Hou Yunlong. (2014) Alibaba Accelerates the Globalization of Financial Business. *Economic Information Daily*, 11 – 19 (003).

[59] Dou Yingying. (2014) Ant Financial Accelerate the "Sea" Intended to the Domestic Market. *China Economic Times*, 11 – 25 (007).

[60] Li Ping. (2012) Summary of 20 Years of GMS Cooperation. *Around Southeast Asia*, (2): 34 – 38.

[61] Ma Chen. (2015) *The Development and Future Counter Measures of China's Cross-Border Electricity Supplier.* University of International Business and Economics.

[62] Yan Xinmiao. (2015) *The Situation and Suggestion to Chinese Cross Border E-Commerce.* University of International Business and Economics.

[63] Zhu Kai. (2015) *The Research on the Application of Cross-border E-Commerce of SMEs.* Hangzhou Dianzi University.

[64] Zhang Hui. (2015) SWOT Analysis and Countermeasure of Cross-Border Electric Business Development. *Journal of Shandong Institute of Business and Technology*, (3): 88 – 93.

[65] Gu Ruoqi. (2016) Yunnan Actively Layout Cross-Border Electricity Business. *International Business Daily*, 05 – 30 (B04).

[66] Ma Miao. (2016) GMS Cross-Border Electric Business Platform Enterprises Alliance was Established. *Kunming Daily*, 06 – 12 (002).

[67] Guo Man. (2016) GMS Economic Corridor from Concept to Reality. *Kunming Daily*, 06 – 15 (T02).

[68] Zhao Maomao and Yan Jianxue. (2016) Reflections on the Development of Cross-Border Electric Businessmen's Export Business in Yunnan Province. *E-business Journal*, (10): 29 – 30.

[69] China and Thailand "Vegetables for Oil" Project Chinese Exports of

Vegetables Worth Billions of Dollars (2009). *International Business Daily*, 11 - 10 (005).

[70] Ni Guangqing. (2009) Vegetables for Oil Shop on a Win-win Road. *Yunnan Economic Daily*, 2009 - 12 - 01 (D02).

[71] Lu Yu. (2015) A Study on the Development of Yunnan Barter Trade-Taking "Vegetable for Oil" as an Example [J]. *Theory Research*, (10): 103 - 104.

[72] Wu Chengsan. (2012) The Agreement that Vegetable for Oil between China and Thailand Set Sail Officially [N]. *China Water Transport*, 11 - 07 (002).

[73] Zhang Zizhuo. (2012) Vegetable for Oil Project Set Sail. *Yunnan Economic Daily*, 11 - 01 (001).

[74] Mi Hua. (2010) "Vegetables for Oil" by the Political Turmoil in Thailand Hindered. *China Business News*, 06 - 11 (B02).

[75] The project China-Thailand Vegetables for Oil has Great Potential. *Times Finance*, 2014 (19): 44 - 45.

[76] Yunnan "Vegetable for Oil" Project Progressing Smoothly. *Vegetables*, 2014 (07): 13.

[77] Yun Xun. Yunnan Vegetables Into Thailand Changing for Oil. *China Co-Operation Times*, 2014 - 05 - 16 (A03).

[78] Ma Hongmin. (2000) Utilize Futures Market to Improve Management Level of Enterprises Actively-Talking about the Hedging Experience of Tongling Nonferrous Metals (Group) Company. *Nonferrous metals industry*, (11): 44 - 46.

[79] Dou Dengkui. (2011) *Empirical Research on Hedging of Listed Companies Using Derivative Financial Instruments*. Southwestern University of Finance and Economics.

[80] Wang Zhigang. (2014) *Study on Strategic Hedging of Copper Enterprises in China*. China Agricultural University.

[81] Yuan Xinhui, Yao Liqun, Cao Ruobing. (2005) Tongling Nonfer-

rous Metals: Successful Cases of Overseas Commodity Futures Trading. *Foreign Exchange*, (10): 59 -60.

[82] Liang Hongliu, Shu Yajun. (2010) The Influence of RMB Exchange Rate Change on Tongling Nonferrous Company and the Countermeasures. *China Non-Ferrous Metals*, (S1): 167 -170.

[83] Zhang Jin. (2013) Research on the Relation of Hedging by Derivatives and Enterprise Value. *North China University of Technology*.

[84] Zhu Jigao, Sui Jin, Tang Guliang. (2014) Why do Listed Companies Withdraw from the Market-Based on the Grand Interaction and Alibaba Case Study. *China Industrial Economics*, (1): 127 -139.

[85] Yang Di. (2014) A Study on the Innovation of Ownership Structure of Listed Companies-From the Perspective of Alibaba Group's Listing. *Modern Economic Research*, (2): 43 -47.

[86] Zhang Shiyang. (2015) *The Enlightenment of Alibaba Group's Listed Cases in China on the Legal System of Listed Companies in China.* Shanxi University.

[87] Zou Longfeng. (2016) *A Critical Discourse Analysis of News on Alibaba's IPO in China Daily and The New York Times.* Ludong University.

[88] Wen Yimo. (2013) Alibaba Listing Dilemma: the Infighting of Control? . *Accounting Learning*, (11): 10 -12.

[89] Qi Tong. (2016) On the Improvement of Global Financial Governance System by Asian Infrastructure Investment Bank. Law Science Magazine, (6): 13 -21.

[90] Xu Qiyuan. (2015) Asian Infrastructure Investment Bank How to Take the Next Step. *People's Tribune*, (12): 58 -59.

[91] Bai Xiulan, Zhao Feisu. (2015) Realistic Analysis for Asian Infrastructure Investment Bank. *International Finance*, (3): 75 -80.

[92] Zhang Monan. (2015) Asian Infrastructure Investment Bank Hasten the Global New Financial Governance Structure. *Party & Government Forum*, (12): 25 -25.

[93] Zhu Hongchun. (2015) How to Deal with the Challenges of Asian Infrastructure Investment Banks' Management and Operation for China? . *South China Finance*, (6): 10 –13 +54.

[94] Wang Xiaoqiu. (2012) To Enhance the International Financial Speaking Right of China in the Post-Crisis Period and the Countermeasures. *Reformation And Strategy*, (3): 71 –74.

[95] Sun Siyuan. (2015) *Research on Wanda Group Acquisition of AMC Economic Consequences.* Harbin University of Commerce.

[96] Chen Yafei. (2015) *The Study on Transboundary Transformation Development of Wanda Group under the Changing Market.* Shanghai Normal University.

[97] Xie Wei. Wang Jianlin: The Internal Logic of Internationalization of Wanda Group, *China Economic Weekly*, (20): 35 –37.

[98] Gao Zhanshiqi, Shi Jingru, Jiang Hanting, etc. (2016) An Analysis of the Effect of Wanda Group's M&A on American Legendary Film Industry. *Foreign Economic Relations & Trade*, (7): 51 –52 +63.

[99] Wanda Group: Focus on Creating an International and Open Modern Enterprise Groups [N]. *Dong Ying Daily*, 2011 –12 –12 (003).

[100] Zhang Yuling. Whether Wanda Group's Internationalization is Too Aggressive? *Guang Ming Daily*, 2012 –09 –11 (014).

[101] Wang Jianlin Talk about International Transformation in Harvard: Wanda Will Continue the Sports Industry Mergers and Acquisitions [N]. *Beijing Business Today*, 2015 –11 –03 (B02).

[102] Guo Tengjiang. (2014) The Study of BYD Motors' Competitive Advantages and Generic Competitive Strategies. *East China University of Science And Technology*.

[103] Wang Hongsheng and Zhang Yuming. (2015) Cloud Innovation: New Development Model for New Energy Automobile Industry-Based on BYD New Energy Automobile Industry. *Science and Technology Management Research*, (23): 195 –199 +222.

[104] Wang Hongqi, Wang Yinghua, Wu Jianlong, etc. (2016) Evolution Mechanism of Innovation Ecosystem for New Energy Vehicles: Case of BYD New Energy Vehicles. *China Soft Science*, (4): 81 –94.

[105] Xiang Man. (2016) Market Competitive Environment and Strategic Analysis of BYD New Energy Vehicles. *China Market* (32): 187 –188.

[106] Guo Yanqing, Shi Hongmei. (2010) Research on the Innovative Way in the Development of BYD New Energy Vehicle. *Journal of Managment Case Studies*, (6): 469 –478.

[107] Yong Jun. The change of BYD strategy [J]. Hong Kong and Shanghai Economics, 2014 (6): 64 –65.

[108] Xiao Taiming. Analysis of development strategy of BYD electric bus market [D]. Shanghai Jiao Tong University, 2013.

[109] Zeng Li. (2016) Project System, so that ZTE Organization "Self Operation". *Sino Foreign Management*, (8): 112 –113.

[110] Qiao Yinghe. (2009) *Design and Implementation of Dongjiang Design and Implementation of Software Outsourcing Project Management Workflow Engine in Neusoft.* Northeastern University.

[111] Han Lei. (2010) Study on the Selection of Enterprise Logistics Outsourcing Supplier. *Ocean University of China*, 8 (3).

[112] Lei Jia, Wei Yang and He Jianhong. (2016) Restrictive Factors and Motivation of Constructing Global R&D Network in Chinese Enterprises: A Case Study of Changan Automobile Company. *Modern Business*, (14): 123 –124.

[113] Two Convergence: Innovation of Chang'an Automobile R&D Cooperation Model [J]. *Enterprise Management*, 2015 (9): 12 –15.

[114] Zhang Baolin. (2014) Government, Industry, Research and Production, Collaborative Innovation, to Build the Independent Brand of China's Auto Industry. *Science & Technology Industry of China*, (1): 15.

[115] Liu Yige. (2016) Research on the Synergetic Effect of Enterprise Strategy and Human Resource Management Based on Entrepreneurial Thought – A

Case Study of Tencent Company. *Human Resources development of China*, (18): 92 -98.

[116] Li Jianfeng. (2014) New Thinking of Human Resource Management in Internet. *Human Resources development of China*, (16): 6 -9.

[117] Li Wei. (2010) *Tencent's Development Research.* Shanghai Jiao Tong University.

[118] Ren Li. (2013) *The Research On The Total Compensation Motivation Forknowledge Workers In Internet.* China University of Political Science and Law.

[119] Zhang Jie. (2012) Research on Financial Diagnosis of Enterprise. *Assets and Finances in Administration and Institution*, (8): 57 -58.

[120] Wu Shinong. (2013) *Financial Analysis and Decision Making of CEO.* Peking University Press.

[121] Wang Zhuquan, Sun Ying, Zhang Xianmin, etc. (2014) Investigation on Working Capital Management of Chinese Listed Companies: 2013. *Accounting Research*, (12): 72 -78 +96.